D0949655

Reaching Across Boundaries of Culture and Class

Widening the Scope of Psychotherapy

edited by
RoseMarie Pérez Foster
Michael Moskowitz
Rafael Art. Javier

JASON ARONSON INC.
Northvale, New Jersey
London

This book was set in 11 pt. Bodoni by Alpha Graphics of Pittsfield, New Hampshire and printed and bound by Book-mart of North Bergen, New Jersey.

10 9 8 7 6 5 4 3 2 1

The editors gratefully acknowledge permission to reprint material from the following sources:

"Countertransference in Cross-Cultural Psychotherapy," by Michael Gorkin, in *Psychiatry*, vol. 49, pp. 69–79, copyright © 1986 and used by permission of The Guilford Press.

Lyrics from "Redemption Song," by Bob Marley. Copyright © 1980 Bob Marley Music, Ltd. All rights reserved. Used by permission of Polygram Music Publishing Corporation.

Library of Congress Cataloging-in-Publication Data

Reaching across boundaries of culture and class : widening the
  scope of psychotherapy / edited by RoseMarie Pérez
Foster, Michael Moskowitz, Rafael Art. Javier.
     p. cm.
  Includes bibliographical references and index.
  ISBN 1-56821-487-1 (alk. paper)
  1. Psychodynamic psychotherapy—Social aspects. 2. Psychiatry,
Transcultural. 3. Psychoanalysis and culture. 4. Minorities—
Mental health services. I. Pérez Foster, RoseMarie.
II. Moskowitz, Michael. III. Javier, Rafael Art.
    [DNLM: 1. Psychotherapy. 2. Cultural Diversity. 3. Socioeconomic
Factors. WM 420 R281 1996]
RC489.P72R43   1996
616.89'14—dc20
DNLM/DLC
for Library of Congress   95-52039

Manufactured in the United States of America. Jason Aronson Inc. offers books and cassettes. For information and catalog write to Jason Aronson Inc., 230 Livingston Street, Northvale, New Jersey 07647.

Para Ramón, Alberto, Chefito, y Rafael:
desaparecidos pero no olvidados.
R.M.P.F.

To Paul Moskowitz and Gail Moskowitz, in memory.
M.M.

To my brother, Marino, and my sisters,
Margarita, Rosa, Ana, Doris, and Lucy.
R.A.J.

CONTENTS

Part III
LANGUAGE AND OTHER CLINICAL CONSIDERATIONS

ACKNOWLEDGMENTS

We wish foremost to acknowledge the inspiration and enduring influence of Bernie Kalinkowitz, Director of the New York University Postdoctoral Program in Psychoanalysis from its inception in 1961 until his death in 1992. He was a model for us all. It was Bernie who brought us together in 1989 when he constituted the NYU Committee for a Multicultural and Multiethnic Psychoanalysis. We also want to thank our colleagues on that committee as well as our fellow members of the Multicultural Committee of Division 39 of the American Psychological Association for their collaboration and camaraderie. We want to give special thanks to Kirkland Vaughans for his steadfast leadership as co-chair of the NYU committee for its first five years, and to Dolores Morris for her continuing passionate commitment to both committees as well as to the newly founded Bernie Kalinkowitz Scholarship Fund.

Much thanks is also due to Jason Aronson, our publisher, for his steady encouragement and generosity, and the staff at Jason Aronson Inc., most especially Sharone Bergner, copyeditor, Judy Cohen, Senior Production Editor, Nancy D'Arrigo, Art Director, Catherine Monk, Acquisitions Editor, and Norma Pomerantz, Director of Author Relations, for their kindness and attention both to large themes and small details.

I want to thank special teachers and guides: Esther Menaker for the wisdom of her historical perspective, Adrienne Harris for hearing and supporting my voice, and Ben Wolstein for shifting my priorities in the consulting room. Deep thanks to my guide, the NYU Ehrenkranz School of Social Work, for widening the scope of my thinking. I am grateful to Pat Fava for her patience during the preparation of my manuscripts. And to Jeff, Lauren, and James, the loving centers of my life, thank you for being such wonderful partners in our multicultural adventure.

R.M.P.F.

I feel most fortunate to have had the support of many friends and colleagues over the years. Of those who have most influenced my work, three stand out as constant sources of inspiration for the past twenty-five years, Steven Ellman and Anni Bergman, my first clinical supervisors, my mentors and friends, and Sally Moskowitz, my collaborator in life. And to John and Peter Moskowitz, for all their patience and fun, thank you.

M.M.

Although there are many individuals deserving recognition for their support of this work, special mention should be given to the assistance provided by my staff, Margaret Schwartz and Carolyn DeCesare, as well as the contribution made by my students, Philip Yanos and Angela Martinez. I would also like to thank Dr. Willard Gingerich for continually encouraging me to explore issues of culture, ethnicity, and language in my writing. The support provided by Drs. Louis Primavera, Jeffrey Fagen, Florence Sisenwein, and my colleagues at the psychology department is also appreciated. My students at St. John's University are a tremendous source of inspiration and hence a special acknowledgment should be given to them. And finally, my son, Joshua, deserves a special recognition for his encouragement and for being so proud of what I do.

R.A.J.

CONTRIBUTORS

Neil Altman, Ph.D., is a faculty member and supervisor at the New York University Post Doctoral Program in Psychotherapy and Psychoanalysis and an Associate Editor of *Psychoanalytic Dialogues*. His work in public mental health clinics is described in a recent book, *The Analyst in the Inner City: Race, Class and Culture through a Psychoanalytic Lens*. He has a private practice in New York City.

RoseMarie Pérez Foster, Ph.D., is an Associate Professor at the New York University Ehrenkranz School for Social Work, Clinical Instructor of Psychiatry at New York University Medical School, and faculty member at the NYU Postdoctoral Program in Psychotherapy and Psychoanalysis. She is currently writing a book for clinicians on the role of bilingualism in personality development and its impact on the treatment process.

Michael Gorkin, Ph.D., was formerly Chief Psychologist at the North Suffolk Mental Health Center in Smithtown, New York. He has taught at the Institute for Psychotherapy, Sackler Medical School, Tel Aviv University, and at the Student Counseling Services of the Hebrew University, Jerusalem. He has published in psychotherapy and psychoanalytic journals and is the author of *The Uses of Countertransference*. He maintains a private practice in Jerusalem, where he lives.

Rafael Art. Javier, Ph.D., is a Clinical Professor of Psychology at the St. John's University Doctoral Program in Clinical Psychology and Director of the Center for Psychological Services and Clinical Studies. He is also on the faculty of the Object Relations Institute in New York City. Dr. Javier conducts research in the areas of language, memory, and bilingualism, and is currently writing a book on thinking, feeling, and speaking in two languages.

Michael Moskowitz, Ph.D., is in private practice in New York City, and is an editor at Jason Aronson Inc., Publishers. He is also an Adjunct

Associate Professor in the City University of New York Doctoral Program in Clinical Psychology and a member of the Institute for Psychoanalytic Training and Research.

Mario Rendon, M.D., is Director of the Department of Psychiatry at Lincoln Medical and Mental Health Center and Professor of Clinical Psychiatry at New York Medical College. He is also a Training and Supervising Analyst with the American Institute of Psychoanalysis and in private practice. He is currently investigating the relationship between depression and culture.

Alan Roland, Ph.D., is faculty and member of the Board of Trustees of the National Psychological Association for Psychoanalysis. He is the author of *In Search of the Self in India and Japan*, and most recently, *Psychoanalysis in a Global Age: The Asian and American Experience*. He has a private practice in New York City.

Cheryl L. Thompson, Ph.D., is an Associate Professor of Clinical Psychology at Seton Hall University and a faculty member of the Institute of Psychoanalysis and Psychotherapy of New Jersey. Dr. Thompson researches the role of racial factors in development and its impact on the clinical process. She has a private practice in Milburn, New Jersey.

George Whitson, Ph.D., is co-founder of the Suffolk Institute of Psychoanalysis and a member of the teaching and supervising faculty of the Manhattan Institute for Psychoanalysis. His special interests lie in the impact of the therapist's anxiety on clinical work. He practices in Long Island, New York.

Addette Williams, M.A., is a doctoral student in Clinical Psychology at The City College, City University of New York. She is studying the role of skin color in psychic development for her doctoral dissertation.

INTRODUCTION

Psychoanalysis—Freud's mapping of the universal human unconscious with its repository of hidden desires, and his creation of a general method of psychological inquiry which facilitates its exploration, has stood the test of time across the discipline's diverse and always evolving theoretical perspectives. Relatively unrecognized, however, in the history of the psychoanalytic movement, are the potent ethnocultural factors that have also come to shape the complex body of psychoanalytic thought. As the original movement migrated from nineteenth-century Central Europe to establish new homes in twentieth-century Britain and the United States, it acquired indelible cultural markers from both its native and host cultures. While today's evolving spectrum of theoretical viewpoints spawns avid debates about what drives the human condition, the psychoanalytic literature rarely considers the meaning of these debates in the context of their enthnopsychological origins. It is sobering to consider the observations of contemporary social anthropologists: that psychological theories which carry the strongest power are those that rationalize and extend a culture's most deeply rooted and dearly held traditions and beliefs. These theories basically elaborate and formalize a culture's implicit views on how to function within it as a desirable and capable human being (Bruner 1986). Thus, notions about what moves people to do what they do, or how one defines the idea of self in the context of the world, are intrinsically enmeshed with how a culture views the living process.

Psychoanalysts are moved to consider these issues now because of a growing awareness in the United States that there is a serious problem with the application of psychoanalytic/psychodynamic treatments to the general population. Moreover, the burgeoning era of managed health care and "universal coverage" brings the psychoanalytic community to task, no longer allowing it to practice quietly and discreetly with the privileged few while remaining unchallenged by others. We are well aware that American residents span a unique range of cultural, racial, and socioeconomic groups. What we have not been so willing to acknowledge is that this diversity leads to questions about the generalization of psychodynamic theories beyond their original patient population—the educated person of European descent. Are we to question the analyzability/treatment fit of the population, or are we willing to consider problems with our method when faced with the disturbing research data that cultural and racial minority groups in the United States tend not to take advantage of mental health treatment? In addition, those minorities who do use treatment show the highest premature termination rates of any social group. Something is clearly wrong.

The main contributors to psychoanalytic thinking have been middle class and of European heritage. It is the viewpoint of some in contemporary analytic circles that the movement—despite its claims of comprehensive universality—has not enjoyed as much success outside its native culture groups, because of three principal factors: (1) First, ethnocentric valences always find their way into theory. In psychoanalysis cultural influences have molded psychodynamic theories, various aspects of clinical technique, and the implicit goals that are set for the therapeutic process. The body of psychoanalytic thought has much to offer in its observation of some human universals, such as the presence of unconscious processes. However, embedded in its theory are aspects of Western cultural lore about human nature that are not necessarily cross-ethnic in their applicability. (2) Second, there has been a prejudice on the part of the psychoanalytic community in general against giving cultural factors their due weight when considering the developmental experiences and psychic distress of their patients. Some analytic clinicians believe that cultural explanations are not "intrapsychic enough." However, they do not pause to consider that the primary object experiences so intimately involved in the formation of internalized psychic structures are in fact the dynamic bearers of the cultural surround. For groups establish unique, ethnocentric parameters about such things as self-definition, self–other differentiation, permeability of ego boundaries, and the titration of impulse/emotional life (Roland 1991, Chapter 4). (3) Third, the mutual anxiety and discomfort that are often shared by members of cross-cultural therapeutic dyads have had a tremendous impact on the analytic movement's circumscribed cultural application. One of the least acknowledged barriers to treatment is not what we usually think of as culture per se, but rather, on the one hand, the emotional impact of class and the feelings of suspicion and shame about difference that often characterize immigrant and oppressed cultures, and on the other, feelings of superiority and guilt that characterize members of the dominant culture. The immigrant patient in treatment has typically expressed this anxiety through silence, resistances, or premature termination. The dominant-culture therapist has, more often than not, ignored this anxiety in disavowed countertransference.

These attitudes are beginning to undergo dramatic changes in this postmodern era. We clinicians in urban areas know that the shifts in our consciousness have in large part been spurred by the increasing work we do with people from different cultural groups, as well as people whose lives are characterized by repeated and massive psychic trauma. We are using trauma here in the psychodynamic meaning of the term, referring to an event so out of the ordinary that it distorts the course of development and leaves effects that are usually readily apparent to the trained observer. Like the individual who has suffered the loss of a parent, life-threatening illness or physical or sexual abuse, so do we consider the immigrant patient who has lost his or her family, homeland, and environmental surround, to be injured and potentially derailed in his or her pursuit of a full life. In addition, our clinical work has broadened our awareness and we now recognize a second group of traumatized individuals—members of oppressed cultural groups. While they additionally may have experienced their share of early psychic trauma, the circumstances of their daily lives are such that their sense of self worth is more or less constantly assaulted. No single event necessarily distorts development; there is, instead, cumulative impact of chronic narcissistic injury caused by poverty, emotional neglect, environmental violence, and inferior status in society. Members of oppressed cultures experience this kind of trauma. Many of us believe that to grow up dark-skinned, and, especially, poor in this culture, is to live under such constant assault.

Faced with the painful reality of these patients' lives, we analytic clinicians no longer have the luxury of holding on to a non-dialectically formulated theoretical rationale for non-analyzability, especially when, as we have recently come to discover, this assessment often derives from our own subjective countertransference (Bromberg 1992, Ehrenberg 1992, Ellman 1991, Hirsch 1984). We are now being confronted with our own psychological resistances to widening the spectrum of human experience and co-experience for work in the analytic frame. Thus, if we are seriously committed to expanding the clinical use of the analytic method as a meaningful and valid mode of psychological inquiry and psychic repair, we have a formidable task ahead of us as we train a new generation of analytic clinicians.

To begin, we must address the cultural and historical roots of the theory, and question some of those basic assumptions in psychoanalytic thinking that may in fact reflect ethnopsychological rather than universal phenomena (Section I). Then, we must study the dynamics of the cross-cultural, cross-racial, and cross-class therapeutic dyad, assess these clinical situations with care, and note just how the analytic process both succeeds and falters when the therapeutic interaction unfolds between two people who may hold different views and different experiences of the living process (Section II). Finally, we must address aspects of our method, meaningfully questioning whether certain approaches to therapeutic technique inadvertently foreclose rather than expand the field of psychological inquiry (Section III). In this book we attempt an initial approach to these complex tasks.

This work is a cross-cultural effort on various levels. The editors and contributors are all clinical practitioners in the New York metropolitan area who themselves come from diverse cultural, racial, linguistic, religious, and theoretical backgrounds. While we all currently live and work in the United States, our ethnic roots and personal experiences span divergent world views. And while we are all trained psychoanalysts (with the exception of Williams, who is a doctoral student in clinical psychology at The City College) who consistently use the analytic method of psychological inquiry, we lean toward different theoretical views of human nature, ranging from the contemporary Freudian, to Interpersonal, and Object-relational viewpoints. For some, like Moskowitz, Javier, and Altman, differing metapsychological viewpoints lie at the heart of broader sociopolitical perspectives. No fervor is spared in articulating their positions. For others, like Roland and Perez Foster, the frustrations with psychoanalytic theory are more cross-cultural in nature and descriptive of the cultural binds that can drive or derail therapeutic work. Despite our conceptual differences, we share a commitment to psychoanalysis as an effective method of exploring and resolving psychic distress, and a deep human concern—the desire to expand its use to an ever-growing multicultural American population.

A note on the title:

We have chosen not to use the word race in our title. Recent studies have confirmed that there is no acceptable genetic basis for the concept of race (Cavalli-Sforza et al. 1994). It is especially important that we confront the fact that the division of the world into black and white is a delusion of civilization. People are not black or white. Where the line is drawn is politically and psychologically motivated. The fact that "race" is the only ethnic grouping in this culture that does not allow for the possibility of dual identity belies its delusional rigidity. While "race" clearly has powerful psychological meanings that are discussed in many of the chapters in this volume, we felt it was important not to lend it continuing scientific respectability by using it in our title.

RoseMarie Pérez Foster, Ph.D.
Michael Moskowitz, Ph.D.
Rafael Art. Javier, Ph.D.

REFERENCES

Bromberg, P. (1992). The difficult patient or the difficult dyad? *Contemporary Psychoanalysis* 28:16–30.

Bruner, J. S. (1986). Value presuppositions of developmental theory. In *Value Presuppositions in Theories of Human Development*, ed. L. Cirillo and S. Wapner, pp. 19–28. Hillsdale, NJ: Lawrence Erlbaum.

Cavalli-Sforza, L., Menozzi, P., and Piazza, A. (1994). *The History and Geography of the Human Gene*. Princeton, NJ: Princeton University Press.

Ehrenberg, D. (1992). On the question of analyzability. *Contemporary Psychoanalysis* 28:16–30.

Ellman, S. (1991). *Freud's Technique Papers: A Contemporary Perspective*. Northvale, NJ: Jason Aronson.

Hirsch, I. (1984). Toward a more subjective view of analyzability. *American Journal of Psychoanalysis* 44:169–182.

Roland, A. (1991). *In Search of the Self in India and Japan: Toward a Class Cultural Psychology*. Princeton, NJ: Princeton University Press.

I

Fundamental Issues

This section will discuss the fundamental issues raised in applying psycho-dynamic treatment to the wider multicultural population. At the heart of this challenge lies the inescapable human tendency toward construct-ing meaning from the centerpoint of one's own experience, and the in-evitable societal tendency toward selectively enforcing the meaning sys-tems of those in power. Psychoanalysis, despite its attunement to the non-conscious derivatives of human action and the multiple determinants of conscious meaning-making, remains nevertheless encumbered by the formidable weight of the value presuppositions embedded within its be-liefs. Analysts have had difficulty appreciating the powerful relationship between their theories and the socio-cultural environments within which they were conceived. As a result, therapists are now confronted with nu-merous pitfalls as they try to cope with the psychic distress of increas-ingly diverse patients who present systems of meaning about their lives that markedly differ from the therapist's own.

In Chapter 1, Perez Foster explores the presence of Euro-American be-liefs within psychoanalytic theory and practice, noting through case ex-amples how these cultural assumptions are integrated into definitions of psychological health, pathology, and the goals set for the analytic process. In Chapter 2, Moskowitz takes us back to the roots of psychoanalysis as a progressive force for social change. He charts the divisions that have under-mined the wider application of psychoanalysis and reminds the psycho-analytic community of its own role in its increasing marginalization. In Chapter 3, Rendon places the development of psychoanalysis in a historical-economic perspective, noting how the unacknowledged forces of social and fiscal concerns have shaped psychoanalytic thought and the delivery of its clinical interventions. Rounding out this section, Roland studies the defi-nition of the self in psychoanalytic thought in Chapter 4, questioning its universality and describing just how its construction is reflective of its in-digenous Western origins, and different from other psychologies of the individual represented in the Eastern cross-cultural panorama.

1

What is a Multicultural Perspective for Psychoanalysis?

RoseMarie Pérez Foster, Ph.D.

As psychoanalytically trained clinicians, we carry a secret shame. While being members of a field that prizes the value of all human life, and people's efforts to realize their fullest potentials, analysts also know that they, in fact, touch a very narrow range of people. As private practitioners, many of us assuage our guilt by reducing our private fees so that we can see the student, less privileged, or immigrant patient. Some of us work in clinics and city hospitals where we offer ethnic minority patients a brand of psychodynamic psychotherapy. But this does not address the real problem. Our hidden shame is that psychoanalysis has a very defined view of life and how it should be lived, and it is this perspective that determines who is to be treated, who is analyzable, who has adequate ego strength, who can meaningfully relate to objects, and who is capable of exploring his or her deep inner self. We see those who do not fit into our life program as "simpler people" who have limited or narrower life goals, "poor people" who are too consumed with the reality-based problems of daily survival, or "foreign people" who come from alien cultures or alien neighborhoods and simply do not fit the picture of self-actualization as we define it in our psychoanalytic culture. The bold fact is that for the most part, we work best with those people who are most like us, the middle class and educated who basically think and live the way we do.

Author's note: I am grateful to Dr. Benjamin Wolstein's guidance in my pursuit of a multicultural perspective and indebted to his generosity for allowing me to cite his work in this chapter.

When we stand back and assess the health of the psychoanalytic movement in the United States and its efficacy as a clinical approach to the mental conditions of American people at large, we cannot deny our increasing marginalization.

In the last two decades, the American mental health field as a whole has been engaged in a great deal of self-criticism over the effectiveness of therapeutic services for poor and ethnically diverse groups (Abramowitz and Murray 1983, Atkinson 1985, Sue 1988). Criticism has focused on discriminatory practices directed toward the poor, therapists' lack of knowledge and understanding of the cultural contexts of their ethnic patients, and the inaccessibility of services available to the non-middle class. As a result, studies have uncovered therapist prejudice, clinical bias in diagnosis, and premature termination rates among non–middle-class patients (Sue 1988). Questions have even been raised about the value of using psychodynamically oriented therapies with minority patients clinically described in some literature as lacking the ability to explore the meaning of their experiences (Olarte and Lenz 1984).

Something has clearly gone wrong with the treatment of those people who are not highly educated, middle class, or of European origin. Given this grim state of affairs, it is rather striking that the psychoanalytic community has, for the most part, remained silent. This theoretical community, which has always attempted to describe, understand, and treat the emotional conflicts of the human condition, seems to have fallen woefully behind its own critical self-examination of the crisis at hand. The crisis may very well be that psychoanalysis as it stands today is simply not made for Everyman and Everywoman (Foster 1993). It is proposed here that psychoanalysis' only limited success in expanding its applicability beyond the European group it originally addressed is due to a complex set of ethnocentric biases and methodological parameters that impact on its work—from the foundations of its theoretical metapsychology to its applications as a clinical technique.

While I would like to address some of these issues in this chapter I wish first to note that by suggesting an expansion of the psychoanalytic method into the wider multicultural arena I am not talking about modifications in technique, or the use of so-called parameters in treating the poor, less educated, or culturally diverse patient. I intend to suggest no such value-laden or condescending compromise of the real "analytic thing." Instead, I am proposing a basic reconsideration of how we use our metapsychologies, as well as a re-emphasis on the co-experiential human action that lies at the base of our clinical technique. The goal is to develop a method of psychic inquiry that would accommodate a much wider spectrum of living activity as viable and workable data for the therapeutic frame. The large number of people judged as non-treatable by our method must push us as humanistically oriented clinicians to question our theoretical and clinical paradigms. The press here is not the intellectual excitement of new ideas or the thrill of challenging traditional models but rather, simply, the fact that too many people are not being cared for (Foster 1993). Just as psychoanalysis clinically matured and widened its range of application to the spectrum of treatable psychopathology, so must it now consider impediments to its application that are specific to its standing in the wider multicultural/multiracial context.

I would like to go about this task by highlighting two contemporary thrusts in psychoanalytic thinking that have occupied the stage of recent theoretical debate. These ideas represent shifts in the tide of psychoanalytic understanding and practice that are key to broadening the application of both its theory and its methodology. The first theme concerns our epistemological approach to clinical data and our use of theoretical metapsychology. The second concerns clinical technique and the new emphasis on the co-experiential and intersubjective action of the therapeutic field (Foster 1993).

ON THE THEORETICAL METAPSYCHOLOGY

We are told that all across the intellectual landscape, epistemological currents have shifted from the dogmatic emphasis on certainty and theoretical accuracy to the position that mental images are, in fact, the creations of people and thus speak of a constructed reality (Howard 1991, Spence 1982). Recently, psychoanalytic theory has been taken to task as perhaps one of the most persistent and dogmatic theoretical frameworks in the social sciences today (Lamb 1991). Pressured by the wave of these intellectual times, psychoanalysis is being asked to look inward, to reflect upon itself and take note of its own participation in how it goes about understanding psychic operations. As clinicians, we have traditionally used our metapsychological formulations as frameworks to help us understand what makes people do what they do. There is the instinct story, the object relations story, the power story, to name only a few. We are passionate about and intellectually invested in our stories of choice. They are the templates through which we see our patients and evaluate their strengths, weaknesses, and ability to undergo our method of psychic inquiry.

But voices from outside our field have been quite adamant of late in pointing out that our theoretical affinities suffer from considerable short-sightedness. Social anthropologists (Carrithers et al. 1985, Kirschner 1990, McNamee and Gergen 1992, Shweder and LaVine 1984) argue that we have been unable to see the powerful relationship between our theoretical metapsychologies and the cultural environments that created them. They point out that the psychological theories that seem to carry the strongest power are those that rationalize and extend a culture's most deeply rooted and dearly held traditions and beliefs. Psychological theories basically elaborate and formalize a culture's implicit views on how to function within it specifically as a desirable and capable human being. Jerome Bruner (1986) does not mince words when he speaks of modern psychological theories as being, in effect, canonized cultural values!

It has been well documented in the literature how the personal, historical, and contextual elements of Freud's immediate world were powerfully interactive elements in the construction of his theory of mind. Born out of the intellectual momentum of the European Enlightenment, Freud's theory of human behavior also reflected the social mores of nineteenth-century Vienna. He lived in a Victorian world that placed particular emphasis on social class distinction, appropriate behavioral comportment, and affective restraint. His instinct metapsychology reflected this sociocultural story. He saw the control of impulsive life as the primary imperative of the human condition at that moment in time. Herein, he concluded, lay the source of psychic conflict and psychic pathology.

Freud and every theorist after him were the products of their respective cultural surrounds. We know that when psychoanalysis migrated to the United States it continued to develop, now in the midst of a very different ethnopsychology. Initially, under the influence of American medicine, it attempted a concertedly scientific approach to psychic functioning (Jacoby 1983). American psychoanalysis branded the analytic movement with its own specific stamp—its own unique view of the human condition. Whether emerging from the more quantifiably oriented American ego psychology, later Sullivanian interpersonal theory, or Kohutian self psychology, the analytic movement in the United States elaborated a view of the individual and his or her functions that essentially described the ideals of the American cultural ethic: self-sufficiency, self-actualization, forward mobility, and conflict-free action in the world. Thusly informed is our psychodynamically oriented work in the United States and thusly defined are the criteria by which we assess our patients. As American psychotherapists, we are part and parcel of the society that views assertion and independent self-direction as the veritable *essence* of good life. And these are the treatment goals that we either explicitly or implicitly establish for our patients.

And let us not forget the force of the current zeitgeist—the object relations movement—a British psychoanalytic psychology adopted by the American mental health field for its very syntonicity with the American way. Bred within religious and secular values that hold individual self-responsibility in high regard, this particularly Anglo-American view of humanity prizes autonomy of the self above all human attributes (Kirschner 1990). This self is one that develops from dependency with another to ultimate individuated autonomy. We measure the pathology of this self by its ability to titrate the wish for merger with the desire to stand alone. So enmeshed are we as American therapists in this view of the human condition that we hardly stop to question whether this definition of the self is applicable to all people. There are some cultures in which to be a separate differentiated self, as we know it, would be anathema. There are other cultures where the deep inner self, upon maturity, does not separate but finally merges with the cosmos (Roland 1988). While this is a deeply spiritual concept, which is foreign to us in the West, we have only to analytically treat a patient from an Eastern culture to be struck by the fact that our metapsychological concept of the self in the Anglo-American West is by no means universal, but highly ethnocentric and circumscribed to our own unique view of humanity (See Roland in this volume).

Psychoanalysis must begin to understand that cultural values have found their way not only into its general theory, but into the explicitly constructed definitions of adequate ego functions, psychopathology, and the psychic criteria required for undergoing its particular method of inquiry.

Viewed from a historical, epistemological perspective, psychoanalysis would appear to sit squarely in the middle of the postmodern era's intellectual dilemma—we are seeking to establish systematic, meaningful, and comprehensive bodies of thought and action, only to be reminded of the myriad exceptions to the rule. Can psychoanalysis make its way out of such a paradox? Can it maintain a basic system of beliefs, as well as meaningfully broaden its clinical method of inquiry into a larger, varied, and

more divergent cultural milieu? I believe that it can, and propose a perspective based on the philosophical traditions of pluralism, which held
to the multiplicity of lived experience even before the dawn of social-
constructivist sensibilities (James 1977).

THE PLURALISM
OF THE METAPSYCHOLOGIES

Over the course of his writings, Benjamin Wolstein (1967, 1971, 1973,
1990, 1992a,b, 1994) has defined certain conceptual and operational
parameters in psychoanalytic thought that I believe have fundamental
bearing on integrating the discipline's assumptions with its sociocultural
context. According to Wolstein, psychoanalytic literature describes two
sets of operations conducted by the psychoanalytic enterprise. On one
side, psychoanalysis operates as a method of empirical psychological inquiry—a clinical approach aimed at solving psychological distress. No
matter what their analytic school of thought, all psychodynamically oriented clinicians—be they Freudian, object relational, ego psychological,
interpersonal, or self psychological—believe in a few core notions: (1) the
existence of unconscious processes, (2) the basis of anxiety symptoms
in some kind of psychic conflict, (3) the presence of transference and
countertransference as processes that repeatedly occur in the therapeutic situation, (4) and, most important, the unique psychic connection
that is created with each patient in the process of the analytic work.
These leading terms of observation are coordinated in the overall structure of psychoanalytic inquiry and treatment, their guiding premise
being the belief in unconscious psychic experience. Psychoanalysis has
selected these leading elements of observation out of the complex totality
of the psychic domain because of their observed ability to expand and
deepen self-awareness beyond its initial conscious boundaries (Wolstein
1994).

However, there is the other side of psychoanalysis—the theoretical
interpretive order of inquiry. Therapists and their patients shape and
understand the data gathered from their empirical observations in different ways, depending on which metapsychological visions of human
nature they find most appealing. Here, theorists, therapists and patients
exercise speculative intelligence and the freedom of creative imagination.
They put a deeply private stamp on their enduring choices of myth and

metaphor to interpret the analytic narrative. No single choice is intrinsically better than all others. Wolstein (1994) has written that within psychoanalysis, "even a cursory review of the wide variety of metapsychologies now in favor would reveal its many and mutually enriching divergences. With therapists uniquely individual no more, or less, than their patients, one central point of convergence for all is still hard to imagine" (p. 495). For some therapists, it is the discharge of the instincts that drives people to action. For others, it is the search for objects that constitutes the driving imperative of human nature. It is this side of psychoanalytic thinking—the interpretive metapsychological side—that is so rooted in the assumptions, beliefs, and expectations of one's personal, environmental, and cultural surround. Furthermore, no two therapists, by virtue of their distinct individuality, approach metapsychological interpretation in quite the same way, despite the consistent metaphors directly received from the various traditional schools of psychoanalysis. Wolstein (1994) states that this reflects each analyst's uniqueness and deeply personal perspectives:

> From this new self-awareness follow certain unavoidable premises about making interpretations: first, that the various perspectives on metapsychology are not distinctive of psychoanalytic therapy (to know them, you don't have to practice it); second, that the empirical observation of transference and countertransference, and so on, and the systematic theory of unconscious psychic experience, sets psychoanalytic therapy apart from the other psychotherapies (to know them, you do have to practice it); and third, when psychoanalysis is constructed as ego, object, or interpersonal relations, it is also, so to say, inter-metapsychological; every therapist and every patient, like everyone else, has the makings of a metapsychology at some level of abstraction and complexity. All this is, in sum, to propose that any two individuals doing psychoanalytic therapy together bring to it two distinct psyches, which probably goes now without saying; but they also bring to it two distinct metapsychologies, which undoubtedly has too long gone without saying. [pp. 497–498]

Thus, the relevant meaning and understanding of the analytic work is created in the intimate and unique dialectical discourse between the two members of the therapeutic dyad—each of whom is guided by his or her own experiential and theoretical view of life. Thus it would seem that the more disparate the respective worlds of the members of the dyad, the more the work must be undertaken as a joint quest for understanding, with the therapist needing to exercise particular cautions against rushing to apply his or her personal assumptions and metapsychology about minds at large.

Consider the following case vignettes, the clinical use of particular interpretive metapsychologies, and their relevance to understanding the inner experiences of each patient.

Willie[1]

Willie R. was an 11-year-old Spanish–English-speaking boy, native of the Dominican Republic, who had migrated to the United States with his parents at age 5. He was referred to an outpatient child and adolescent clinic for defecating in his clothing, a symptom that had developed shortly after his move, but that had recently worsened. Willie's soiling had now progressed to occasionally relieving himself outdoors in a deserted area on his way to or from school "if I need to go." The boy was ashamed of his habit, feared that he would be seen as "dirty" by his peers, and conscientiously washed himself and changed clothes after soiling himself.

Willie was a handsome, sturdily built boy whose gentle and smiling social manner only momentarily covered a sad and preoccupied face when at rest. He was quite tense and had difficulty speaking freely with me, such that we almost entirely interacted through symbolic play. His fantasies described lost people, houses, and animals swept away by destructive forces, and soldiers parading in uniform.

Willie had become a cause célèbre at the clinic, which was part of a large teaching hospital. He was presented at both pediatric and psychiatric grand rounds. Diagnosed with a secondary encopresis of functional etiology, the patient was viewed psychodynamically as a textbook case of an early anal personality. His soiling, accompanied by compulsive cleanliness (he washed after his accidents), militaristic interests (he played with GI Joes), and emotional constriction (Dominican children rarely initiate conversation with authority figures) were supposedly sure signs of his repressed wishes to explode with rage upon the world that has overzealously imposed anal and behavioral controls on him.

After about six months of biweekly treatment in which Willie's only change was an increased sense of comfort in my presence, his mother told me that Willie was not her biological child. She adopted him from a poor family in the LaRomana province of the Dominican Republic before com-

---

[1] This case was previously reported by the author in *Psychoanalytic Dialogues* (1993) 3:69–84. Copyright © 1993 *Psychoanalytic Dialogues*. Used by permission.

ing to the United States. The biological parents had willingly given up this child, who was one of twelve, in the hopes of enhancing his socioeconomic environment—not an uncommon practice in the international culture of poverty. It so happens that I have traveled in the area of Willie's original home. Families in this part of the Dominican Republic are mostly share-croppers who live at a subsistence level. Illiteracy is high, electrification is primitive, and horses are still a common mode of transportation. Verdant plains are dotted with grazing cattle and shacks. Toddlers amble unclothed in the heat. There is minimal running water, and there are no indoor toilets.

Willie's case frustrates and shames me when I think of the misplaced emphasis of my early theoretical formulations. While busy searching for the anal-aggressive data that would substantiate my psychodynamic for-mulation (and intellectual narcissism!), I had missed the painful elements of Willie's reality. Adopted by caring people who had unquestionably im-proved his physical standard of living, Willie had nevertheless been termi-nally separated from his mother and the world that he knew. As I would later hear from him, Willie's letting go, especially during times of stress, was his way of returning to Mother and his early life, which for him had included the option to relieve himself outdoors at will. Abandonment, feel-ing like a lost child in a strange world, and the sense that everything he knew around him could disappear suddenly, were the inner psychic real-ity in which Willie lived. Though I had not been made privy to Willie's early history from the beginning of treatment, in thinking back, I am sure that he had communicated it to me in some symbolic form in session. Unfortu-nately, however, this information had fallen on ears deafened by fixed theo-retical assumptions about latency-age boys who defecate in places other than indoor toilets!

Notwithstanding the reactive anger that surely resided in Willie, the point here is that his own sense of trauma about his life was derived not from the imposed controls around anal issues but the imposed separa-tion and loss of life as he had known it. Although his open defecation may have, indeed, comprised a form of anal auto-stimulation, as held by the classical view (Freud 1905), defecating—as Willie himself eventually came to explain—was part of an attempt to reconstruct his early world. "I used to live in a place," he said, "where people let me do this. I want those people and that place back."

Willie's case demonstrates a real clinical pitfall arising from my assump-tion of a rather positivistic theoretical posture early in his treatment. First, I imposed a metapsychological interpretation onto his life that was taken from Freud's (1905) construct of the classical anal phase of psychosexual development—a psychoanalytic formulation designed for those who by definition engage in modern, Western, European toilet habits. The validity of applying the presumed vicissitudes of this developmental phase and its impact on character formation to a boy from LaRomana is questionable, or limited, at best. Second, firmly entrenched in my conviction regarding the truth of my own theory about Willie's life, I had barely left room for any kind of real dialectical discourse—albeit through play—with *him*. In the interest of building what Quine and Ullian (1970) would call a "seamless web of belief," I rushed toward the elements in the patient's narrative that supported *my* story of his life, foreclosing any additional data from the real author—the boy himself.

Aside from the use of a metapsychological interpretation that came to have questionable clinical relevance to Willie's inner life, the main pitfall in this case was my holding fast to an old and admittedly respectable tradition in the execution of the psychoanalytic method: that of placing prime focus on the intellectual interpretive power of metapsychological theory. This tradition by definition relegated the human co-experience of the therapeutic field to secondary status, as if the knowledge garnered from my living action and interaction with Willie in the process of the therapeutic inquiry could not stand on its own in the process of reconstruction and psychic healing (Wolstein 1992, 1994). I will return to this matter later in this chapter.

Manash

Consider the questions posed by the next patient, whose case reflects more contemporary metapsychological formulations about the articulation of the structure of the self and its degree of differentiation.

Manash was a 29-year-old man, a political refugee from a middle-eastern country. He spoke English—his second language—fluently. His homeland had been taken over by a foreign power and was now under oppressive military rule. The patient entered treatment after about one year in this country, feeling severely depressed and stating that all meaning to his life had vanished. In his country, Manash had belonged to a semi-religious social caste dedicated to public and community service. Given the current political situation in his country, he felt that hopes of fulfilling his function were lost. Following the tradition of all men in his family, Manash had been groomed for his life's work since childhood, having been educated in special schools. He believed that his destiny would now not be fulfilled, and that he was nothing without the community group that he was meant to live with, educate, and serve. "I feel so empty and worthless within myself as a man, I am shameful to my father and ancestors."

I struggled to understand Manash's inner sense of loss for many months, while also noting that he was a resourceful man who had managed to start a small import business that was affording him an income. I also struggled with personal and theoretical assumptions about what makes people feel stable and whole. Manash appeared resilient and creative. Surely he would soon find other ways of repairing his sense of narcissistic injury. But he didn't.

These were some of my psychoanalytically informed questions: Was I to view this patient along the lines of Western personality development, possibly using some contemporary metapsychological formulations about the self? Should I consider notions of a pathological self structure (Kohut); of early derailments in separation-individuation (Mahler); of pathological differentiation from the primary object (Fairbairn)? Or might I consider that my theories about how people go about the psychic task of becoming able-minded and able-bodied are simply creative descriptions of how to be a functional self in a particular kind of Western Euro-American cultural life? My patient's culture might very well conceive of the self—and consequently its value, wholeness, robustness, health, and developmental metamorphosis—quite differently. As Manash eventually came to show me, the ideal of mental health in his world was not the socially autonomous, externally oriented, self-actualized individual, but rather a person centered in spiritual consciousness, the confluence of will and fate, and the emotional bonding of family and group kinship wherein one's sense of self is deeply involved, throughout life, with others.

As an American-trained clinician I found these values difficult to understand, since my own life and metapsychological views of human nature were intrinsically connected with Western individualism and a deep belief in the autonomy and will of the individual. Unlike Manash, who sought his uniqueness within the life of his group, my values were those of current American culture. Individuals in our world, particularly those of the educated middle class with whom psychoanalytic culture is so enmeshed, push to become free from family of origin, and create their own unique meaning in life through self-sufficiency and separateness (Roland 1988). Manash's sense of what made a person esteemed and whole proved to be a world away from mine.

ON THE LIVING INTERACTION
OF THE THERAPEUTIC FIELD

I would like to turn now to some issues of technique and their impact on the culturally unmatched therapeutic dyad. The cross-racial, cross-cultural, or cross-class therapeutic dyad, despite our often humanistic, or "politically correct" leanings, is never a quiet enterprise. Beginning with the first contact, the obvious chasm of disparity between life experiences can throw both patient and analyst, consciously or unconsciously, into a veritable whirl of potential estrangement, distrust, or basic anxiety born of a sense of being in the presence of a stranger (Basch-Kahre 1984). Historically, the analytic method has always provided the clinical protocol for the patient to explore these feelings. But what is the fate of the therapist's subjective reactions? And what does the patient do with observations and inferences that he or she may have drawn about the therapist's real attitudes—especially as they relate to the cultural disparity? If necessary, how can patient and therapist begin systematically to deal with the co-experience of their mutual anxiety in each other's presence?

For psychoanalysis, the resistance to this avenue of inquiry is deeply embedded in its history, and the primacy placed on the intellectual interpretive thrust of metapsychology. In brief, Freud's original reduction of the strivings, affects, and cognitive experiences that occurred within the psychic connection of patient and analyst to the instinctual domain, relegated all experience and behavior to conjectured subpsychic origins and speculated derivation from a biological basis. The interpersonal gap or split that this formulation introduced between the two participants was an arbitrary personal limit that was built into the early model of the therapeutic experience. Most relevant to the present discussion, however, was the decision to reduce as much as possible any processes and patterns that might be explored under the conditions of direct therapeutic relatedness. All interactions were seen as based upon the instinctual derivatives of the id (Wolstein 1992).

Aside from early experiments conducted by Ferenczi (1921) on the analyst's psychology and its potential impact on the therapeutic work, Freud's seminal tradition of separating the living mutual experience of the analytic field from meta-psychological interpretation was followed by later psychoanalytic contributors such as Rank, Klein, Fairbairn, Winnicott, and Kohut, who used their own brands of meta-psychological interpretation to define the subpsychic origins of current life experience. As Wolstein (1992) has written:

> It is as though the psyche, under its own conditions, lacked the substance, structure and functions to supply the boundaries of a self-sufficient field of scientific knowledge; as though, in its own terms, the analysis of the psyche were not capable of generating the elements of a coordinated empirical and systematic inquiry within those boundaries; and as though, on its own grounds, the manifold experience of the ongoing co-participant connectedness that makes the actual therapeutic inquiry, were a psychic wasteland, itself beyond visioning, reconstruction and healing. [p. 321]

In these contemporary psychoanalytic times, tides seem to be shifting, however, as more reports bring the lived co-experience of the therapeutic field to center stage. We are being told, for example, that the therapist's own subjectivity, and what the patient comes to know of it, is a vital and often unheeded aspect of the therapeutic work (Aron 1990, Gill 1983, Greenberg 1991, Hoffman 1983, Racker, 1968, Wolstein, 1988). Contemporary writers speak here not of transference distortions, parapraxes, or endogenously determined fantasies about the therapist, but of solid observations that the patient is able to make over time about the therapist's own character and inner psychology. The fact is that analysts are neither neutral screens nor simple clay for transferential transformation. They are, in fact, formidable characters who often have robust prejudices.

As noted, given the traditional primacy lent to theoretical interpretation, the trend in most analytic work has been to avoid exploration and weighted consideration of a patient's views of the therapist, outside of their transferential context. Furthermore, therapists are aware that inquiry into this part of the patient's mental life is anxiety-provoking, potentially embarrassing, and quite stimulating of their own psychic resistances (Gill 1983, Racker 1968). As recently described by Aron (1990) and Greenberg (1991), this avoidance can drive patients to sidestep and accommodate aspects of the therapist's psychology. Patients can become quite sensitive to their therapists' real vulnerabilities and come unconsciously to fear that what they observe may endanger the therapists' own well-being, as well as the very stability of the work.

In the case of marked cultural or racial differences in the dyad, where the disparities are often such a source of mutual subjective arousal, sidestepping exploration of the patient's observations inevitably leads to severe impasses in the work. The following is a case example:

Norma[2]

Norma is a 30-year-old chemical engineer I saw in psychodynamic therapy for four years. She is Panamanian and originally sought treatment with me because of my own Latin-American background. Norma is a particularly striking young woman with light cocoa skin, brown eyes, and very curly, shoulder-length hair. About one year into the work, I noticed that the patient had never brought up the issue of color or race in session. This is surprising as Latin Americans in general are very cognizant of their mixed racial heritage. Indian, Caucasian, and black lineages are all part of a rich genetic pool in which there is much intermarriage.

For a person of Latin-American heritage, I am viewed as light-skinned. I have blue eyes and curly hair. The patient, on one rainy day, commented that my hair looked shorter, as if I "had gotten a haircut." I decided to say, "No, it's just curlier today in the humidity." I asked her more about this. As it turns out, the patient had been an astute observer of my hairstyle over the year, noting that I probably blow-dry my hair to make it less curly. I nervously inquired on. She had also surmised that I probably did not like my hair, because it is the thing that made me look the most Hispanic. Her exploration of the inner me continued: she described the physical charac-teristics of my parents and grandparents, the percent distribution of the various races in my blood by virtue of my features, the coloring of my hus-band and children, and how I felt about all of them. Inevitably this explo-ration finally turned to Norma's own family. She had been the darkest-skinned of all her siblings. Not only had she been mocked for this and accused of not being her fair-skinned father's child, but also, because of her color, she was offered no hope of succeeding in a white-dominated world. Norma had hidden her racial pain, assuming that I would also dis-like her for being a dark-skinned girl.

The exploration of Norma's thoughts about what might be my own sub-jective issues brought powerful personal poignancy and served a strong facilitating function. It finally opened vital areas about the patient's self-image, her parents' reaction to color, and the emotional distance that they had maintained with her. Norma would often mention this "permission to get into your head" as a nodal point in her treatment. I am convinced that had I not allowed her—to use a Kleinian metaphor—to climb inside my body and explore the objects within me, she would have resigned herself to a somewhat forced suppression of this material. Norma's perception of my own unspoken conflict, and her effort not to threaten my equilibrium would

[2] This case was previously reported by the author in *Psychoanalytic Dialogues* (1993)3: 69–84. Copyright © 1993 *Psychoanalytic Dialogues*. Used by permission.

have truncated open exploration of her own sense of racial inferiority. In other words, she would have come to know my secrets, but at great expense to herself silently permitted me to hide them.

The recognition of the contributing role of the therapist's own psychology in psychodynamically oriented work could not be more vital than in the treatment of patients whose culture, race, or class markedly differs from that of the therapist. We must no longer delude ourselves and assume that the psychotherapeutic frame can cloak the analyst's inner life. I would add that the myriad of subjective reactions that are aroused in the socioethnic unmatched dyad are a general fact of life—they are in the air, a part of the social-environmental fabric in which we all live. Whether the therapist's attitudes fall within the range of despondency, sadness, or guilt over the circumstances of the patient's life, or whether the therapist's reactions run the gamut of puzzlement, fear, ethnic prejudice, or dislike, they will all eventually be discernible to our clients. A client's silent recognition of a therapist's unspoken, forbidden attitudes will, at the very least, create an impasse in the work, foreclosing exploration of particular dynamic areas; at the very worst, it will lead to premature termination (Foster 1993).

The psychoanalytic treatment method is poised at a crossroads. We can no longer ignore its admittedly limited application beyond the cultural group of its origins. The unicultural nature of the analytic enterprise is borne out in the statistics that describe large numbers of cultural and racially diverse people who quickly terminate therapy, as well as in the personal experiences we have in our consulting rooms where the more psychologically, ethnically, and experientially diverse patients routinely fail our criteria for treatment.

Our method clearly needs remediation if we are to catapult it into the multicultural arena. We are heartened, however, by these contemporary intellectual times which offer, as it were, therapeutic interventions for both our theory and our practice. First, with regard to our metapsychology, we are reminded that psychoanalysis need no longer carry the unrealistic (and presumptuous) burden of explaining the universal driving imperative of the human condition. Postmodern academic writers note the shifting, mercurial, and context-bound nature of this enterprise as individuals, shamans, philosophers, psychoanalysts, and artists across cultures, historical eras, and geographic locales, have all attempted thoughtful and inevitably personalized explanations for the meaning of their lives. Psychoanalysis must learn to admit that it knows the people of its own culture well and those of non-European cultures less well. Analysts need to become less positivistic in their assertions about human nature, and more willing to shape psychodynamic meaning through reciprocal interaction with their patients, especially when their worlds are so markedly different.

This brings us to psychodynamic technique and practice. The contemporary era in psychoanalysis is, thankfully, bringing the analytic method back to what some of us view as basics, that is, a refocusing on the processes that emerge under the conditions of direct therapeutic relatedness. Aside from our common and fundamental belief in the unconscious as the source of manifest psychic distress, we all have at our disposal the manifold experience of the ongoing co-participant connection with our patients. Whether we choose at any given moment to address this interaction at a conscious, preconscious, or unconscious level, the evidence now shows that these human co-experiences are capable, within themselves, of generating a self-sufficient empirical field of systematic inquiry. A multicultural perspective for the psychoanalytic movement is not yet another theoretical-methodological shift in its trajectory, but the functional yield of modern currents that seek to cast a more sober light on theoretical construction and a brighter beam on the living human connection of the therapeutic field.

REFERENCES

Abramowitz, S. I., and Murray, J. (1983). Race effects in psychotherapy. In *Bias In Psychotherapy*, ed. J. Murray, and P. Abramson, pp. 215–255. New York: Praeger.

Aron, L. (1990). One-person and two-person psychologies and the method of psychoanalysis. *Psychoanalytic Psychology* 7:475–485.

Atkinson, D. R. (1985). A meta-review of research on cross-cultural counseling and psychotherapy. *Journal of Multicultural Counseling and Development* 1:138–153.

Basch-Kahre, E. (1984). On difficulties arising in transference and counter-transference when analyst and analysand have different socio-cultural back-grounds. *International Review of Psycho-Analysis* 11:61–277.

Bruner, J. S. (1986). Value presuppositions of developmental theory. In *Value Presuppositions in Theories of Human Development*, ed L. Cirillo, and S. Wapner, pp. 19–28. Hillsdale, NJ: Lawrence Erlbaum.

Carrithers, M., Collins, S., and Lukes, S., eds. (1985). *The Category of the Person*. Cambridge: Cambridge University Press.

Ferenczi, S. (1921). *Further Contributions to the Theory and Technique of Psycho-analysis*, 3rd. edition. London: Hogarth, 1969.

Foster, R. P. (1993). The social politics of psychoanalysis. Commentary on Neil Altman's "Psychoanalysis and the Urban Poor." *Psychoanalytic Dialogues* 3:69–84.

Freud, S. (1905). Three essays on the theory of sexuality. *Standard Edition* 7: 125–245.

Gill, M. (1982). *Analysis of Transference. I. Theory and Technique*. New York: International Universities Press.

—— (1983). The interpersonal paradigm and the degree of the therapist's involvement. *Contemporary Psychoanalysis* 19:200–237.

Greenberg, J. R. (1991). Countertransference and reality. *Psychoanalytic Dialogues* 1:52–73.

Hoffman, I. Z. (1983). The patient as interpreter of the analyst's experience. *Contemporary Psychoanalysis* 19:389–422.

Howard, G. S. (1991). Culture tales: a narrative approach to thinking, cross-cultural psychology, and psychotherapy. *American Psychology* 46:187–197.

Jacoby, R. (1983). *The Repression of Psychoanalysis*. New York: Basic Books.

James, W. (1977). *A Pluralistic Universe*. Cambridge: Harvard University Press.

Kirschner, S. R. (1990). The assenting echo: Anglo-American values in contemporary psychoanalytic developmental psychology. *Social Research* 57: 822–857.

Klein, M. (1930). The importance of symbol formation in the development of the ego. In *The Writings of Melanie Klein, vol. I*. London: Hogarth, 1975.

Lamb, S. (1991). Comment: An objectivist in social constructionist clothing. *American Psychology* 47:80.

McDougall, J. (1980). *Plea for a Measure of Abnormality*. New York: International Universities Press.

McNamee, S., and Gergen K. J. (1992). *Social Construction and the Therapeutic Process*. London: Sage.

Olarte, S.W., and Lenz, R. (1984). Learning to do psychoanalytic therapy with inner-city populations. *Journal of the American Academy of Psychoanalysis* 12:89–99.

Quine, W. V., and Ullian J. S. (1970). *The Web of Belief*. New York: Random House.

Racker, H. (1968). *Transference and Countertransference*. New York: International Universities Press.

Roland, A. (1988). *In Search of Self in India and Japan: Toward a Cross Cultural Psychology*. Princeton, NJ: Princeton University Press.

Shweder, R. A., and LaVine R., eds. (1984). *Culture Theory*. Cambridge: Cambridge University Press.

Spence, D. P. (1982). *Narrative Truth and Historical Truth*. New York: Norton.

Sue, S. (1988). Psychotherapeutic services for ethnic minorities. *American Psychologist* 43:301–308.

Wolstein, B. (1967). *Theory of Psychoanalytic Therapy*. New York: Grune & Stratton.

—— (1971). *Human Psyche in Psychoanalysis*. Springfield, IL: Charles C Thomas.

—— (1973). The new significance of psychic structure. In *Interpersonal Explorations in Psychoanalysis*. New York: Basic Books.

—— (1988). Introduction. In *Essential Papers on Countertransference*, ed. B. Wolstein, pp. 1–15. New York: New York University Press.

—— (1990). Five empirical psychoanalytic methods. *Contemporary Psychoanalysis* 26: 237–256.

—— (1992a). Aspects of contemporary pluralistic psychoanalysis. In *Relational Perspectives in Psychoanalysis*, ed. N. J. Skolnick and S. C. Warshaw. Hillsdale, NJ: Analytic Press.

—— (1992b). Resistance interlocked with countertransference. *Contemporary Psychoanalysis* 28:172–190.

—— (1994). The evolving newness of interpersonal psychoanalysis. *Contemporary Psychoanalysis* 30: 473–498.

2

The Social Conscience of Psychoanalysis

Michael Moskowitz, Ph.D.

Free yourself from mental slavery.
None but ourselves can free our minds
—Bob Marley, "Redemption Song"

When I taught in the City University of New York (CUNY) clinical psychology program, I often was asked, overtly and implicitly, to defend the relevance of psychoanalysis to the needs of the poor, the immigrant, and the oppressed. When I did demonstrate my concern and method of approach, I was often told, "You are not really psychoanalytic, certainly not Freudian, not one of them." Friends and colleagues working at that training clinic and in other public clinics and institutions have described similar experiences. Because I have always seen psychoanalysis as a radical procedure—derived from an even more radical theory—that could have a decisive influence on both individual and social structures, I was and am troubled by the common perception of it as irrelevant.

Psychoanalysis has a long history as a progressive social movement dedicated to the alleviation of common misery. Like all such movements, its revisionist and reactionary elements have at times dominated some part of the field. While these trends have been powerful, we should neither overestimate their influence nor allow them to blind us to the history or reality of much of the progressive focus of present-day psychoanalytic work. Most of all, these conservative developments should not blind us to the inherently progressive theoretical imperatives of every strain of psychoanalysis. Without doubt, every perspective has within it aspects that can be used with reactionary, repressive intent, but the basic thrust of a psychoanalytic position is progressive.

For a theory to be progressive it must hold foremost a belief in the potential for positive change. It must posit that while people are not perfectible, they are improvable, capable of being both happier and more moral than they are. This belief is based on several assumptions:

1. Many people live much of their lives in states of psychic suffering.
2. People generally and individually are capable of living more satisfying lives than they currently do.
3. Though much suffering is inevitable, much is avoidable.
4. Social structures are in part a product of an effort to keep the privileged privileged and thus less unhappy than those they exploit, although they pay a price in guilt and fear.
5. Social structures can be made better than they are.

In this chapter I will try to show that psychoanalysis as a progressive social force has been undermined by its continuing division along several different fault lines. The first is the bifurcation of critical social theory from both everyday clinical practice and the theory that informs it, which is to say that while critical theory developed and continues to develop as a radical critique of culture, its impact on practicing therapists has been minimal. As a consequence, clinical practice and theory can be justifiably criticized for having an insufficient appreciation of social factors, while social theory can be criticized for being clinically remote.

Within the clinical field itself there are other divisions relevant to this discussion. The first is the one between the repressively rigid, authoritarian, elitist, and moralistic version of psychoanalysis that gained ascendance as the official psychoanalysis in the United States and remained dominant until recently, and a looser, more egalitarian and accessible psychoanalysis that is now coming to the fore. When I refer to the clinical field, clinical theory, and clinical practice I am referring to the whole body of knowledge on which the typical psychoanalytically informed clinician relies. It includes what is found in all the major psychoanalytic journals and books to which clinicians refer, and developmental theory and research that are clinically relevant. It does not include social theory and research, which almost never find their way into the major psychoanalytic journals. The second division to be addressed here is the split between intrapsychic and interpersonal perspectives, with the former perspective (over)emphasizing constitutional and internal factors while neglecting the impact of interpersonal reality, and the latter one (over)emphasizing external factors while ignoring or underemphasizing intrapsychic reality.

While the motivations underlying these divisions are undoubtedly complex, I propose that one major contributing factor is the fact that a cohesive socially conscious psychoanalysis would amount to a powerful progressive social force that would challenge the cultural status quo. Because of this potential power, as psychoanalysis has moved in this progressive direction it has engaged socially conservative forces that now threaten its suppression.

THE BIFURCATION OF SOCIAL THEORY AND CLINICAL PRACTICE

When psychoanalysis and Marxism came of age together in Central Europe in the first part of the twentieth century, they shared a common goal and a common means. The goal was the understanding and alleviation of human misery. The means was the analysis of false consciousness. Both posited that humans participate in processes of self-deception that perpetuate both individual unhappiness and authoritarian social structures. Though Freud saw this process as internally motivated and Marx saw it as a response to external oppression, their commonalities drew the attention of socially conscious intellectuals throughout Europe and Russia.

The social implications of Freud's psychoanalysis are at once apparent and difficult to grasp. Freud saw culture as a vast compromise formation between the forces of love and aggression. Neurosis was an individualized internalization of that conflict, with individualized compromise formations built on a cultural template. Some compromise formations, particularly those undertaken under developmental immaturity or the impact of trauma, are less satisfying and more painful than others. Clinical psychoanalysis was conceived of as a procedure for developing a relationship that allowed for understanding and changing the impact of those internalizations. Though many early analysts believed in making treatment accessible to the poor and thus worked in low fee public clinics, they also recognized that any individual treatment could have only limited social impact, and that it could only partly repair damage that had already been done. In a letter to the Harvard neurologist James Jackson Putnam, Freud wrote, "the recognition of our therapeutic limitations reinforces our determination to change other social factors so that men and women shall no longer be forced into hopeless situations" (Turkle 1978, p. 142). In *Future of an Illusion* (1927) he wrote:

> One thus gets the impression that civilization is something which was imposed on a resisting majority by a minority which understood how to obtain possession of the means to power and coercion. [p. 6]

And further:

> It is to be expected that these underprivileged classes will envy the favored ones their privileges and will do what they can to free themselves from their own surplus of privation. Where this is not possible, a permanent measure of discontent will exist within the culture concerned. [p. 12]

Elsewhere (1919) he wrote:

> We shall probably discover that the poor are even less ready to part with their neuroses than the rich, because the hard life that awaits them if they recover offers them no attraction, and illness gives them one more claim to social help. . . . whatever form this psychotherapy for the people may take, whatever the elements out of which it is compounded, its most effective and most important ingredients will assuredly remain those borrowed from strict and untendentious psycho-analysis. [pp. 167–168]

While clearly seeing that culture extracted a price in suffering, and from some more than others, Freud proposed no comprehensive program of social change. He did write about the pernicious effects of religious and overly restrictive education and advocated openness of sexual discussion with and sexual education of children. Yet Freud remained a pessimist when it came to implementing social change that would have meaningful long-term effects. He saw most Marxists as hopelessly naive. Freud's perspective was a Hobbesian one, which sees people as naturally selfish in the pursuit of desires, with aggression and sexuality needing to be tamed for culture to develop. Though he believed the situation could be better, since some people were much less unhappy than others, he seemed to reject the possibility of dramatically altering the balance between nature and culture, since culture reflected nature.

The French literary historian and critic Emile Faguet wrote that if Rousseau's claim that man is born free but is everywhere in chains is true, then "it would be equally correct to say that sheep are born carnivores and everywhere eat grass" (O'Brien 1991, p. 60). Freud was actually more crass in his assessment. Responding to Wilhelm Reich's report of utopian communal experiments in the then new Soviet Union, Freud said that trying to do away with the oedipal conflict by eliminating the family is like attempting to cure an intestinal disorder by stopping up the anus (Berman 1988).

Still, psychoanalysis and social activism made natural allies. Pre-Stalinist Soviet Union was the site of psychoanalytically informed experiments in child rearing. However, after visiting one such experimental environment, Reich (1974) prophetically concluded that if more was not done in the area of loosening sexual morality, the great experiment would soon deteriorate into a repressive bureaucracy.

In Germany, a more or less loose association of liberal intellectuals, all in some way affiliated with the Frankfurt Institute of Social Research, devoted their attention to understanding the unconscious meaning of social processes and institutions, particularly domination, oppression, and the failure of revolutions. This group and its students have come to be known collectively as the Frankfurt School, and their method of analysis as critical theory. (The original group included Walter Benjamin, Horkheimer, Adorno, Marcuse, Fromm, and to some extent Reich and Fenichel. The second generation included Habermas and Foucault and the influence of the Frankfurt School is seen clearly in the work of Lacan and Fanon.)

Though it has had profound influence on legal and literary theory, the impact of critical theory on mainstream clinical psychoanalysis has unfortunately been minimal. Only recently, in the work of feminist analysts such as Jessica Benjamin and Nancy Chodorow, has it exerted any real influence on mainstream psychoanalytic theory.

Unlike Freud's, Marx's theory was predictive and utopian. It stated the conditions for revolution and the evolution toward a utopian state. The failure of the 1918 German revolution and the rapid reinstitution of domination and repression following the Russian revolution led Horkheimer, Fromm, Adorno, Marcuse, and others to apply psychoanalytic insights to the question of why people allow themselves to be oppressed and in fact often identify with their oppressors. Their work led in significant theoretical directions and included seminal research on the authoritarian personality.

Freud's theory lacked a utopian dimension. He saw civilization as, at best, an unhappy compromise between the desires of the individual and the requirements of the larger group. In order to develop a utopian vision Marcuse (1955) proposed the possibility of what he called non-repressive sublimation. It involved some way of loving society as an extension of one's self, that is, loving narcissistically. He did not, unfortunately, address the question of how one can love others narcissistically while at the same time allowing them the right to a separate existence. Marcuse's vision was that of a polymorphously sexual utopia in which people work very little and live in unity with nature. His work provided the theoretical backdrop for many of the utopian experiments of the late 1960s. Other important psychoanalytic critics of American culture who wrote in the '60s included Norman Brown, Franz Fanon, Grier and Cobbs, and Marcuse's student Angela Davis.

An especially important outgrowth of critical theory was the major psychoanalytic research project on the authoritarian personality, which was headed by Adorno (Adorno et al. 1982) in the late 1940s and early 1950s. Its source and implications have been overly simplified in secondary sources. This research was funded by the American Jewish Committee, and its explicit goal was to identify potential fascists and to define potential modes of intervention. A primary assumption of the Frankfurt School was that "every social organization produces those character structures which it needs for its preservation. In class society, the ruling class secures its position, with the aid of education and the institution of the family, by making its ideology the ruling ideology of all members of the society" (Reich 1972, p. xvii).

The authoritarian personality—here meaning someone who willingly follows the dictates of a cruel authority—was hypothesized to be nurtured by a particular oedipal constellation common to industrial-capitalist society. In this constellation, the father is either relatively absent and ineffectual or relatively absent and punitive. The child turns away from the father to the state-culture to provide structure and ideals. He turns away with anger and guilt, having in fantasy destroyed the father. In his search for a new ideal father, the person easily falls under the sway of authorities who control the individual and direct his anger and projected self-reproaches at enemies and outgroups. Because of the appeal of its simplicity and inclusiveness, variations of this theme were incorporated by Fanon (1963, 1967) to explain racism and more recently by Chodorow (1978) to explain men's lack of empathy. While the model has been critiqued in terms of its oedipal focus and male centeredness, and while an adequate model of the female authoritarian personality has yet to be articulated, the authoritarian personality research findings seem to apply to women as well as men.

Adorno's research group developed a simple questionnaire designed to measure authoritarianism. Known as the F scale, which has been shown to be valid in forms as short as fourteen questions (Ray 1979), it also proved to be a good measure of racist tendencies. In fact, the most powerful finding in forty years of F scale research has been the consistent relationship of authoritarianism, as measured by the scale, to racist tendencies and ideology. The relationship has been described as "one of the most enduring in the social science literature" (Ray 1988, p. 673). Although Adorno's methodology has been roundly attacked, and his psychoanalytic formulations critiqued, reviewing the more than 1200 studies on authoritarianism conducted through 1983, Meleon and colleagues (1988) concluded that the concept of authoritarianism is valid and that the hypothesized relationships among authoritarianism, racism, conservatism, and sexism have been repeatedly confirmed.

There are several reasons for recalling this research and reviewing its findings. One is the fact that this psychoanalytic research is almost never described in the psychological literature as psychoanalytic, and that the dynamic developmental hypotheses on which it is based are also typically ignored. The research is thus stripped of its deep meaning and described as social psychology research. This is an example of a pattern that repeats—psychoanalytic research is either attacked or ignored by the academic psychologists. When its findings are too powerful to ignore they are removed from the theory and given explanations that are devoid of the stipulation of unconscious meaning. Psychoanalysts themselves, for the most part, also ignore the research.

Another reason to recall Adorno's work is—and this seems to be the case with most psychoanalytic research—that its social policy implications have been ignored. While many these days seem eager to jump on the biological bandwagon that proposes to identify genetically violence-prone youth, we seem unable to take seriously even the possibility that we could develop tools for identifying authoritarian and racist attitudes and the familial-cultural structures that nurture them.

An awareness of this historical-theoretical background is useful in trying to understand why psychoanalysis in the United States has come to be viewed by many as politically conservative and socially impotent. The powerful tools for social research, cultural analysis, and change that psychoanalytic theory offers have been largely ignored by both the mainstream clinical profession and in public policy debate. Psychoanalytic social theory hangs in midair unattached to an official organization. To make matters worse, the clinical field has been subject to internal and external forces and resultant phenomena that further diminish its social relevance and even threaten its survival as a therapeutic modality accessible to more than the elite few. These phenomena can be summarized as: the repression of psychoanalysis, the splitting of psychoanalysis, and the suppression of psychoanalysis.

REPRESSION

Like Russell Jacoby (1983) I am using the term repression as an analogue of the individual intrapsychic process of repression. In the social context, repression is understood to be an interorganizational phenomenon, motivated by fear, that entails the forgetting of aspects of memory and desire and leads to inhibitions and unsatisfying compromises (symptoms) evidenced in the way that groups relate to each other.

Jacoby (1983) traces the transformation of the culture of psychoanalysis as it moved from Europe to the United States. Jacoby views this move as a virtual abandonment of a culture that was intensely social, radical, Bohemian, and political, and feels that almost nothing of the original project has survived. The main figures in the movement, which included prominent analysts Otto Fenichel and Edith Jacobson, essentially actively hid their political beliefs in order to fit into a conservative and anti-communist time. Jacoby traces the transformation of this politically radical group into a frightened and hidden one that continued to be clinically influential but stripped itself of political content, one that became identified with the group that stood for mainstream psychoanalysis— The American Psychoanalytic Association otherwise known as the American. While Jacoby's analysis is eye opening, persuasive, and sad, it is also thankfully, incomplete.

In equating American psychoanalysis with the American Psychoanalytic Association Jacoby, I think, unfortunately takes part in the repression that he so powerfully documents. For Jacoby identifies all that went on outside of the American with revisionist psychoanalysis, a psychoanalysis divorced from its radical roots. This was not the case, as I will later show.

Nostra Culpa

Still, the impact of the actions of the American cannot be overestimated. Many analysts, myself included, have asked, what have we done to deserve our conservative and socially irrelevant reputation? In truth, we have done a great deal. I use the word we here in order to refer to a sense of collective responsibility in the same way that a young German might say, "We take responsibility for the actions of our grandparents." I am suggesting that one should bear responsibility for the cultural heritage to which one is heir. We have a responsibility to examine our past in order both to preserve the best of it and avoid repeating the worst of it.

The American Psychoanalytic Association dominated psychoanalysis in the United States from 1911 until very recently. Although it never numbered more than 3000 members, its rigorous training/indoctrination methods and technical procedures set a standard others either tried to emulate or against which they rebelled. It set criteria for analyzabiltiy that excluded most people in need of help. Homosexuals were seen as unanalyzable and thus were denied training (Lewes 1995). Under the cover of high standards and scientific objectivity, a puritanical American morality very different from the Bohemian cosmopolitanism of the European analytic community was imposed. Dissension was not tolerated. The resulting lack of vitality and originality led a historian of psychoanalysis to write, "Psychoanalysis had finally become legitimate and respectable perhaps paying the price in becoming sluggish and smug, hence attractive to an increasing number of minds which find security in conformity and prosperity" (Oberndorf 1953, p. 207).

With rare exception, the American sanctioned only the training of psychiatrists and under conditions so monastically rigorous that most people with any hope of having a family life before age 40 found it intolerable. When non-medical people were allowed in for training they had to sign a waiver promising not to practice clinical psychoanalysis. Women, who made up about 30 percent of the analysts immigrating to the United States, accounted for only 9 percent of the students in training at approved institutes in 1958 (Jacoby 1983).

The attitude of the American with regard to homosexuals and non-medical analysts directly contradicted Freud's. Freud even considered expelling the American from the International Psychoanalytic Association over the issue of training non-medical analysts, but the political uncertainties of Europe forced him to look toward the United States as a safe haven. The battle over the medicalization of psychoanalysis has been well documented (Gay 1988, Schneider and Desmond 1994). Reeling from the findings of the Flexner report of 1910, which chastised American medicine for shoddy training and the production of charlatans and snake oil sellers, medical psychoanalysts wanted to establish respectability for a profession already tainted by sexuality and Jewish cosmopolitanism. But it is worth reiterating that not only did the American exclude non-medical doctors from membership—and threatened their members with expulsion if they trained outside of official channels—it also promulgated the most rigid and elitist form of psychoanalysis as the only true method. These elitist practices are well described by Rendon in Chapter 3 of this volume.

The rigid clinical approach that was presented as the only true psycho-analysis had a particularly insidious effect. All work that was different from the official model was seen as lesser than, watered down, unortho-dox, merely psychotherapy. Even Leo Stone's groundbreaking work on treating more disturbed patients—which was really only groundbreaking within the context of the American—was seen by many as soft, a depar-ture from the real thing. Parameters were seen as unfortunate, even if necessary. The fact that many of Freud's patients were extremely dis-turbed, and that his practice deviated from rigid technique more often than not (Ellman 1991, Roazen 1995) was distorted or ignored. Since few real patients and treatment situations met the psychoanalytic ideal, people often lied about or incompletely described what they did, not revealing their practice of reducing fees, supportive interventions, working with families, reducing the frequency of sessions and so on, further perpetu-ating the myth that these interventions were not part of analysis. Thank-fully this has since changed, but damage has been done. As I will show in Chapter 9, the ideal patient in classical treatment who does not require parameters is largely a social aberration.

While analysts were advertising strict standards for the conduct of analysis four or five times a week on the couch, no social contact with patients, and sternly criticizing therapists who did otherwise, those pa-tients with sufficient money or power were often treated in whatever way they desired. This was rarely acknowledged and never discussed in the professional literature. While hypocrisy may be the norm in professional organizations it seems particularly troubling in a group devoted to the analysis of self-deception. Despite professing that their exclusionary criteria were necessary to ensure high standards of practice, the evidence suggests that technical and ethical principles were violated by analysts in the American with a frequency similar to those of outlaw psychoanalytic organizations. Some of the more infamous violations of analytic protocol are depicted by Farber and Green (1993).

In the meantime, most psychoanalytic treatment went on outside the context of the American. A plethora of different psychoanalytic training sites and clinics developed. Some were modeled after the American; others were quite different. Many of these places had clinics that offered therapy for non-traditional patients at low fees, successfully applying psychoanalytic principles to underserved and disadvantaged populations. Yet because the practice was unofficial, it never got the recognition it deserved. Often, trained psychoanalysts worked or supervised in those settings, yet it was rarely written about, and even more rarely researched. And the social application of psychoanalysis went unrecognized.

As a result of a long legal battle in 1989, the American Psychoanalytic Association agreed to admit non-medical candidates into training and to pay substantial costs and legal fees ($650,000) to the plaintiffs (Schneider and Desmond 1994). In the meantime, the International Psychoanalytic Association has begun the process of fully accrediting several non-American institutes. Most training still goes on outside the auspices of these organizations. While many in the American opposed its policies and taught and supervised in non-member institutes, many others still seem unable to acknowledge the harm that has been done. Some appear incredulous that psychologists and social workers are not now eager to join the American. They expect the excluded and ignored to come to the aid of the now ailing exclusionary organization. While some psychologist-psychoanalysts are eager for reconciliation, others remain opposed, and much of academic clinical psychology, once open to psychoanalytic ideas, has moved into an actively antipsychoanalytic position.

Having said all of this, I want to make clear that I do not think the largest factors motivating the American's policies were greed or the desire for personal power. I am convinced that those who battled to uphold the exclusionary and rigid requirements of the American thought they were doing what was best for psychoanalysis. Repressively moralistic forces always think they are right, and they always are, in part. A progressive socially involved psychoanalysis probably could not have flourished in pre-sixties America. So official psychoanalysis was molded into a moralistic, puritanical, materialistic organization that was accepted by our culture and was, for a time, well rewarded by the ruling class that it served.

SPLITTING

Splitting is used here in both its non-technical literal sense to refer to actual organizational splits, and as a metaphorical analogue to the individual process. As in the individual process, the term refers to the coexistence within a single entity of two or more contrary and independent attitudes, and it is inferred that the persistence of splits in the face of their obvious illogical and self-defeating qualities belies a defensive process.

The actual social structure of psychoanalysis has been characterized by splits almost from the beginning. Like the now frequently encountered and often diagnosed borderline patient, psychoanalytic organizations have had a hard time maintaining contradictory ideas and multiple perspectives. The early splits of Jung and Adler from Freud have been variously analyzed as having been due to either a rejectingly authoritarian father or an unappeasably rebellious son. The truth probably lies somewhere. Yet the recent interpretations of the work of Ferenczi and his relationship to Freud offer the tantalizing possibility of a loving psychoanalytic relationship that contains disagreement and conflict. Still the half-life of psychoanalytic societies, particularly in their heyday, often seemed to approach trans-uranium elements in their brevity. For example, Horney's group split off from New York Psychoanalytic in 1941, and within three years had split into three other groups—the original Horney group, the William Alanson White Institute, and an institute at New York Medical College (for a further discussion see Rendon Chapter 3).

The prestige and power of the American did seem to enable it to contain some splits. Few wanted to leave an organization that wielded such authority. Yet within this organization, unofficial splitting continued, resulting in factions that stopped interacting. The Chicago institute's division into Kohut's self psychological group, which stood apart from the more traditional analysts, is a good example (Gedo, in press).

Outside of the American Psychoanalytic Association, groups splintered along lines of uncertain definition, sometimes leading to the formation of rival groups with similar ideologies that often shared key faculty. Other groups developed under the auspices of charismatic leaders like Robert

Langs and Hyman Spotnitz. The nitpicky issues that sometimes divided psychoanalysis seemed to give full meaning to Freud's notion of the narcissism of small differences. Although an eclectic and flexible psychoanalytic training institution such as the New York University Postdoctoral Program in Psychotherapy and Psychoanalysis absorbed dissension more successfully, it too became home to many informal and two formal splits in the time since its inception. Yet the overall structure and holding environment inspired by Bernie Kalinkowitz, one of the foremost clinical psychologists and psychoanalytic educators in the United States, did serve to keep the communicative flow of ideas going, resulting in the closest thing psychoanalysis has had to an open academic environment.

While it is possible to analyze the personal rivalries and eccentricities that led to these various splits, the persistence of this phenomenon should lead one to infer a powerful underlying dynamic. The group psychology of psychoanalysis is undoubtedly as complex as that of any group—perhaps the numerous irrational rivalries are reflective of the theories' relative lack of attention to sibling issues—but I would propose that at least one powerful factor is the movement's resistance to confronting its relationship to contemporary culture. A unified psychoanalysis would be forced into the uncomfortable position of questioning its place in the overall social context rather than focusing on the relationship among its various and warring parts.

There is today a sense of progressive and evolving integration. Its motivations are difficult to disentangle, but it does bring with it feelings of hopefulness, tempered by the realization that mainstream, institute-based psychoanalysis has—in part by virtue of its splits—made itself increasingly irrelevant to the mental health needs of contemporary culture. Still, it is heartening to see that previously doctrinaire journals such as the *Psychoanalytic Quarterly* and the *Journal of the American Psychoanalytic Association* are now open to authors of all orientations, and that object relations viewpoints have become part of the mainstream. It is now hard to believe, and seems like a bad dream, that Kleinian thought was at one time dismissed by most American institutes as crazy, that Winnicott was treated with disrespect, and that even Loewald and Stone were held as heretical by many. It is to the enduring credit of Stone, Loewald, and others like them that they persisted in the face of a withering orthodoxy, holding on to the core of a Freudian viewpoint. Much credit is also due to Kernberg who introduced a Kleinian viewpoint to many for the first time.

While applauding current trends toward mutual respect and integration we must recognize the persistence of one particular split that runs through the history of psychoanalysis and still threatens to create an unbridgeable divide supported by antagonistic professional organizations. Now that the American has lost its power, and hopefully its desire to promote a particularly restrictive and elitist version of psychoanalysis, other organizational entities that have emerged are attempting to define what is "true" analysis, while others have continued to work in opposition, an opposition that, in a different way, threatens to strip the theory of its progressive potential.

To reiterate a previous point, the progressive and even revolutionary implications of psychoanalytic therapy were not lost on Freud, many early analysts, and the Frankfurt School. Yet their revolutionary zeal was blunted by the enormity of the undertaking. The development of a less repressive society would necessitate the undermining of many of the core structures of culture. Such change was only articulated in the utopian visions of Marcuse (1955) and Brown(1959). With the transformation of Freudian analysis into a politically conservative medical subspecialty, its revolutionary implications were repressed, but they remained embedded in the theory, which continued to posit basic human needs that remain chronically unsatisfied.

Other early analysts, perhaps starting with Adler, saw Freud's theory as positing too much in the way of an inevitable conflict between biological desires and cultural constraints. Human nature was seen as more pliable and thus more easily satisfied by smaller adjustments in social conditions. Ironically, it was perhaps this non-revolutionary view that turned out to be politically empowering, since the undertaking it pointed to did not seem so enormous.

The Intrapsychic-Interpersonal Divide

Though this line of demarcation is blurry, a significant theoretical division developed, which continues to split psychoanalysis. One side of the divide has been variously described as: Intrapsychic, Freudian, Classical, Conflict Theory, Drive Theory, Kleinian, Biological, Essentialist, Nativist, Object Relational. The other side has been identified as: Neo-Freudian, Revisionist, Sullivanian, Interpersonal, Social Constructionist, Cultural, Relational, and

Object Relational. While there is a danger of losing meaning in trying to simplify this divide—which has been so persistent in psychoanalysis—for purposes of this discussion it can be made short and stark.

Early revisionist critics of Freud saw his theory as too biologically determined. Innate forces of sex and aggression were seen as less consequential, and what Freud saw as an inevitable conflict between drives and culture was seen rather as an expression of a particularly puritanical cultural environment. As this side of the divide developed—through the work of people such as Horney, Sullivan, Thompson, and most recently Mitchell and Altman, notions of conflicting desires gave way to ideas of conflicting relationships. The innate was viewed as unimportant or nonexistent.

For example, Mitchell (1988)writes, "Relational-model theories view mind as fundamentally dyadic and *interactive*; above all else, minds seek contact, engagement with other minds. Psychic organization and structures are built from patterns which shape those interactions" (pp. 3–4). For reasons that remain unclear, Mitchell maintains that a model that posits endogenous, biological, inborn propensities and motivations for satisfaction, which in psychoanalysis have been called drives, is incompatible with a model that pays sufficient attention to interpersonal processes and their role in the construction of personal meaning. He for instance (Mitchell 1993) misinterprets Parens' (1979) research to argue that there is no aggressive drive, when in fact, Parens explicitly concludes quite the opposite. Mitchell, like other interpersonal theorists, seems to believe that a theory must choose between environment and biology, that these are and must remain unintegratable dichotomies (see Peace and Newton 1963 for an earlier version of this position).

This lack of attention to—or even disavowal of—the innate has been a source of great consternation to those on the other side of the divide, and, interestingly, particularly for those who had some interest in social issues. (Most clinical Freudians ignored the important work of the interpersonalists, which has probably only added to the continuing venom.) Marcuse (1955, 1956), reacting to what he viewed as Fromm's apostasy, wrote several devastating attacks on the interpersonalist perspective. Jacoby (1975), Juliet Mitchell (1974), and others who were influenced by the Frankfurt School, expanded and continued the assault. Succinctly stated, their critique says that a theory that does not posit a fundamental nature cannot speak to the fundamental dialectic between nature and culture, which means that no cultural practice can be viewed by such a theory as a fundamental violation; therefore, all cultural forms are tolerable. This leads to a tendency to adaptationalism—the triumph of the therapeutically palliative over the analytically radical.

Fromm replied to Marcuse, I think correctly, that his position implied that anything short of utopia was revisionist hell. Marcuse in this context did in fact reject clinical work as "mere therapy." This debate between two clearly progressive psychoanalytic theorists demonstrates that the line between conformist adaptationalism and realistic compromise is a difficult one to draw.

In the meantime, name calling continues on both sides. Some writers from the relational perspective, a position first named and articulated by Greenberg and Mitchell (1983), have made a special point of attacking the Freudian position whenever possible. The assertion that drive and object relations models are irreconcilable is repeatedly made without logical or factual support. Since Greenberg and Mitchell first made this assertion it has been reiterated in various forms, such as Altman's (1993a,b) claim that "drive/structure" and "relational/structure" models can in no way be integrated. Yet it has never been shown that Freud or any other significant theorist put forth a drive model that is not at the same time also a relational model. It is also hard to know what to make of Mitchell's and Altman's insistence on the irreconcilability of drive and relational models, given the fact that such an integration has been the main thrust of modern Freudian and object relations positions in the psychoanalysis articulated in the work of such writers as Bach (1994), Ellman (1991), Loewald (1980), Ogden (1994), Poland (1996), Steingart (1995), and Stone (1984).

Altman (Chapter 10, this volume) goes out of his way to attack his socially conscious Freudian colleagues. He paints a picture of a one-person psychology that is a caricature of analytic understanding and technique and bears no relationship to the work advocated by contemporary analysts of any intellectual stature. Similarly, in a previous paper, Altman (1993b) attacks Bergman's (1993) position that ego psychological and object relational positions are indeed compatible and complementary. Bergman presents a clinically rich statement describing her integration of ego psychological and object relational perspectives. Her work is in the direct tradition of the Freudian model of early intervention and prevention, a tradition that includes the work of Anna Freud, Spitz, Fraiberg, Mahler, and Parens. It is in a tradition of social activism that is consistent with the approaches of Fenichel, Jacobson, and the Frankfurt School.

Illustrating an integration of psychoanalytic perspectives, she writes: "The approach is developmental as well as psychodynamic. This means that it is based on knowledge of early development within the caretaker–child dyad as well as the knowledge of the beginnings of intrapsychic conflicts. Our aim is to create a facilitating environment in Winnicott's sense. We attempt to create an environment that allows for the creation of mind and the creation of meaning" (1993, p. 57). Still, Altman berates Bergman for adopting "a frame of reference that is essentially ego psychological" (1993b, p. 86), as if that were enough to consign it to social irrelevance.

It is a paradox worth pondering that a clearly socially conscious analyst like Altman (see Chapter 10, this volume) should attack other clearly socially conscious analysts such as Bergman, Holmes, and Schachter and Butts. Yet he stands in a long psychoanalytic tradition of one socially conscious analyst attacking another. Perhaps, in fact, the anger of Mitchell, Altman, and some others of the relational school—who are the heirs of the tradition of Sullivan and Fromm—is made understandable by the scorn with which their forebears were treated by mainstream American psychoanalysis. But I think there is more to it than that. The multiple splits within the field, in particular the everpresent one between nativists and culturalists, function to keep psychoanalysis from turning its attention to the outside world and furthering and developing its critique of culture.

Freud tried hard to turn the attention of psychoanalysis to the pathologies of civilization. In 1927, he wrote:

> [I]t is understandable that the suppressed people will develop an intense hostility towards a culture whose existence they make possible by their work, but in whose wealth they have too small a share. In such conditions an internalization of the cultural prohibitions among the suppressed people is not to be expected. On the contrary, they are not prepared to acknowledge the prohibitions, they are intent on destroying the culture itself, and possibly doing away with the postulates on which it is based. [p. 12]

Freud was writing here, at least in part, about himself and psychoanalysis. This statement appears in *Future of an Illusion*, a work in which Freud attempted to undermine one of the basic postulates of Western civilization—religion and the belief in God. Elsewhere (1910) he wrote: "Since we destroy illusions we are accused of endangering ideals" (p. 147). For Freud the task of psychoanalysis was not only to liberate the individual from the illusions of childhood but also to liberate us from the illusions of civilization. It appears too that Freud is making explicit a motivation for revolution when he speaks to the futility of mainstream culture's attempt to force its values upon those that it oppresses.

This liberation is a frightening task and one that many analysts consciously disdain. Bergler (1951), for example, writes, "Psychoanalytic psychiatry has neither reformatory, political nor propagandistic aims" (p. xvi). Others such as Fairbairn (1952) have offered simplistic and reactionary analyses of revolutionary forces. As Javier and Herron (1992) write, "In fact, it is as though all the prominent psychologies of present-day psychoanalysis—drive, ego, object, and self—fixate on individuals and repress their own inspirational roots. Early analysts were after all a militant lot, not just among themselves, a tradition that has regrettably been maintained, but they also used to joust with society, a tradition that is being sorely neglected" (p. 460). Even those analysts who have achieved wide general recognition as cultural critics—such as Erikson and Coles—receive remarkably little notice within the clinical field, and radical social critics such as Kovel, Marcuse, Brown, and Koenigsberg are positively ignored.

THE SUPPRESSION OF PSYCHOANALYSIS

Isn't it interesting that psychoanalysis was most influential and culturally mainstream when it was at its most reactionary and moralistic? During the heyday of psychoanalysis in the United States sentiments such as Bergler's, cited above, predominated. More than one analyst trained in the prime of the American has said something like "Psychoanalysis is like custom tailoring. It's only for those who appreciate it and can afford it." I will not belabor this point about the obviously elitist, classist core of mainstream psychoanalysis in the United States. What I wish to highlight and to stress is that alongside the elitist psychoanalysis there developed a shadow, a progressive, socially involved, clinically diverse psychoanalysis that was first repressed, and is now, having been brought into the light, being massively suppressed. I am suggesting that the present suppression of psychoanalysis—under the auspices of managed care and biological psychiatry, is due not to the failure of psychoanalysis but to its success.

In many ways psychoanalysis was admirably successful in fulfilling Albee's (1969) project of bringing psychology to the people. While the American Psychoanalytic Association restricted training to the few, alternative psychoanalytic training institutes bloomed like wildflowers especially in major metropolitan areas. In New York City alone, there are approximately seventy-five such places. Many people trained at these places—social workers, psychologists, and others—went on to work and train at clinics, hospitals and other public institutions. Through most of the '70s, inner city hospitals and clinics provided psychoanalytically informed treatment to their patient populations. For example, the New Hope Guild, the largest outpatient treatment facility in New York State, offers approximately 250,000 patient hours a year in psychoanalytically oriented treatment for fees as low as fifty cents.

The CUNY clinical psychology program at City College, which has a small, student-run clinic, currently sees over 140 mostly poor and minority patients in over 10,000 hours annually of psychoanalytic or psychoanalytically informed psychotherapy for very low fees or even no fee at all. Also at City, Anni Bergman ran a comprehensive treatment program for severely disturbed children, mostly from very poor and minority backgrounds. This program was maintained with intermittent funding and minimal institutional support for nearly twenty years. These are but a few examples of many. Mosher and Gunderson (1979) and Karon and VandenBos (1994) have reported on the successes that similar intensive treatment programs have had with people diagnosed as psychotic.

Psychoanalysis and psychoanalytic therapy are now available to more people at lower fees than ever before and their availability will undoubtedly expand (Karon 1994). Psychoanalytic thought has become embedded in modern culture and psychoanalytic treatment is now widely accepted and valued. A recent Consumer Reports study (Seligman 1995) found not only that people substantially benefit from psychotherapy but also that, generally, the longer the treatment the better its results.

Yet there is a sense of fear, disillusionment, and doubt, partly due to the fact that the psychoanalytic perspective is under sustained attack by regressive forces within this culture. Ever since the cultural upheavals of the '60s there has been an overall societal effort to reverse progressive trends and re-restrict access to psychoanalytic treatment to the elite. The intrusions of government and insurance companies threaten the very basis of psychoanalytic treatment—its confidentiality—as they turn psychotherapists into government agents (Bollas and Sundelson 1995). Studies confirming both the human effectiveness and the cost effectiveness of psychotherapy—particularly in reducing medical use and costs—are routinely ignored, and biological psychiatry attempts to regain its power backed by the enormous funding of the pharmaceutical companies. Any scholarly work that raises serious questions about the effectiveness of biological treatments (see Fisher and Greenberg 1989) and in fact demonstrates that their utility, while real, is limited, gets shunted aside, while books such as *Listening to Prozac* (Kramer 1993), which offer anecdotal testimonials of questionable virtue (see Nuland 1994), achieve cultic status. Meanwhile a growing number of children (now well over one million) receive powerful drugs after being labeled with a diagnosis of dubious validity, reflecting the thinking of many in this culture who would rather drug and suppress our children than care for them (Breggin and Breggin 1994, McGuinness 1989, 1991).

Psychoanalytic approaches are frequently criticized for being unsupported by research (see for example Crews 1994) and even fundamentally unscientific (Hook 1959). For this, psychoanalysts bear some considerable blame. When government money was available and psychoanalysts were flush with income, much of it was squandered. Institutes used very little of it to build structures for research and scholarship. Research was often held in disdain and the psychoanalytic situation was seen as unresearchable by many. Research done outside of mainstream psychoanalysis was often ignored and not integrated. Still, psychoanalytic theory has received extensive empirical support, and the theory itself has evolved in response to new empirical findings.

It would be futile to attempt to reference even a small portion of the research that lends support to the psychoanalytic perspective (but see Barron et al. 1992, Fisher and Greenberg 1985). It should also be noted that much research—such as the authoritarian personality research cited previously and much current developmental research that is psychoanalytically informed—is often not characterized as psychoanalytic. A piece in the *APA Monitor* (Azar 1995) on attachment theory provides a good example of academic psychology's suppression of psychoanalysis.

In some ways psychoanalysis has fulfilled Freud's prophecy that its greater value would lie not in therapy but in the possibilities for early intervention and prevention, that is, in progressive social change. Many psychoanalytically informed child researchers find themselves becoming child advocates making social policy recommendations as their research points to the need for high quality child care. Many child policy experts such as Spock, Brazelton, and Bowlby are psychoanalytically trained. Once again this goes unacknowledged.

The parallels between the reception of developmental research and the authoritarian personality research of the Frankfurt School are uncanny. Findings that support the theory—and in particular the progressive implications of the theory—are either ignored or stripped of their progressive connection.

Where To From Here?

Despite all these difficulties, the progressive intent of the psychoanalytic perspective keeps asserting itself. It is our only comprehensive theory of human liberation. It is the only theory that considers the interplay between biological needs and the social forces that either satisfy or frustrate them. It is the only theory so far that posits both a conceptualization of the mechanism for the all too common internalization of oppression and self-loathing, as well as a potentially liberating treatment. In other countries, such as France (Turkle 1978), Germany (Kachele 1995) and Nicaragua (Langer 1989) psychoanalysts have been more publicly involved in social policy debate (see also Thoma and Kachele 1994 for a discussion of psychoanalysis and government health insurance), but there is no doubt that the impact of psychoanalysis on American culture—particularly on the liberation movements of women, children, and sexual minorities—has been enormous. While the sexual revolution in part has been inspired by psychoanalysis it continues to go on largely without comment by the psychoanalytic community (Koenigsberg 1989). Child-rearing practices have changed markedly, in part inspired by psychoanalysts like Spock and Brazelton, yet again this goes on largely unrecognized in the psychoanalytic literature. Regressive forces within the culture and repressive forces within ourselves are powerful. It seems dangerous to take credit for something when by doing so we also place ourselves in the position of taking the blame. Yet if we are to have a voice in the public arena and not lose the gains we have made, it is time to stand together and assert what we stand for and what are values are.

A Question of Values

Psychoanalysts have come a long way toward dismantling the elitist and repressive structure of institutional psychoanalysis and healing divisive internal splits. In this volume a diverse group of us have tried to articulate socially conscious treatment approaches. We have taken a progressive stance that offers psychoanalysis as a universally applicable tool for human liberation. But the split between those of us mainly labeled Freudian and those labeled relational still needs further attention. The attack of some in the relational position on the Freudian position has largely been an attack on the former's hypothesizing of innate needs, propensities, and desires. While many specifics of the critique of various aspects of the Freudian drive model are undoubtedly warranted, such a wholesale rejection of any model of innate desire is potentially extremely regressive. As has already been stated in connection with a Frankfurt-School-based critique of the interpersonalist position, if people have no innate needs, then any social organization is morally defensible and any treatment modality that succeeds in fostering adaptation is acceptable. This point is beautifully made by Chomsky (1976) who writes:

> The question "What is human nature?" has more than scientific interest. As we have noted it lies at the core of social thought as well. What is a good society? Presumably one that leads to the satisfaction of intrinsic human needs, insofar as material conditions allow. To command attention and respect, a social theory should be grounded on some concept of human needs and human rights, and in turn, on the human nature that must be presupposed in any serious account of the origin and character of these needs and rights. Correspondingly, the social structures and relations that a reformer or revolutionary seeks to bring into existence will be based on a concept of human nature however vague and inarticulate. [p. 195]

The Freudian position has tried to articulate a theory of human nature; the relational one has not yet. Psychoanalysis, Marcuse (1955) wrote, "elucidates the universal in the individual experience. To that extent, and only to that extent, can psychoanalysis break the reification in which human relations are petrified" (p. 254). It is its recognition of the primacy of love and aggression that gives psychoanalysis the potential to transcend cultures. It is also this recognition that leads to therapeutic pessimism. If innate desires are so powerful, and the forces of repression necessary to maintain the cultural status quo so strong, unhappiness is the norm and change leading to some autonomy both from internal and external pressures will be very difficult to attain. It is no accident that a Freudian point of view stipulates that therapy often need be intensive and long. Freudians are frequently criticized for insisting on three or more sessions per week. This is seen as elitist and exclusive, motivated by the therapist's desire for financial benefit. While this may be a motive for some analysts, many Freudians substantially reduce their fees to enable a proper analysis rather than maintain their full fees and rationalize that once a week is sufficient. The reason for the insistence on a three or more times per week analysis is a recognition of the importance of the intensity of the analytic relationship, which is called upon to help alter the patient's internal and external realities. Such a perspective takes the analytic relationship seriously without caving in to the materialistic and schizoid pulls of contemporary society. It means challenging social reality in a meaningful way.

It might be argued that the relational position sees the need to relate as primary in a manner analogous to the primacy of Freudian drives. But when Mitchell (1988), for example, writes that "minds seek contact, engagement with other minds. Psychic organization and structures are built from patterns which shape those interactions" (pp. 3–4), the centrality of the need to relate seems quite vague. Important questions remain unaddressed: What are the forces that would oppose such engagement? Why can't people engage freely and be happy? Some relational theorists, such as Benjamin (1977), offer a much more complex view of human nature that may allow bridges to be built engaging their position with the Freudian viewpoint. The work of developmentalists such as Stern (1985) and the attachment theorists may also provide such a bridge.

As we move toward an integration, the question of values should not be forgotten. Unfortunately, in today's world many of us work in a grossly underfunded system that does not come close to providing for the needs of the people it supposedly serves. Given such social and economic realities, many of us make do with the conditions of terribly flawed institutions. Particularly now, when we are faced with so much pressure to adapt to oppressive financial realities—such as those presented by clinics with limited resources or in the context of managed care—it is important that we develop a firm grip on our core beliefs about what people need for satisfaction and what they require for real change to occur.

REFERENCES

Adorno, T. W., Frenkel-Brunswik, E., Levinson, D. J., and Sanford, R. N. (1982). *The Authoritarian Personality*. New York: Norton.

Albee, G. W. (1969). Who shall be served? *Professional Psychology* 1(1):4–7.

Altman, N. (1993a). Psychoanalysis and the urban poor. *Psychoanalytic Dialogues* 3(1): 29–50.

—— (1993b). Reply to Bergman and Foster. *Psychoanalytic Dialogues* 3(1):85–92.

Azar, B. (1995). The bond between mother and child. *The APA Monitor* 26(9):28.

Bach, S. (1994). *The Language of Perversion and the Language of Love.* Northvale, NJ: Jason Aronson.

Barron, J. W., Eagle, M. N., and Wolitzky, D. L., eds. (1992). *Interface of Psychoanalysis and Psychology* Washington, DC: American Psychological Association Press.

Benjamin, J. (1977). The end of internalization: Adorno's social psychology. *Telos.* Summer, 32:42–64.

Bergler, E. (1951). *Money and Emotional Conflicts.* New York: Doubleday.

Bergman, A. (1993). Ego psychological and object relational approaches—Is it either/or? Commentary on Neil Altman's "Psychoanalysis and the Urban Poor." *Psychoanalytic Dialogues* 3(1): 51–67.

Berman, E. (1988). Communal upbringing in the kibbutz: the allure and risk of psychoanalytic utopianism. *Psychoanalytic Study of the Child* 43:319–336. New Haven: Yale University Press.

Bollas, C., and Sundelson, D. (1995). *The New Informants: The Betrayal of Confidentiality in Psychoanalysis and Psychotherapy.* Northvale, NJ: Jason Aronson.

Breggin, P. R., and Breggin G. R. (1994). *The War Against Children.* New York: St. Martins.

Brown, N. (1959). *Life Against Death.* New York: Vintage.

Chodorow, N. (1978). *The Reproduction of Mothering: Psychoanalysis and the Sociology of Gender.* Berkeley: University of California Press.

Chomsky, N. (1976). Equality: language development, and social organization. In *The Chomsky Reader,* ed. J. Peck, pp. 183–202. New York: Pantheon.

Crews, F. (1994). The revenge of the repressed: part II. *NY Review of Books,* Dec 1, pp. 49–58.

Ellman, S. (1991). *Freud's Technique Papers: A Contemporary Perspective.* Northvale, NJ: Jason Aronson.

Fairbairn, W. R. D. (1952). The sociological significance of communism considered in the light of psychoanalysis. In *Psychoanalytic Studies of the Personality,* pp. 233–246. London: Routledge.

Fanon, F. (1963). *The Wretched of the Earth.* New York: Grove.

—— (1967). *Black Skin White Masks.* New York: Grove.

Farber, S., and Green, M. (1993). *Hollywood on the Couch: A Candid Look at the Overheated Love Affair Between Psychiatrists and Moviemakers.* New York: William Morrow.

Fisher, S., and Greenberg, R. (1985). *The Scientific Credibility of Freud's Theories and Therapy.* New York: Columbia University Press.

—— eds. (1989). *The Limits of Biological Treatments for Psychological Distress: Comparisons with Psychotherapy and Placebo.* Hillsdale, NJ: Lawrence Erlbaum.

Freud, S. (1910). The future prospects of psycho-analytic therapy. *Standard Edition* 11:139–151.

—— (1919). Lines of advance in psycho-analytic therapy. *Standard Edition* 17:159–168.

—— (1927). The future of an illusion. *Standard Edition* 21:1–56.

Fromm, E. (1955). The human implications of instinctivistic "radicalism." *Dissent* 2: 342–349.

Gay, P. (1988). *Freud: A Life for Our Time.* New York: Norton.

Gedo, J. (in press). *Spleen and Nostalgia: A Psychoanalytic Memoir.* Northvale, NJ: Jason Aronson.

Greenberg, J., and Mitchell, S. (1983). *Object Relations in Psychoanalytic Theory.* Cambridge, MA: Harvard University Press.

Hook, S., ed. (1959). *Psychoanalysis: Scientific Method and Philosophy.* New York: New York University Press.

Javier, R., and Herron, W. (1992). Psychoanalysis, the Hispanic poor, and the disadvantaged: application and conceptualization. *Journal of the American Academy of Psychoanalysis* 20(3): 445–476.

Jacoby, R. (1975). *Social Amnesia: a Critique of Contemporary Psychology from Adler to Jung.* Boston: Beacon.

—— (1983). *The Repression of Psychoanalysis.* Chicago: University of Chicago Press.

Kachele, H. (1995). Personal communication.

Karon, B. P. (1994). The future of psychoanalysis. In *A History of the Division of Psychoanalysis of the American Psychological Association,* ed. R. C. Lain and M. Meisels, pp. 351–365. Hillsdale, NJ: Lawrence Erlbaum.

Karon, B. P., and VandenBos, G. R. (1994). *Psychotherapy of Schizophrenia: The Treatment of Choice.* Northvale, NJ: Jason Aronson.

Koenigsberg, R. A. (1989). *Symbiosis & Separation: Towards a Psychology of Culture.* New York: Library of Social Science.

Kramer, P. (1993). *Listening to Prozac: A Psychiatrist Explores Mood-Altering Drugs and the New Meaning of the Self.* New York: Viking.

Langer, M. (1989). *From Vienna to Managua.* London: Free Association Press.

Lewes, R. (1995). *Psychoanalysis and Male Homosexuality.* Northvale, NJ: Jason Aronson.

Loewald, H. W. (1980). *Papers on Psychoanalysis.* New Haven, CT: Yale University Press.

Marcuse, H. (1955). *Eros and Civilization.* Boston: Beacon, 1966.

—— (1956). A reply to Erich Fromm. *Dissent* 3: 79–83.

McGuinness, D. (1989). Attention deficit disorder, the Emperor's clothes, animal pharm, and other fiction. In *The Limits of the Biological Treatment for Psychological Distress,* ed. S. Fisher and R. Greenberg. Hillsdale, NJ: Lawrence Erlbaum.

—— (1991). Stimulants and children. *Mothering,* Summer, p. 108. Compuserve reference #A10927431.

Meleon, J. D., Hagendoorn, L., Raaijmakers, Q., and Visser, L. (1988). Authoritarianism and the revival of political racism: reassessments in The Netherlands of the reliability and validity of the concept of authoritarianism by Adorno et al. *Political Psychology* 9(3):413–431.

Mitchell, J. (1974). *Psychoanalysis and Feminism.* New York: Vantage.

Mitchell, S. (1988). *Relational Concepts in Psychoanalysis.* Cambridge, MA: Harvard University Press.

—— (1993). *Hope and Dread in Psychoanalysis.* New York: Basic Books.

Mosher, L. R., and Gunderson, J. G. (1979). Group, family, milieu, and community support systems treatment for schizophrenia. In *Disorders of the Schizophrenic Syndrome,* ed. L. Bellak, pp. 399–452. Northvale, NJ: Jason Aronson.

Nuland, S. B. (1994). The pill of pills. *NY Review of Books,* January 9, pp. 4–7.

Oberndorf, C. P. (1953). *History of Psychoanalysis in America.* New York: Harper & Row.

O'Brien, C. C. (1991). Paradise lost. *The New York Review of Books*, April 25, pp. 52–60.

Ogden, T. (1994). *Subjects of Analysis*. Northvale, NJ: Jason Aronson.

Parens, H. (1979). *The Development of Aggression in Early Childhood*. New York: Jason Aronson.

Pearce, J., and Newton, S. (1963). *The Conditions of Human Growth*. New York: Citadel.

Poland, W. (1996). *Melting the Darkness: The Dyad and Principles of Clinical Practice*. Northvale, NJ: Jason Aronson.

Ray, J. (1979). A short balanced F scale. *The Journal of Social Psychology* 109:309–310.

—— (1988). Why the F scale predicts racism. *Political Psychology* 9(4):671–680.

Reich, W. (1972). *Sex-Pol: Essays 1929–1934*. New York: Random House.

—— (1974). *The Sexual Revolution: Toward a Self-Regulating Character Structure*. New York: Farrar, Straus & Giroux.

Roazen, P. (1995). *How Freud Worked: Firsthand Accounts of Patients*. Northvale, NJ: Jason Aronson.

Schneider, A. Z., and Desmond, H. (1994). The psychoanalytic lawsuit: expanding opportunities for psychoanalytic training and practice. In *A History of the Division of Psychoanalysis of the American Psychological Association*, ed. R. C. Lain and M. Meisels, pp. 313–335. Hillsdale, NJ: Lawrence Erlbaum.

Seligman, M. E. P. (1995). The effectiveness of psychotherapy: the *Consumer Reports* study. *American Psychologist* 50(12): 965–974.

Steingart, I. (1995). *A Thing Apart: Love and Reality in the Therapeutic Relationship*. Northvale, NJ: Jason Aronson.

Stern, D. (1985). *The Interpersonal World of the Infant: A View from Psychoanalysis and Developmental Psychology*. New York: Basic Books.

Stone L. (1984). *Transference and Its Context*. New York: Jason Aronson.

Thoma, H., and Kachele, H. (1994). *Psychoanalytic Practice: vol 2, Principles*. Northvale, NJ: Jason Aronson.

Turkle, S. (1978). *Psychoanalytic Politics: Freud's French Revolution*. New York: Basic Books.

3

Psychoanalysis in an Historic-Economic Perspective

Mario Rendon, M.D.

INTRODUCTION

The nineteenth century saw the birth of modern psychology. In philosophy Hegel published his monumental *Phenomenology of the Mind*, the first blueprint of a psychoanalytic theory at the beginning of the century. Later Johannes Peter Muller described reflex action and nerve impulses, and von Helmholtz contributed the theories of color vision and resonance in hearing. In 1879 Wundt established the first psychological laboratory at the University of Leipzig, and published the first handbook of psychology. In North America William James initiated experimental psychology at Harvard and published his *Principles of Psychology*. The dual origin of psychology in philosophy and physiology would mark its development and define its conceptual parameters throughout the next century. In the early years of describing and classifying abnormal psychological states, psychopathology and mental illness fell within the purview of the medical field, as neurology had originally described some abnormal mental phenomena related to physical disease states. However, Western Europe at the end of the nineteenth century was confronted with a new phenomenon heretofore unexplained by medical knowledge: the problem of hysteria. Charcot, Janet, Bernheim, and Freud, the early chronologers of this phenomenon, fought centuries of theological domination to bring about a scientific understanding of this and other mental conditions. However, it was Freud's germinating theory of unconscious processes and their link to manifest symptomatology that paved the way for another leap. His elaboration of a depth psychology rooted in basic human desire and experience would later replace the initial psychological explanations framed in the physical metaphors of electricity and magnetism.

Psychoanalysis not only revolutionized psychology and severed psychiatry from neurology, but because of its claim to universality, it also raised high hopes for the availability of a rational remedy for emotional or mental disease for all. In the Hegelian tradition followed by Darwin and Marx, who attempted to explain evolutionary and social history as unified processes governed by systematic laws, Freud also conceived of his psychoanalysis as a macrosystemic theory. He attempted to explain the universal mind—ontogeny and phylogeny, civilization and cultures, and the normal and the deviant, in an attempt to create the most ambitious psychological system ever. One of the effects of the Freudian system was its equalization of the categories that heretofore had been seen as different brands of human—such as the sane and the insane, the refined and the brute. Across culture and class, health and illness, common and alien, psychoanalysis promised to provide a universal understanding of human nature and human malaise.

Freud, a naive Hegelian, would be caught in the contradictions emerging from the old Cartesianism he had learned and the dialectical method his findings were pushing him toward. In their conjoint publication *Studies on Hysteria* (Freud 1895) Breuer seems to reprimand Freud for his failed neurological "project" and states that they will be using psychological language and refraining from "neuronal hypothesis" that for him are just "psychological concepts in disguise." Freud and Breuer's joint project inaugurated a paradigmatic transition for psychology, from the Cartesian method of the natural sciences into a dialectical method more fitted to the social sciences and human interactive behavior. Freud's early explorations led him to conclude that encapsulated memories were at the foundation of hysterical phenomena. The concept of a memory that exists and does not exist at the same time presented the challenge to formal logic that led to Freud's ultimate formulation of the unconscious (Rendon 1986).

Freud's noble intent was confounded, however, by several factors. During the time of the birth of psychoanalysis at the turn of the nineteenth century, psychiatry in Western Europe was already divided along social class lines. Hospital psychiatry was neurologically oriented and limited to such physical treatments as hydrotherapy and sedatives. Public hospital institutions provided these biological treatments to the poor mentally ill. But it was the psychiatrists in private practice who were struggling to find methods of treating the growing ranks of patients who came from the expanding middle class and could pay a private fee. While Charcot and Freud conducted their original studies of hysteria within hospital settings that cared for a socioeconomic cross section of patients, we know that the original psychoanalysts focused and pursued their psychological explorations with the patients in their consulting rooms: the educated middle and upper-class.

This social and economic reality established a trend in the development of the psychoanalytic movement that has been neither sufficiently noted nor well understood in the literature. It is suggested here that both the state of the respective economies in which psychoanalysis flourished, and the market population for whom psychoanalysis developed its product, have probably exerted a significant mutative impact on both theory and praxis. While striving to understand universal human phenomena at a theoretical level, psychoanalysis has been much less aware of how the concrete demands of its immediate economic milieu may have molded its body of thought to suit its unique consumers and the private doctor-clinician. Developed by, tested on, and mainly sold to the educated classes, psychoanalysis remains to this day a product subjected to limited market experimentation. The research data that has in fact been generated in the United States over the last decade alarmingly reveals that the poor and non-middle-class have the highest psychotherapy dropout rate of any socioeconomic group (Sue 1988). Whether the fault lies in the consumer not fitting the product, the product not suiting the needs of the general consumer, or the practitioner simply gearing his or her services to the market that renders the highest economic remuneration—no matter. The point is that claims of a universal macrosystemic theory and approach to human distress may be overstated. Ironically, after a century of psychoanalysis, the care of the mentally distressed is still divided along social class lines just at it was in Freud's, Charcot's, and Breuer's time. The sickest and the poorest remain in public hospitals or clinics, which are tended by medical treatments and are seemingly unsuited to the psychological invention called psychoanalysis.

This chapter will attempt to explore the complex roots of this state of affairs within an economic context—an area that has been only marginally integrated into any discussion of the psychoanalytic movement. The discussion will follow the clinical trajectory of psychoanalysis as it migrated from Europe to the United States. In North America the history of psychoanalysis can be divided roughly into three phases, each covering about one third of the present century. During these periods, psychoanalysis clearly adjusted to the new culture, and particularly to its economic nature. Intensely growing as the economy did during the first half of the century, it seems to have partially retreated with it during the second. Most important, psychoanalysis has shown its inability to reach across social class lines to the strata of the poor, in spite of efforts to customize it.

THE FIRST PHASE—TO THE THIRTIES: ENTRANCE TO AMERICA

The close of the nineteenth century marked several important events that placed the United States in the position of a world power. The era of "Manifest Destiny," the rationalization of the acquisition of territory in order to spread democracy, was coming to an end with the winning of the Hispanic-American War and the acquisition of the Panama Canal a few years later. A new industrialization wave—the second Industrial Revolution—was at its height with petroleum as its fuel. Ford had just built his first automobile and many other technological advances, such as airplanes, were appearing at a fast pace. In his famous sermon, "Acres of Diamonds," Russell Conwell exhorted Americans to "get rich" at the break of the new millennium. The United States had become the land of opportunity, and conspicuous consumption was replacing the Protestant ethic. As a result, the flood of immigrants from many parts of the world kept growing, with people coming in search of the realization of their economic dreams, as well as seeking political freedom.

Yet, the new century would also see the unfolding of contradictions that modern American imperialism had inherited from Europe. During the first decade of the century, racism, the American equivalent of European anti-Semitism, had engendered African-American ferment leading eventually to the creation of the NAACP. Pauperization fears, based on class chauvinism and racism, brought immigration to an almost complete halt in the early '20s, and radically altered immigration laws. This is reflected in Terman's published reports that the country was admitting too many "high grade defectives" thus placing not only the race but also the economy in grave danger. Using the Binet-Simon instrument at Ellis Island, Terman would find about four fifths of immigrants mentally defective, particularly Jews and Eastern and Southern Europeans (Laosa 1984). This was a categorization inherited later by so-called minorities, the American euphemism for the politically powerless. Although Roosevelt opened the new century by announcing the principles of "fair play and a square deal," and although the First and Second World Wars offered a perfect opportunity for the acceleration of American industry, the grandeur of the first third of the century eventually ended with the bang of the Great Depression in the thirties.

Psychiatrists in the United States were struggling with the same problems as their European colleagues. There had been high demand for private practice in order to treat the emotional ailments of the well to do—such as neurasthenia or "excessive stress of the nervous system"—and little in the form of treatment. The emergent theory of psychoanalysis, coming from Europe, provided a welcome response to the need. It has been said that with the exception of pragmatism, no other system of thought has had the influence that psychoanalysis had in American culture. An heir of Vienna, psychoanalysis was to become America's adoptive child (Wells 1964); however, this new culture and economy would come to press its own indelible stamp on the psychoanalytic movement.

Upon the official invitation of G. Stanley Hall in 1909, Freud visited the United States and gave five lectures at Clark University. This event, attended by William James, E. B. Titchener, Franz Boas, Adolf Meyer, E. B. Holt, and other members of the local intelligentsia, marked the grand opening of the Freudian era in the United States. Upon saying good-bye, the American philosopher and founder of psychology William James ambivalently told Freud that the future of psychology was essentially in his hands (Roback 1952). Of course, psychoanalysis had a revolutionary gradient, not only in its implicit critique of sexual repression and the Protestant ethic, but, more important, in postulating a universal psyche across all previous social boundaries with repression as its hallmark. That was the reason for Freud's famous statement that he was bringing Americans "the plague." Although there was always resistance to psychoanalysis, little by little its influence began to be felt as reputable professionals such as Morton Prince and S. Weir Mitchel lent their support, and physicians began to explore its theories and practice through didactic self-analysis. However, the inherent contradiction of psychoanalysis—its claim to universality despite its own embeddedness in the narrow ideological segment of the middle class—would become more and more manifest as time went by.

After Freud's visit, groups of neurologists, psychologists, and psychiatrists started to organize professional groups around the new psychoanalytic ideas. The better positioned physicians monopolized the new method for a good part of the century. In 1910, Putnam presented a paper about his experiences with the Freudian psychoanalytic method to the American Neurological Association (Wells 1964). The International Psychoanalytic Association was founded the same year in Salzburg. In February 1911, the New York Psychoanalytic Society was established by Brill, Jellife, and Oberndorf, and May of the same year saw the beginning of the American Psychoanalytic Association. As a comparison, the Berlin Psychoanalytic Association, one of the most influential in Europe and the United States, was created only in 1920. After World War I quite a few people had begun going to Europe to study psychoanalysis. Between 1921 and 1925 there was a group that went from New York to be analyzed by Freud and his students. Among them were Esther and Thomas Menaker and Abram Kardiner. A little later people began to go to Berlin where Alexander was the head of the Berlin Institute. The flow was soon reversed with Alexander moving to Chicago in 1930 and Rado coming to New York in 1931. Rado, Kardiner, and others founded the Columbia Presbyterian Institute as a member of the American Psychoanalytic Association. Robert Waelder went to Philadelphia, Hanns Sachs went to Boston in 1935 as did Helene and Felix Deutsch. Ernst Simmel and Otto Fenichel went to Los Angeles, and many others such as H. Hartmann, E. Kris, R. Loewenstein, G. Silboorg, B. Lewin, and W. Silverberg came to New York. At Alexander's invitation, Karen Horney arrived in Chicago in 1932. In 1934 she came to New York. Fromm came in 1934. The same year Fromm-Reichmann settled at Chestnut Lodge. The Washington-Baltimore Psychoanalytic Society was formed in 1930 (Thompson 1955). In 1931 the psychoanalytic institutes of New York (Jacobs 1983) and Chicago (Pollock 1983) were established and modern psychoanalytic training was basically being shaped along the lines of the Berlin training model. The Boston Institute came into being in 1932. During the thirties the complete institutionalization and formalization of psychoanalysis in the United States would thus be completed (D'Amore 1981). At the University of Chicago, Franz Alexander was the first university chairman to be named "Professor of Psychoanalysis." He founded and remained director of the Chicago Institute for twenty-five years.

A pivotal force in these early years of American psychoanalytic development was its adoption by the medical establishment. In contrast to

Europe, where psychoanalysis was barred from the medical mainstream, the United States appropriated it from approximately 1915 to 1935. This had a deeply influential, double-edged impact on its American course of development. On the one hand, medicine's embrace offered a degree of validity and social acceptance to a new discipline. In fact, American physicians now trained and recognized as psychoanalysts came to stand on solid financial ground as their principally educated upper-class patients consented to fee structures already long established by the American medical community. This is a tradition that is still maintained by American psychoanalysts of all academic disciplines. However, it is now recognized that this medical aegis simultaneously curtailed many critical and revolutionary aspects of psychoanalytic thinking. This effect emerged from a confluence of economic, social, and ultimately theoretical factors. First, as had been the case in the early Freud-Charcot era, American psychoanalysis, inadvertently fell in lockstep with the economic/social class lines delineated in Vienna—it was administered to the educated classes in the private practice sector. By the 1930s there was a proliferation of American psychiatrists who were trained as psychoanalysts working in large public teaching hospitals. While they trained in private institutes fueled by independent practice or selective clinics, they developed a diluted version of psychoanalysis for hospital patients who tended to come from a broader cross section of middle, working-class, and poor people: psychodynamic therapy. This might be seen as a regrettable social example of the less affluent receiving less potent medicine; however, as we will see below, American clinical practice would also add its own unique stamp to the psychoanalytic base, creating a perspective on the human condition that was consistent with American cultural values.

THE SECOND PHASE—
TO THE SIXTIES: EXPANSION

From the end of the Second World War to the sixties, psychoanalysis thrived in an American socioeconomic atmosphere marked by great social programs. In part, as a national response to the Depression of the thirties, the National Labor Relations Act, the Fair Labor Standards Act, the Social Security Act, the GI Bill, banking and farming reforms, and public work programs were all implemented. Though unsuccessful, a National Health Insurance program was also first proposed in the late 1930s (Means 1953).

The Second World War placed the United States in a leading world position with the exclusive control of atomic weapons and an economy that had been remarkably stimulated by war production. The combination of war neurosis and war veterans, as well as the new acquisitive capacities of the middle class, would enhance both the need and the market for psychotherapeutic services in the country. At this time, broad treatment programs for mental disorders were initiated by the Veterans Administration, and eventually such legislation as the Mental Health Act of 1948 was produced. Clinical psychologists, whose services had proven indispensable in the assessment and treatment of military personnel in the Second World War, were now functioning in hospital settings and individual practices within the private sector.

The postwar era also saw significant shifts in the social balance of the American population. The Civil Rights Movement of the 1950s was a glaring statement of class differences in the country. This period, as we know, culminated in the Civil Rights Act and the end of school segregation.

The socioeconomic phenomena of this era were reflected in the microcosm of psychoanalytic practice. While not a time of consolidation, this was nevertheless a period of continued intense growth for the psychoanalytic movement. By the end of the Second World War, North America was already in numerical control of the International Psychoanalytic Association. However, the medicalization of psychoanalysis in America, the opening of psychoanalysis to a larger segment of the middle class, and the development of psychoanalytic psychotherapy for hospital trainees were factors that would impact on both psychoanalytic theory and practice. During its early years of development in the United States, psychoanalysis lost some of its unique power as a depth psychology. First, the needs of the modern American man and woman were seen as different and more pragmatic than the issues presented by the European patient predecessors. Second, forceful theoretical changes were evolving as American ego psychology, the school that inherited Freud's mantle, placed focal emphasis on adaptation and optimal levels of human functioning. This was a psychology immersed in the American ethos of self-sufficiency and upward-striving mobility. Later, critics such as Laing and Cooper would consider American psychoanalysis a reactionary instrument of the contemporary social order. More recently Lacan, in his well-known criticism of the ego psychology school, would deem American psychoanalysis deluded in its belief in an alleged "model" ego. Initially a conflict theory deriving from a dialectical method founded in the tension between nature and society, expression and repression, mainstream American psycho-analysis eventually turned into a deficit theory reflecting largely capital-ist accumulation laws, a trend also seen in the work of the Neo-Freudians.

Being sown in a pragmatic milieu in America, it did not take long for different disciplines to start testing psychoanalytic hypotheses through the old methodology of the natural sciences. According to Wells (1964), the publication in 1942 of Robert Sears's compilation of years of research on child development was one of the factors that influenced a change in psychoanalytic direction toward revisionism. Subjected to the critical lens of Cartesian logic, which was blind to psychoanalysis's dialectical nature, psychoanalytic hypotheses proved difficult to test. Psychoanalytic anthropologists also tried to carry theory into the field, attempting to fit the behavior of varied cultures into a rigidly constructed theoretical procrustean bed. As observations began to emerge on cross-cultural differences in family structure, sexual behavior, and social customs, psychoanalysis—now metamorphosed into an adaptive psychology—had seemingly lost its ability to grasp the deep human experience. Many anthropologists interpreted the new observations as proof against the discipline.

It is of interest to note that despite psychoanalysis's position outside the measurable parameters of traditional science, it nevertheless contin-ued to grow during this period, progressively acquiring large segments of the mental health market over time. The American Psychoanalytic As-sociation alone grew from thirty-three members in 1925 to 273 in 1946 (Wells 1964). While these early years of the discipline in the United States were marked by its affiliation to medicine/psychiatry, it was not long before the burgeoning fields of anthropology, sociology, and linguistics began to show their impact and declare their logical affiliation to human developmental theory. Traditionally, psychologists had already been deeply immersed in diagnostic evaluation and developmental research. Since the proliferation of psychologist-clinicians after World War II, some were also training at psychoanalytic institutes, albeit with restrictions placed upon them because they were not physicians.

Within psychoanalytic circles at this time, the road was also being paved by new clinical observations and innovative queries that began to chal-lenge traditional Freudian ideas. Karen Horney, a member of the New York Psychoanalytic Institute in the late 1930s, was beginning to grow progressively discontented with both the classical biologic drive model and the Freudian view of female sexuality. Influenced by the new anthropological work of Malinowsky, Mead, Benedict, and others, Horney began to develop her views on the integral pivotal role of cultural influence on character development (Horney 1939). Her published works openly questioned many fundamental principles of Freudian thinking. The psychoanalytic establishment responded by eventually revoking her status as training analyst. With this action, she resigned, together with several other members of the New York Psychoanalytic faculty and fourteen candidates. Erich Fromm joined this group, which became the Association for the Advancement of Psychoanalysis and the American Institute for Psychoanalysis in 1941. In a new split in 1943, seven of the Association members, together with Clara Thompson and others, founded the William Alanson White Institute; they left the original dissident group because Horney would not accept Fromm's nonmedical status and his view that psychoanalysis belonged to sociology rather than to medicine. The White group opened branches in New York and Washington. They became chartered as a separate organization in 1946. Now freed from the interpretive absolutism of American Freudianism, they began to speculate about alternative metapsychologies and the clinical implications of new thought in practice. In 1944, a number of members and candidates left the Horney group to start the Comprehensive Course in Psychoanalysis at New York Medical College. This led to yet a new division. Later in 1956, the dissident groups came together and founded the American Academy of Psychoanalysis, the non-orthodox version of the American Psychoanalytic Association (Horney-Eckardt 1979, Kelman 1968, Marmor 1968, Moulton 1968, Thompson 1955).

These fragmentations reflected not only theoretical and perhaps personality differences, but also the presence of a strong market demand for a new discipline in a climate of intense competitiveness and private enterprise. Against the original decree of the American Psychoanalytic—that each city have only one Institute—New York City alone now had five schools, including the Columbia School headed by Rado. Thus, the forties, fifties, and sixties saw psychoanalysis replicated, all of this in the exclusive hands of the psychiatric elite.

As for the consumers of psychoanalysis, in 1948, 38 percent of the patients were medical professionals, 21 percent were business people, and most of the remainder were professionals, intellectuals, and those "engaged in cultural activities." One third of analysands earned an average of $30,000 and over one quarter between $20,000 and $30,000 with the rest at about $10,000. The yearly cost of analysis was estimated to be about $5,000 (Wells 1964). Encouraged by the demand, institutes opened clinics that aimed at treating expanded segments of the middle class. The application of psychoanalysis to members of the lower socioeconomic ladder and to so-called minorities still remained an occasional curiosity (Gould 1967).

In summary, the second phase of psychoanalysis in the United States saw an accelerated growth, the movement's firm institutionalization within the psychiatric community, and its full incorporation in academia and hospital training. Although by the end of the period psychoanalysis reigned unchallenged as a psychological approach to mental disorders (Neill and Ludwig 1980), it also saw a salvo of theoretical and empirical challenges from researchers and anthropologists. During this period, one reason for the earlier optimism—the exploration of the possible application of psychodynamic therapy to lower socioeconomic patients in hospital settings, began to be eroded by adverse research findings. Also, the impressive growth of psychoanalysis itself during this period was not entirely healthy. A combination of factors led to the splintering and creation of a number of divergent schools. These schools fell grossly into one of two major camps represented by the American Psychoanalytic Association and the American Academy of Psychoanalysis. At an international level, this would later be mirrored by the formation of the International Federation of Psychoanalytic Societies as a counterpoint to the International Psychoanalytic Association.

As to the medical appropriation of psychoanalysis, initially some member institutes of the American Psychoanalytic Association trained psychologists and foreign doctors with exchange visas on the condition that training was for research or academic purposes only, not for clinical practice. It was not until the 1980s, in response to a lawsuit initiated by the American Psychological Association, that the New York Psychoanalytic Institute opened its doors on equal grounds to doctors of psychology and social work. Charging the psychiatric establishment with monopoly and restraint of trade, American clinical psychologists had legally broken through the contrived medical appropriation of Freud's original legacy.

THE THIRD PHASE—THE SIXTIES TO THE MID-NINETIES: UNCERTAINTY

During the period from 1960 through the early 1990s, complex and shifting socioeconomic factors converged to influence the expansion and utilization of psychoanalytic treatments in the United States. Running counter to the basic growth trend of the previous decade, psychoanalysis was deeply impacted by nationwide capitalistic trends that halted its dissemination into the larger cross section of the American population, even further solidifying its usage by the relatively smaller numbers of the educated middle class. Psychoanalysis now had strong competition from cost-effective psychopharmacologic and behavior-focused treatments, which could indeed be easily offered to masses of the public sector and monitored by the expanding power of an industrialized health care machine.

Ironically, this third phase of psychoanalysis's evolution in the United States was opened in the 1960s by a period of hopeful revolutionary fervor throughout the world. This was expressed in wide student and worker movements from China to Mexico. In France, revolts in the academic sector led to a growing recognition of the role of psychological factors in physical disease, as well as a popularization of psychoanalysis among the growing mental health segments (Hawkins and Hawkins 1979, Turkle 1978). The rebellious mood in the United States was reflected in the anti-Vietnam and Civil Rights efforts. In the American mental health field it saw its equivalent in the Community Mental Health Movement.

Supported by the large federal funding efforts of the Kennedy administration in the 1960s, the Community Mental Health Movement was America's short-lived answer to broadening the distribution of mental health care. It operated, however, on the belief that mental disorders and deviant behavior emanated in large part from social conditions: poverty, poor nutrition, discrimination, and community breakdown. The therapy then lay in the implementation of social policy changes and the use of therapeutic processes as social operations. This was a far cry from viewing psychodynamic psychotherapy as a technique aimed at uncovering the unconscious determinants of human behavior and distress. This era thus saw the proliferation of behavioral, cognitive, group, and family therapies. Applied in the context of community-based clinics, these interventions were viewed as solutions through which the individual could rectify his relationship with himself, the family, and the group. This era had the interesting political effect of somewhat decreasing medicine's stronghold on mental health care by the proliferation of new modalities practiced by other trained mental health professionals (Neill and Ludwig 1980). However, this era also marked a dangerous and most unfortunate turn in the history of American mental health: the focus on behavioral and social change was largely presented as antagonistic to psychoanalysis's psychodynamic model and its emphasis on the meaning of human experience.

Changes on the American economic front, however, would soon cut short the funding of large scale Community Mental Health efforts. President Kennedy's massive federal funding project for social programs never reached full fruition. The worsening Cold War of the '60s and '70s saw the results of an expensive and deadly weapons race. While the Soviet Union eventually capitulated in bankruptcy, the American economy, which already had suffered creeping inflation and stagflation starting with the Vietnam War, was also deeply affected, with symptoms of a sustained recession as a consequence. Federal spending deficits reached trillion dollar figures for the first time. Pawnbroking the country and passing the debt onto future generations, an alternative to taxation, was just one of the symptoms of a social empathy disorder, the psychological mode of the period. As the government desperately tried to reduce the mammoth deficit, a logical result was a reduction in social services. Pauperization of the middle class, and a strong shift in ideology in health care delivery from service to profit, had an additional impact on the practice of psychoanalysis. The revolutionary spirit of the '60s and '70s, which briefly spirited a social/community orientation to mental health, would be supplanted with the capitalistic, yuppie ideology of the '80s. In the psychoanalytic world, this social trend would be reflected in much theorizing about narcissistic disorders. At a world level the failure of socialism and the resultant erosion of political class consciousness resulted in the eruption of ethnic conflict throughout. Ethnic strife now disguises a capitalistic crisis as countries vie for new market realignments.

In this economic climate, the American psychoanalytic movement is impacted by its greatest challenge of all: the industrialization of mental health care. Resting on the growing popularity of symptom-targeted, cost-effective psychopharmacotherapy, the early hegemony of psychoanalysis in American mental health seemingly has been unseated by the ominous era of expedient biological treatments. In addition, a massive shift from the traditional human service ideology in health care delivery to an industrial orientation places psychoanalysis and psychotherapy at a great disadvantage. The main objective of industry is to maximize profit, and one way to achieve this is by reducing cost. The costlier element in production is the human element. While in the '80s the private-for-profit and the technological segments of health care were among the most lucrative industries in the country, cost-effectiveness, utilization, problem-oriented record, management by objectives, peer review, quality assurance, and so on, are the new linguistic hand-me-downs for the discipline. Managed care, with its medical gatekeepers and national health reform, looms larger every day, glossed over by the unquestionable altruistic motive of universal coverage. The traditional therapist–patient relationship has been slowly replaced by a growing number of parties that make their presence felt in what is left of the analytic hour. Since the 1960s some important data have been collected by various psychoanalytic associations, institutes, and practitioners concerning the status of psychoanalytic practice in the United States. While methodological differences make formal comparisons difficult, two major trends do seem consistently to emerge. First, there has been a clear shift in the identity of psychoanalytic practitioners as physicians have lost their initial franchise on the discipline. Numerous authors as well as surveys conducted by the American Psychoanalytic Association (Dorwart et al. 1992, Hamburg et al. 1967, Namnum 1980) note that medical psychoanalysts in private practice have shown a decrease in analytic patient hours over the years. They attribute this to the proliferation of non-medical psychoanalysts as well as to the growing use of psychotropic medication and competing symptom-focused therapeutic modalities. Second, the most striking statistic to emerge concerns the characteristics of the analytic patient and the glaring lack of heterogeneity within this group. Namnum (1980) reports that when one looks at those special interest group characteristics, which are important to nationally planned programs, differences in the psychoanalytic patient population stand out. These include the absence of minority racial groups, with more than 98 percent of analytic patients being white. Patients are predominantly highly educated, over one half with a graduate or professional degree, and males—atypically—predominate in treatment. These demographics certainly argue toward an elitism in psychoanalysis.

Looking at the characteristics of psychoanalytic clinic patients we find a similar picture. Examining the demographics of 1,585 patients in psychoanalysis and psychoanalytic psychotherapy at the Columbia Psychoanalytic Center from 1945 to 1971, it was found that subjects were likely to be Jewish, young, white, highly educated, employed in professional or technical jobs, and high vocational achievers. Although the clinic was set up for patients who could not afford private office psychoanalysis, and some had no declared income, their family background was of wealth. Subjects specifically referred for analysis were better educated and more likely to have status jobs as well as to be unmarried or divorced (Weber et al. 1967, Weber et al. 1985). In these samples only 4.5 and 5 percent of patients were black at a time when the Census had 17 and 26 percent of New Yorkers in this category at the two periods of data collection. The latter is, however, a progressive figure compared to other psychoanalytic reports that showed 1–2 percent blacks (Hamburg et al. 1962, Shapiro et al. 1980) or zero of blacks in analytic treatment (Siegel 1962, Weintraub and Aronson 1968). Weintraub and Aronson (1968) comment that this finding is particularly significant in view of the fact that many of the analysts who participated in the study practiced in communities with large minority populations.

A study of patients of members of the American Psychoanalytic Association, which looked at the characteristics of patients in psychoanalysis, concluded that the patients—mostly physicians and other professionals, business people, housewives, and students—appeared to resemble a middle-class group in its formal occupational structure (Siegel 1962). Similar characteristics are described by Erle (1979) in her report of forty consecutive patients at the New York Psychoanalytic. The Menninger Clinic study (Wallerstein 1986) reveals an analogous pattern—there were no minority patients.

In summary, the third phase of psychoanalysis's development in the United States leaves a complex picture. On the one hand, the discipline has expanded outside the confines of the medical establishment into legitimate use and study by other disciplines. It remains to be seen what mutative impact, if any, this will have on psychoanalytic thinking per se, and its clinical application. On the other hand, psychoanalysis seems to have suffered a dangerous retreat from the public sector as the capitalistic industrial health care machine discourages its practice by supporting non-psychodynamic therapeutic models. Unfortunately, this has further entrenched the use of psychoanalysis exclusively by the monied classes who can personally pay a private fee.

PSYCHOANALYSIS OF THE POOR

As we have seen, psychodynamic psychotherapy emerged in the '30s as "the psychoanalysis of the less affluent," its cost being estimated originally to be only one- to two-fifths that of analysis (Wells 1964). Inspired by psychoanalysis and modified to reach more people at a lower cost, psychotherapy experienced a very significant metamorphosis with many groups branching out or verbal therapies appearing during the second part of the century. Additionally, the Community Mental Health movement brought in practitioners from health disciplines such as social work, nursing, counseling, and others increasingly interested in the modality as well as in the advantages of private practice.

In the 1950s, publications began formally to address the relationship between social class and psychotherapy. The problem was clearly highlighted by Hollingshead and Redlich's (1985) report. According to this study, while patients of upper socioeconomic levels seeking treatment for emotional disorders were found to receive psychodynamic psychotherapy, their lower-class counterparts would typically receive supportive psychotherapy, brief therapy, pharmacotherapy, or other somatic treatments. This bias against psychotherapy for the poor has been documented in many studies even dating before the classic New Haven-Hollingshead study (Auld and Myers 1954, Brill and Storrow 1960, Kahn et al. 1957, Lorr 1959, Rosenthal and Frank 1958, Winder and Hersko 1955), along with a number of other related prejudices. It has been found, for example, that even in clinics where upper-class patients are allegedly excluded or where payment is not a factor at all, lower socioeconomic status patients are still not admitted (Siassi and Messer 1976). Also, there is a direct relationship between the social class of the patient and the experience of the assigned therapist, with the less experienced clinicians typically being assigned to the poorer patients. Rejection rates in clinical settings for low socioeconomic status patients reach levels as high as between 69 percent (Schaffer and Myers 1954) and 97 percent (Cole et al. 1962). Duration of psychotherapy similarly has favored the higher economic level subjects while dropout rates occur more frequently among the disadvantaged (Baekeland and Lundwall 1975, Imber et al. 1955, Lief et al. 1961). Furthermore, at discharge, higher-class patients are more frequently catalogued as socially improved (Cole et al. 1962). Although dropout rates in psychotherapy have been associated with the therapist's experience, Imber and colleagues (1955) found that even when controlling for this variable, social class determines length of treatment.

In contrast to common biases, one study that asked poor patients what they expected from the therapist found that they wanted not prescriptions, as generally suspected, but "an active but at the same time permissive attitude" (Overall and Aronson 1963). Another study (Kraft-Goin et al. 1965) found that 52 percent of low socioeconomic patients expect to resolve their problems "by talking and examining their past," a number similar to those who expected the doctor "to do something" for them (48 percent). However, even within the last group, 34 percent expected "advice" and only 14 percent wanted medication. Curiously, patients in this latter study expected treatment to last for only up to ten visits, a finding that would surely satisfy the third party payer (Kraft-Goin et al. 1965).

The concept of psychological mindedness is often used as a criterion for clinic psychotherapy candidates although some have found that the applicability of this criterion is highly social-class biased and that therapists in fact look for patients similar to their own socioeconomic extraction (Ruesch 1953, Yamamoto et al. 1967). Experienced therapists, trainees, and supervisors alike have expressed discontent and lack of motivation to offer therapy to low-income patients (Lorion 1973). This is despite the fact that there are no studies to show that psychoanalytic or psychotherapeutic treatment has adverse effects on the poor.

Regarding the proverbial minorities, some have assumed that traditional psychotherapy is ineffective for them. Others, in contrast, have concluded that it is in fact existing barriers that preclude such patients from full access to treatment, and have recommended ethnic or culturally syntonic services and education. These conclusions follow the repeated observation that there is either lack of utilization or a high dropout rate among ethnic minorities served by white mainstream therapists (Sue 1988). After the President's Commission on Mental Health (1978) essentially took the position of recommending culturally syntonic services, a number of bilingual and/or bicultural clinics have appeared, and most claim success in abolishing barriers and reducing dropout rates (Trevino and Rendon 1994). However, the matter is confounded by a host of social class and political issues, as race and ethnicity are often used to cloud deeper social class contradictions. The fact remains that at present, upper-class patients continue to seek psychoanalytic treatment, and the poor, for the most part, receive a smorgasbord of short-term, behaviorally oriented, or biological treatments.

THE OTHER ECONOMY OF PSYCHOANALYSIS—THE POLITICAL ECONOMY

We have seen how the other economy, the non-libidinal, has essentially shaped the life span of psychoanalysis in the most advanced country in the late phase of capitalism. A central conflict between the goals of psychoanalysis—abolishing repression and decreasing neurotic suffering, and the goal of the present civilization—maximization of surplus value, has radically altered the image of the discipline.

It is generally recognized that Freud originated psychoanalysis in an individual, entrepreneurial, and unregulated mode. Fees came from the pocket of the patient or a family member. These conditions appear to have been very suitable for the development of the new discipline (Chodoff 1987). However, these conditions are hardly suitable to the disenfranchised. As psychoanalysis developed in the American capitalistic society, and its range of applicability extended from office to institutional setting, the fiscal possibilities of the psychotherapies became clear to the corporate sector, and "patients" turned out also to be "clients." This invited the well-intended, namely politicians, administrators, insurers, and auditors to participate in the new enterprise, a development that has changed psychoanalysis from an exploratory venture in the service of humanization to a project with goals and objectives to be approved by a third, commercial party.

Insurance has had no minor effect on the therapeutic relationship since it initially created a powerful illusion of limitlessness. Insurance has been defined as a game of shared risk (see Compton's Interactive Encyclopedia, "Insurance"), which is constructed as a protection against catastrophic loss (7.5 percent of annual adjusted gross income as per tax code). In this regard insurance has clearly failed psychoanalysis, the cost of which is essentially catastrophic for most Americans today. It has also failed the mentally ill. The fact that there are 37 million Americans with no health insurance reflects the sad reality that, de facto, the poor have no access to mental health services, not to speak of basic medical assistance. Unprofitable compared to those specialties that utilize technology, psychotherapy is labor-intensive and therefore unattractive in an industrial climate. However, we know that something beyond material incentives keeps the discipline alive. The passage of the Medicare and Medicaid acts in 1965 was a timid insurance solution that—although allowing the ruling class to save face—clearly continues to discriminate both against the poor and against mental health. In 1986 only 41 percent of people below poverty level were covered by Medicaid. Yet, in the same year, 70 percent of the revenue for mental health organizations came from public sources. This contradiction is food for much thought. As has been mentioned, Medicare, initially more receptive to psychotherapy, has progressively curtailed it. Most insurance programs are following suit and progressively limiting services. In 1987, "bare bones legislation" that permits insurance companies to market minimum benefits excluding coverage for mental disorders and substance abuse was passed in twelve states of the union (Chodoff 1987). The national health care plan recently proposed by the Clinton administration, while committed to comprehensive coverage, allowed only twenty outpatient visits per year for psychotherapy. This is an alarming trend that does not bode well for psychoanalytic treatment.

As practitioners, we have been admonished for the fact that psychotherapy has been traditionally conducted without regard for cost or other economic factors. It is time to address this, we are told (Krupnic and Pincus 1992). However, measurement of cost in psychotherapy is no simple matter. Comparisons of treatment on the basis of cost must, for example, take account of differential effectiveness. Cost effectiveness analysis can be compared only if the outcomes can be measured in the same units. Here such units as "Quality Adjusted Life Years" have been used (McGrath 1994). However, how does one go about defining and measuring quality of life in this highly complex cultural climate?

Astrachan and colleagues (1976) have delineated four major tasks for mental health care: a clinical task such as diagnosis and treatment, a reparative task such as rehabilitation, a social control task that is geared to modify what is considered as deviant behavior, and, finally, a humanistic task related to personal growth. It is the last two tasks that are implicitly in our psychoanalytic domain, although they are so diametrically opposed. Of course if we lived in a dream world in which all human needs could be fulfilled, tasks such as "knowing thyself" would receive higher priority. However, the means of the present world to fulfill human needs are limited, if only by the non-negligible fact that a small minority of people in power run things while maintaining the priority of a reasonable rate of profit. Therefore, we must address needs according to their consensus on hierarchy and priorities.

As for pressures from the industrial sector, there is still the nagging issue of the so-called offset effect of psychotherapy. There is suspicion that psychotherapy may reduce the cost of physical care, for example, by helping patients better handle their chronic illness (Schlesinger et al. 1983). It has been found that psychotherapeutic intervention may improve or even prevent conditions that carry a high medical cost (Trad 1992). This economic fact, if proven beyond reasonable doubt, could provide a comfortable place for psychotherapy within the medical field, as the indications for it within the diagnostic mental health manuals seem to fade. Another puzzling discovery from an economic perspective is that mental illness, depression, or even demoralization have not only a personal but also a systemic impact on the economy. Depressed patients, for example, are underproductive, leave the economic mainstream, and may eventually become a charge to society. The total economic impact of mental disorders in the United States in 1988 was estimated at 129.3 billion dollars (Rice et al. 1991). It is no small matter to note reports that depression emerges only second to heart disease in number of bedridden days, and that it contributes to more disability in daily functioning than chronic lung disease, diabetes, arthritis, or hypertension (Wells et al. 1989).

Of particular interest today are the brief dynamic psychotherapies, which, if we can prove their efficacy, could be especially attractive to insurance companies because they would offer the possibility of covering more clients and reducing the average cost per patient (Crits-Cristoph 1992). However, our literature also notes that length of treatment may be related to therapeutic outcome (Erle 1979, Kernberg et al. 1972). These reports suggest what all analytic practitioners know very well: that psychodynamic treatment is embedded in the sustained dialectical nature of the therapeutic relationship over time.

We are left with many questions. Compared to technological procedures, hospital beds, and other medical treatments, psychoanalysis may not always fare badly in the competitive market. However, the culture is driven by priorities that are not necessarily in the service of progressive humanization. Psychoanalysis, a late result of the Romantic movement and the scientific transformation of philosophy, although born in a typical bourgeois economic climate, was a protest against social repressive factors. In America it suffered a metamorphosis into "a prosperous specialty" (Hale 1978) and turned from an avant-garde cultural phenomenon to an elite specialty within a bureaucratic society (Burnham 1979). America largely transformed psychoanalysis from a humanistic endeavor into an approach focused on ego accumulation. Psychoanalysis also split into a series of antagonistic fragments, unable to integrate its inherent internal contradictions. Process and integrity were lost as a result.

Initially thought to be a plus, the medicalization of psychoanalysis in the United States generated a number of consequences that contributed to radically altering the vision its founder had for the discipline. Compounding this influence, the new hegemony of the industrialized medical health care complex has altered both the vision and the mission of psychoanalysis, as primary concerns have shifted from service and humanistic goals to profit. Modifications implemented for the purpose of improved accessibility have failed to reach the poor.

As it looks at the end of the present century, psychoanalysis, with its multiple schools and diffuse identity, would seem to be at a pre-paradigmatic phase in Kuhn's (1962) topology—it is waiting for a new qualitative jump. The main question that remains, however, is where and when such a jump could occur, given that psychoanalysis, a dealienating procedure, has proven to be poorly compatible with capitalism, which is essentially a form of alienation. That psychoanalysis has failed the poor, who are perhaps those most in need, is the understatement of the century. Even for the middle class and the wealthy, the goals of psychoanalysis seem at odds with the prevailing cultural trends. And the truth is that no one will be free until we all are.

REFERENCES

Astrachan, B., Levinson, D., and Adler, D. (1976). The impact of National Health Insurance on the tasks and practice of psychiatry. *Archives of General Psychiatry* 33:785–794.

Auld, F., and Myers, J. K. (1954). Contributions to a theory for selecting psychotherapy patients. *Journal of Clinical Psychology* 10:56–60.

Baekeland, F., and Lundwall, L. (1975). Dropping out of treatment: a critical review. *Psychological Bulletin* 82:738–783.

Brill, A. A. (1944). *Freud's Contribution to Psychiatry.* New York: Norton.

Brill, N. Q., and Storrow, H. A. (1960). Social class and psychiatric treatment. *Archives of General Psychiatry* 3:340–344.

Burnham, J. C. (1979). From avant-garde to specialism: psychoanalysis in America. *Journal of the History of the Behavioral Sciences* 15:128–134.

Chodoff, P. (1987). Effects of the new economic climate on psychotherapeutic practice. *American Journal of Psychiatry* 144:1293–1297.

Cole, N. J., Branch, C. H., and Allison, R. B. (1962). Some relationships between social class and dynamic psychotherapy. *American Journal of Psychiatry* 118:1004–1011.

Compton's Interactive Encyclopedia. CD ROM for Windows. (1994). Compton's NewMedia, Inc.

Crits-Cristoph, P. (1992). The efficacy of brief dynamic psychotherapy: a meta-analysis. *American Journal of Psychiatry* 149:151–158.

D'Amore, A. R. (1981). Psychoanalysis in America: 1930–1939. *Psychoanalytic Quarterly* 50:570–586.

Dorwart, R. A., Chartock, L. R., Dial, T., et al. (1992). A national study of psychiatrists' professional activities. *American Journal of Psychiatry* 149:1499–1505.

Encyclopedia of Associations. (1994). 28th Edition, vol. 1, part 2, p. 1628. Detroit: Gale Research, Inc.

Erle, J. B. (1979). An approach to the study of analyzability and analyses: the course of forty consecutive cases selected for supervised analysis. *Psychoanalytic Quarterly* 48:198–228.

Freud, S. (1886). Report of my studies in Paris and Berlin. *Standard Edition* 1:1–15.

Freud, S., and Breuer, J. (1895). *Studies on Hysteria. Standard Edition* 2.

Gould, R. E. (1967). Dr. Strangeclass: or how I stopped worrying about the theory and began treating the blue-collar worker. *American Journal of Orthopsychiatry* 37:78–86.

Hale, N. G. (1978). From Berggasse XIX to Central Park West: the Americanization of psychoanalysis, 1919–1940. *Journal of the History of the Behavioral Sciences* 14:299–315.

Hamburg, D. A. Bibring, G. L., Fisher, C., et al. (1967). Report of Ad-Hoc Committee on central fact-gathering data of the American Psychoanalytic Association. *Journal of the American Psychoanalytic Association* 15:841–861.

Hawkins, D. R., and Hawkins, E. W. (1979). The role of psychiatry in Western European medical education. *Journal of Medical Education* 54:408–415.

Hollingshead, A. B., and Redlich, F. C. (1958). *Social Class and Mental Illness: A Community Study.* New York: Wiley.

Horney, K. (1939). *Our Inner Conflicts.* New York: Norton.

Horney-Eckardt, M. (1979). Organizational schisms in American psychoanalysis. *The Forum.* (The Society of Medical Psychoanalysts). 14:2–7.

Imber, S. D., Nash, E. H., and Stone, A. R. (1955). Social class and duration of psychotherapy. *Journal of Clinical Psychiatry* 11:281–284.

Jacobs, T. J. (1983). Dreams and responsibilities: notes on the making of an institute. *Annual of Psychoanalysis* 11:29–49.

Jacoby, R. (1984). The Americanization of psychoanalysis. *Psychology and Social Theory* 4:1–14.

Kahn, R. L., Pollock, M., and Fink, M. (1957). Social factors in the selection of therapy in a voluntary mental hospital. *Journal of Hillside Hospital* 6:216–228.

Kelman, H. (1968). The origins of the W.A.W. Institute—1941. *W.A.W. Newsletter* 3:2–3.

Kernberg, O. F., Burnstein, E. D., Coyne, L., et al. (1972). Psychotherapy and psychoanalysis: final report of the Menninger Foundation's project. *Bulletin of the Menninger Clinic* 36:3–275.

Kraft-Goin, M., Yamamoto, J., and Silverman, J. (1965). Therapy congruent with class linked expectations. *Archives of General Psychiatry* 13:133–137.

Krupnic, J. L., and Pincus, H. A. (1992). The cost-effectiveness of psychotherapy: a plan for research. *American Journal of Psychiatry* 149:1295–1305.

Kuhn, T. S. (1962). *The Structure of Scientific Revolutions.* Chicago: University of Chicago Press, 1970.

Laosa, J. M. (1984). Social policies toward children of diverse ethnic, racial, and language groups in the United States. In *Child Development Research and Social Policy,* ed. H. W. Stevenson and A. E. Siegel, pp. 1–109. Chicago: University of Chicago Press.

Lief, H. I., Lief, V. R., Warren, C. O., and Health, R. G. (1961). Low dropout rate in a psychiatric clinic. *Archives of General Psychiatry* 5:200–211.

Lorion, R. P. (1973). Patient and therapist variables in the treatment of low-income patients. *Psychological Bulletin* 81:344–354.

Lorr, M. (1959). Survey Finding, V.A. Survey of use of tranquilizers for psychiatric patients. *Transactions of the Third Research Conference on Chemotherapy in Psychiatry*, vol. 3, ed. C. L. Lindley, pp. 39–49. Washington, DC: Veterans Administration.

Marmor, J. (1968). Origins of the Institute. *W.A.W. Newsletter* 3:6–7.

McGrath, G. (1994). Economic aspects of psychotherapy. *Current Opinion in Psychiatry* 7:241–244.

Means, J. H. (1953). *Doctors, People, and Government*. Boston: Little Brown.

Moulton, R. (1968). Origins of the Institute. *W.A.W. Newsletter* 3:8–9.

Namnum, A. (1980). Trends in the selection of candidates for psychoanalytic training. *Journal of the American Psychoanalytic Association* 28:419–437.

Neill, J. R., and Ludwig, A. M. (1980). Psychiatry and psychotherapy: past and future. *American Journal of Psychotherapy* 34:39–50.

Overall, B., and Aronson, H. (1963). Expectations of psychotherapy in patients of lower socio-economic class. *American Journal of Orthopsychiatry* 33:421–430.

Pollock, G. H. (1983). The presence of the past. *Annual of Psychoanalysis* 11:3–27.

Rendon, M. (1986). Philosophical paradigms in psychoanalysis. *Journal of the American Academy of Psychoanalysis* 14:495–506.

Report to the President (1978). President's Commission on Mental Health. Washington, DC: US Government Printing Office.

Rice, D. P., Sander, K., and Leonard, S. M. (1991). Estimates of economic costs of alcohol and drug abuse and mental illness, 1985 and 1988. *Public Health Reports* 106:280–292.

Roback, A. A. (1952). *History of American Psychology*. New York: Macmillan.

Rosenthal, D., and Frank, J. D. (1958). The fate of psychiatric clinic outpatients assigned to psychotherapy. *Journal of Nervous and Mental Disease* 127:330–343.

Ruesch, J. (1953). *Social factors in therapy*. Association for Research in Nervous and Mental Diseases, Psychiatric Treatment, vol. 31, ed. S. B. Wortis, M. Herman, and C. C. Hair, pp. 59–93. Baltimore: Williams & Wilkins.

Schaffer, L., and Myers, J. (1954). Psychotherapy and social stratification. *Psychiatry* 17:83–93.

Schlesinger, H. J., Mumford, E., Glass, G. V., et al. (1983). Mental health treatment and medical care utilization in a fee-for-service system: outpatient mental health treatment following the onset of a chronic disease. *American Journal of Public Health* 73:422–429.

Sears, R. (1942). *Survey of Objective Studies of Psychoanalytic Concepts*. New York: Social Sciences Research Council.

Shapiro, D., Jaffe, D., Brauer, L., and Leaf, P. (1980). Final report of the survey of psychoanalytic practice, 1976. Report to Executive Council. American Psychoanalytic Association.

Siassi, I., and Messer, S. B. (1976). Psychotherapy with patients of lower socioeconomic groups. *American Journal of Psychotherapy* 30:29–40.

Siegel, N. H. (1962). Characteristics of patients in psychoanalysis. *Journal of Nervous and Mental Disease* 135:155–158.

Simon, G. E., VonKorff, M., and Durham, M. L. (1994). Predictors of outpatient mental health utilization by primary care patients in a Health Maintenance Organization. *American Journal of Psychiatry* 151: 908–913.

Sue, S. (1988). Psychotherapeutic services for ethnic minorities. *American Psychologist* 43:301–308.

Thompson, C. (1955). History of the William Alanson White Institute of Psychiatry, Psychoanalysis and Psychology. *William Alanson White Newsletter* 3:406, 1968.

Trad, P. V. (1992). Will the health care crisis sabotage the practice of psychotherapy? *American Journal of Psychotherapy* 46:499–500.

Trevino, F., and Rendon, M. (1994). Mental health of Latinos in the United States. In *Latino Health in the United States: A Growing Challenge*, ed. C. Molina and M. Molina-Aguirre, pp. 447–475. Washington, DC: American Public Health Association.

Turkle, S. (1978). *Psychoanalytic Politics. Freud's French Revolution.* New York. Basic Books.

Wallerstein, R. S. (1986). *Forty-two Lives in Treatment.* New York: Guilford.

Weber, J. J., Elinson, J., and Moss, L. M. (1967). Psychoanalysis and change: a study of psychoanalytic clinic records utilizing electronic data-processing techniques. *Archives of General Psychiatry* 17:687–709.

Weber, J. J., Solomon, M., and Bachrach, H. M. (1985). Characteristics of psychoanalytic clinic patients: Report of the Columbia Psychoanalytic Center Research Project: I. *International Review of Psychoanalysis* 12:13–26.

Weintraub, W., and Aronson, H. (1968). A survey of patients in classical psychoanalysis: some vital statistics. *Journal of Nervous and Mental Disease* 146:98–102.

Wells, H. K. (1964). *Quiebra del Psicoanalisis de Freud a Fromm.* Buenos Aires: Editorial Platina.

Wells, K. B., Stewart, A., Hays, R. D., et al. (1989). The functioning and well-being of depressed patients: results from the medical outcome study. *Journal of the American Medical Association* 262:914–919.

Winder, A., and Hersko, M. (1955). The effect of social class on the length and type of psychotherapy in a Veterans Administration Mental Hygiene Clinic. *Journal of Clinical Psychology* 1:77–79.

Yamamoto, J., James, Q. C., Bloombaum, M., and Hattem, J. (1967). Racial factors in patient selection. *American Journal of Psychiatry* 124:630–636.

4

How Universal is the Psychoanalytic Self?

Alan Roland, Ph.D.

DIFFERENT CLINICAL VIEWS OF THE SELF

I would like to present the briefest of vignettes to illustrate how some of our current psychoanalytic assumptions on the nature of the self and on psychological functioning are more loaded with Western cultural meanings than we commonly realize. A Japanese psychoanalyst, who has since returned to Japan after completing five years of training at the National Psychological Association for Psychoanalysis in New York City, told the following incident that had occurred early in his program. In a class on psychoanalytic technique, he presented an initial session with a Japanese patient, a young woman in her early twenties. He related to the class that the young woman was rather hesitant and cautious in telling him of her problems with an American boyfriend. For his own part, he had been mostly silently empathic with her, hardly asking any questions. At the end of the session, he said to her, "Now that we are working together, we shall continue in future sessions."

The instructor, an experienced analyst, was apparently astonished at his closing statement. She questioned, "How come you said 'now that *we* are working together' when there was very little if any verbal exchange or interaction between the two of you?" The Japanese student-therapist became very upset, feeling that, as a Japanese, he was not being understood.

What different assumptions about the self and psychological functioning did the instructor and the Japanese student make, causing this impasse?

The instructor assumed, as most of us would, that in psychoanalytic therapy there are two individuals speaking together with one of them gradually free-associating and the other clarifying what is transpiring. Each has an individualistic "I-self," with more or less firm ego boundaries between them; they are engaged in an "I" and "you" contractual relationship that involves exchanging time and expertise for fee. Although the therapist is obviously thought to be more knowledgeable and of higher status, nevertheless, American egalitarianism encourages both patient and analyst to be seen as essentially equal.

The Japanese therapist assumed a very different kind of self in his patient and himself, as well as very different ways of communicating and relating. He based his way of working on the "we-self" of the Japanese, a self that is primarily experienced in relation to others and is particularly integral to Japanese-style hierarchical relationships, in which subordinate and superior form a "we" relationship that is quite different from American egalitarianism. In vivid contrast to the American experiential sense of an I-self, for Japanese, a sense of I-ness, or even of I want or I wish, rarely exists. Rather, Japanese depend on each other to sense what the other wants. The therapist knew from Japanese-style hierarchical relationships, and from years of psychotherapy experience in Japan, that in order for any therapy to take place he had to foster the development of a close "we" relationship between superior—therapist—and subordinate —patient. In Japan, unlike for the most part in America, the superior is expected to be empathically nurturing and responsible to the subordinate.

He further knew that in their society that so stresses the correct presentation of self (*omote*) in a rigorously observed social etiquette, particularly in the formal hierarchical relationships, Japanese keep a highly private, secretive self (*ura*) in which all kinds of feelings, fantasies, and thoughts are present (Doi 1986, Roland 1988). This is a self that is to be empathically sensed and not intruded upon. Only after considerable time, when a trusting relationship has been formed and the therapy relationship has been gradually transformed from an outsider one (*soto*) to an insider one (*uchi*) will a Japanese begin to share important aspects of his or her inner life. Thus, this Japanese therapist was silently empathic with his patient, a not unusual way of communicating in Japan, where both patient and therapist, as in other hierarchical relationships, expect the other to empathically sense what each is feeling and thinking, often with a minimum of overt communication (Roland 1988). There is after all a saying in Japan, "Nothing important is ever to be communicated verbally."

Notwithstanding these significant differences between Japanese and Americans, it can also be said that the Japanese student-therapist, at this stage in his training, needed to learn more about resistance-analysis and transference-analysis, cornerstones of psychoanalytic work, which he subsequently did. Still, resistance-analysis with most Japanese has to be far less confrontive than is characteristic of most American analysts, even when they are being tactful. As in other forms of Japanese communication, it is often done by innuendo. This is due to a superego and ego-ideal that by American standards is highly perfectionistic, thus leaving Japanese highly vulnerable to any criticism or intimation of failure.

CULTURAL ROOTS OF WESTERN INDIVIDUALISM

Let us now take a step back to reflect and delve more deeply into the cultural roots and philosophical assumptions of psychoanalysis. If such a brief vignette can highlight such different psychological worlds—and many other cases could easily be cited—then it behooves us to examine more closely the current elaboration of psychoanalytic theory in its Western cultural context. Only then shall we be in a position to extend psychoanalysis to others from radically different cultures and develop a comparative psychoanalysis rooted in different cultural, social, and historical contexts. More specifically, we shall have to explore how psychoanalytic theory and practice are profoundly related to the Northern European/North American cultural values and philosophical assumptions involving individualism. I shall touch upon a few of the salient issues involved.

Modern Western individualism grew out of the religious sphere of the Reformation, spread into the secular sphere of philosophers of the Social Contract and then to ones of the Enlightenment, and later into the cultural realm of Romanticism. The Reformation transformed an earlier Christian otherworldly individualism to a this-worldly one in which the onus of salvation is put squarely on the shoulders of the individual who is in a direct, unmediated relationship to a God from whom he or she is essentially separate and whom he or she tries to rejoin. In the Calvinist vision, individuals through independent, active achievement in the world gauge the degree to which they are among the elect and therefore predestined for redemption. Protestant sects have emphasized values of individualism involving taking responsibility for attending to one's conscience and making correct moral decisions, thus being self-directed, self-reliant, self-sufficient, and independent. Rather than being rooted in a hierarchical social collective and cosmic order, the individual is set on his own (Dumont 1986, Kirschner 1992, Nelson 1965).

Seventeenth- and eighteenth-century philosophers such as Hobbes, Locke, and Rousseau, each in his own way, then formulated the Social Contract of essentially self-contained, atomistic individuals who interact with each other in a society with some kind of necessary authority. These philosophers were joined by the Jurists who reinterpreted Natural Law as comprised of self-sufficient individuals who are made in the image of God and are the repository of reason. Then came various Enlightenment philosophers such as Voltaire, Diderot, and Descartes, who, with others, laid the cultural groundwork for modern Western individualism in the social and political spheres, an individual epitomized by the formation of the modern nation state as a union of equal individuals with rights and obligations (Dumont 1986).

The individualism of the religious, social, and political spheres was followed by individualism in the economic realm. Adam Smith and David Ricardo conceived of a rationally ordered economy of separate self-contained individuals with similar interests. These cultural valuations of autonomous individuals who are equal to each other, rather than of the person as encompassed by the social and cosmic realms, have come to underlie all modern Western economic, political, legal, and cultural theories, as well as educational approaches (Allen 1996, Dumont 1986). Nineteenth-century philosophical and literary approaches in Romanticism further consolidated individualism through the ideal of the highly individuated, verbally self-expressive individual in close relationships with other highly individuated individuals.

Thus, the individual came to be considered inviolate, the supreme value in and of itself, with each having his or her own rights and obligations and all being equal. Society is considered to be essentially subordinate to the needs of individuals, who are governed by their own self-interest and who participate in mutually consenting, contractual relationships that facilitate their political and economic strivings.

Enlightenment notions of individualism view the rational, thinking person as what is most real and valued, and analytic-deductive modes of thought that explore causal, logical relationships are seen as primary. Rationality is considered intrinsically superior to the emotions. This rational, thinking mind is viewed as autonomous in each individual and separate from others, and this is considered a universal phenomenon rather than one that is historically or culturally constituted. All other ways of perceiving reality are discredited as superstition or demystified, such as religion, magic, or ritual. The reigning views of the world and the cosmos are primarily secular and scientific, the latter in particular becoming supremely valued.

Reason has taken two major forms of cultural expression: dualism and universalism. Since the Reformation dualistic thinking became deeply ingrained in Western culture, with its separation of spirit from matter, value from fact, and the humanities from the natural sciences. Dualism was further developed during the Enlightenment, particularly by Descartes, in the separation of mind from body, subject from object, idealism from materialism, and the increasing specialization and separation of academic disciplines from each other (Marriott 1990). Cartesian dualism pervades the work of the social sciences and psychoanalysis in their study of Western society and the individual, As a result, there is a sharp differentiation in all of the models of psychoanalysis, as well as in other Western psychological theories of personality, between what is inside oneself and what is in others.

The focus on universals derives originally from the Greek philosophers, such as Plato, and from monotheism. Universalism received particular emphasis during the Enlightenment as Diderot and other Encyclopedists formulated Natural Law, and later in the ensuing pursuit in the natural and social sciences, including psychology, for universal laws. Universalism is such a basic philosophical assumption in Western thinking that it is rarely realized how culturally specific it is. Psychoanalysts, for instance, always assume that each new formulation they make has universal validity.

INDIVIDUALISM AND PSYCHOANALYSIS

Against this backdrop of the progression of individualism from the religious to the social and political, to the economic, and then to the philosophical literary sphere, one can look upon psychoanalysis as the further extension of individualism to the realm of the psychological. In fact, one can easily cite psychoanalysis as the psychological theory and therapy par excellence of modern Western individualism. From the perspective of individualism, one easily sees the self-contained individual in traditional Freudian drive and structural theory where all motivation origi-

nates within intrapsychic drives and structures. The social surround re-
ceives scant attention except for its being the agent for the gratification
or frustration of the drives, the source of superego and especially ego-
ideal contents—internalized from parental carriers of the culture, and the
reality principle, which identifies what an individual can or cannot do in
the social world.

It is not simply that Freud veered from the issue of parental seduction
to focusing exclusively on intrapsychic fantasy. The problem goes much
deeper if one views it from the perspective of individualism. When the
concept of the self-contained individual prevails, there is no place in traditional psychoanalytic theory for the impact of the psychodynamics of
parents and siblings or even the effect of changing family dynamics on
the patient. Even the Oedipus complex, the cornerstone of classical Freudian theory, is more of a stage setting of triangular relationships within a
family than a conceptualization that allows for particular dramatis per-
sonae, each with her or his own character in depth. Or in that other tri-
angle, that of sibling rivalry with the mother usually at the apex, again
the only member of the cast with any real characterization is the patient.
The theory almost exclusively emphasizes intrapsychic fantasy in the self-
contained individual.

This does not necessarily mean that the sensitive, traditional psychoanalytic clinician does not take the social surround into account, particularly childhood familial relationships, in working with a patient. There
are often two different narratives in psychoanalytic writing: the theory
and the case illustration (Schafer 1983). It is the former that delineates
one or another facet of the self-contained individual, whereas it is often
in the latter that the clinician may detail subtle parent–child interactions
that resurface in the transference and belie the paradigm of the self-
contained individual.

What is true of traditional Freudian theory is equally true of the object
relations theory of Melanie Klein and her followers, including Kernberg.
While they see the child—from the earliest age—as more basically related
to the object world of parents and other caretakers, nevertheless, what is
introjected into the child's internal object world is seen as being primarily governed by what has been unconsciously projected onto others.
These introjections are then once again projected onto others, or parts
of the internal object world including those of the self may be projec-
tively identified with others. Kleinians primarily consider parental figures as gratifiers or frustraters of the drives, but, as in classical Freudian

theory, family members are never delineated in any psychological depth. Once again, individualism's narrative of the self-contained individual prevails.

However, in the hands of some of the followers of Klein, especially latter-day ones such as Betty Joseph (1985), their clinical narrative departs even more than the one of traditional Freudians from the paradigm of individualism. Since the 1950s, these Kleinians have explored the transferential meanings of induced countertransference reactions to patients with more severe psychopathology, such as borderline, schizoid, and even psychotic. It is frequently in just these kinds of cases that induced countertransference reactions arise and are so germane. In such cases Kleinian analysts often make sensitive reconstructions of subtle psychological aspects of inner images of the parent or of the patient's self in the child–parent relationship as these resurface in the transference–countertransference interaction between analysand and analyst. In these clinical narratives, where the analyst experiences himself or herself as some part of the patient, the self-contained individual is transcended.

A brief example of this phenomenon is discussed in a paper by Betty Joseph (1985) that describes a presenting analyst in a seminar who is quite dissatisfied with the work of a particular session, and in general with her analysis of a quite difficult schizoid patient. The other members of the seminar then strive to understand more about the patient, but they, too, soon become dissatisfied with their ideas. It finally dawns on them that their very inability to comprehend what is really going on with the patient is central to the transference, and is actually a reflection of the patient's inner world. They see the patient as unconsciously evoking her self-feeling in the analyst, as well as in the others. The patient has felt herself unable to make sense of what is going on in her relationship with a highly unempathic mother who only pretends she is attuned to her daughter. They also see the patient as unconsciously evoking in the analyst the complementary mother-imago of seemingly making sense of the patient's inner world when she fundamentally cannot. In either case, the group recognizes that its inability to comprehend is far more a part of the patient's inner world than of their own individual responses.

Other basic philosophical dimensions of individualism also enter into traditional Freudian psychoanalysis. While much has been made of Freud's undermining of the Enlightenment's idea of man's inherent rationality through his discovery and formulation of the unconscious, the fact is that classical psychoanalysis has always emphasized a resolution of unconscious conflicts so that rationality can once more prevail. "Where id was, ego shall be," Freud wrote, clearly carrying over Kant's ideal of rational autonomy, the ability to regulate one's life by norms of one's own devising (Kirschner 1992). There is no question that rational secondary process thinking has always been evaluated as superior to the primary process, with the latter being seen in a pejorative way as occurring developmentally earlier in the child and in the human race. Only in recent decades has there been a shift in view, represented by such work as that of Deri (1984), Noy (1969), Roland (1972), and Rycroft (1968).

Regarding morality, universal principles of conscience located within the individual were emphasized by the Reformation and later incorporated by philosophers such as Kant in his concept of the categorical imperative involving universal moral laws. Freud took this over in his view of a deeply internalized superego that functions in a principled, consistent way. It is only in very recent decades that this, too, has been challenged both from the standpoint of gender and of cross-cultural studies (Bernstein 1993, Gilligan 1980, Roland 1988).

In another philosophical assumption of individualism, derived from Cartesian dualism that separates emotions from the rational mind, emotions are viewed as derived from bodily sensations or drives centered in the individual. In traditional psychoanalytic terms, emotions and affects are considered to be drive derivatives of sexuality and aggression, and as such they are to be brought under the sway of secondary process rational thinking. They are not thought to be centered in the social world and profoundly related to cultural meanings.

Regarding the highly influential ego psychology of Margaret Mahler (Mahler et al. 1975), Suzanne Kirschner (1992), a psychoanalytic anthropologist, argues convincingly that Mahler's emphasis on autonomy, separation, and individuation strongly reflects Protestant—particularly Pietistic and Calvinist Nonconformist—values of individualism involving self-reliance and self-direction. Mahler, in effect, sets the early childhood developmental program for the secular fulfillment of Protestant values in current American individualism that earlier were essential to the Protestant religious world view.

Kirschner further details Mahler's developmental progression—from symbiosis to separation-individuation to having close relationships while still maintaining a high degree of separateness and an individuated identity—as profoundly reflecting a high Romantic narrative of individualism. In this narrative, there is "a quasi-mystical striving towards a 'higher' reunion of subject and object in which the subject's individuated distinctiveness also is preserved . . . " (Kirschner 1992, p. 187). She also sees the strong valuation that ego psychologists such as Spitz (1959) and Mahler put on verbal communication as reflecting both the high Romantic emphasis on individualistic self-expression and the Protestant values of self-reliance and separateness. Nonverbal communication is then pejoratively viewed as occurring at an earlier developmental level of merger and symbiosis.

PSYCHOANALYSIS AS CRITIQUE AND SUPPORT OF INDIVIDUALISM

Within the Freudian opus, there have been important challenges since 1950 to the paradigm of the self-contained individual. Paradoxically the same critics have also delineated essential psychological processes involved in functioning in a culture of individualism. Perhaps no one stands out in this regard as much as Erik Erikson (1950, 1968). On the one hand, Erikson, more than other psychoanalysts, introduced the social, cultural, and historical milieu as essential to a psychoanalytic consideration of the individual. In his psychosocial concept of self-identity, Erikson saw the individual not as self-contained but as integrally part of this milieu, with roles, values, ideals, and norms of the community profoundly shaping and becoming part of a personal identity.

On the other hand, Erikson, in congruence with the essential psychological insight of Otto Rank on self-creation (Menaker 1982), framed the most central dimension of American individualism: the self-creation of one's identity. In his epigenetic stages of development that stressed autonomy and initiative in the childhood years—in certain ways anticipating and paralleling the contributions of Mahler—lay the groundwork for the adolescent struggle to self-create an identity. Erikson's work perceptively charts the stormy seas that are more often than not encountered in this prolonged act of self-creating—the identity conflicts, confusions, and crises, the frequent need for a moratorium, the occasional syntheses around negative identities, and the eventual resolution of a positive identity synthesis. Such a process does in fact occur within the social milieu of contemporary American culture, which imposes on the individual an enormous degree of autonomy in the adolescent and young adult years to choose a mate or love partner, decide what kind of education and vocational training to pursue, and then what kind of work to do, to make social affiliations, select where to live, and develop an ideology or value system and become committed to it. The frequently enormously difficult intrapsychic task of the individual adolescent and young adult in American society—to integrate these adult commitments with the intrapsychic identifications and self-images developed within the family—is the crux of Erikson's elaboration of self-identity and ego-identity.

Another salient psychoanalytic critic of the paradigm of the self-contained individual is Winnicott, author of the famous statement, "There is no such thing as a baby." In suggesting that one cannot even begin to think of a baby without referring to the baby's profound dependence and interconnectedness with a mother or mothering person, Winnicott (1965) challenges the prevailing norms and models of individualism. At the same time, his (1951) elaboration of transitional objects and transitional phenomena is essentially connected to notions of the individual developmentally functioning more and more autonomously, with the gradual sharp separation between inner images of self and object that is characteristic of the individualism of Northern European and North American societies. Observations of infants and children from cultures radically different from this culture area indicate that where there is a far more prolonged symbiotic mothering in more communal societies, transitional objects are not nearly so much in evidence (Grolnick and Barkin 1978).

As a further step in delineating the psychological processes involved in individualism, Winnicott (1958) depicts the internalization of a comforting maternal presence necessary for the ability to be alone and separate. In a similar vein, Winnicott's (1960) emphasis on the true self/false self duality can be considered a secularization of the Protestant values of self-direction, in which it is essential to be deeply in touch with oneself in order to know morally what to do (Kirschner 1992).

The latest psychoanalytic critique of the emphasis not only on the self-contained individual but also on secularized Protestant values of independence and self-reliance is that of self psychology and its offshoot, intersubjectivity. Kohut's (1984) emphasis on the dependent's lifelong need for mirroring, idealizing, and alterego selfobject relationships, which enhance and maintain self-esteem and self-cohesion, goes completely against individualism's main paradigms and values. Even the stance of empathic inquiry versus objective, rational assessment of the analysand runs counter to Enlightenment reason. One can even assert that self psychology specifically addresses the psychopathology—characterized by problematic selfobject relationships with their resultant deficits in structure-building—that arises from extreme American individualism with its heightened mobility and tenuous relationships.

While these kinds of deficits and problems in selfobject relationships can well be present anywhere, they are certainly not as salient in Asian cultures, where empathic attunement and culturally supported figures for idealization are so emphasized (Roland 1988). There, other kinds of psychopathology predominate. Similar to self psychology, Stolorow and Atwood (1992) in their theory of intersubjectivity, which has philosophical roots in phenomenology, address the myth in psychoanalysis of the isolated individual mind and stress the interrelationship of subjectivities in all human relationships.

On the other hand, in his delineation of the bipolar self, Kohut (1977) began to spell out in self psychological terms individualism's main trajectory of the individual realizing his potential in action and relationships throughout life, a secularization of Protestant values. Ambitions are fostered in the early maternal mirroring selfobject relationship. They then exist in a tension arc with the goals and ideals later developed through an idealizing selfobject relationship, and carried out using skills learned through alter-ego selfobject relationships. The initiative, spontaneity, and creativity of a cohesive self are further spelled out. All of this is obviously in accord with American individualism's secularization of individual achievement in the world, self-direction, and the fulfillment of one's inner potentials.

PSYCHOANALYSIS AND OTHER CULTURES

With this kind of cultural baggage, how has psychoanalysis approached persons from cultures that are significantly to radically different from the Northern European/North American culture belt? And what kinds of problems are engendered by using a theory and therapy so rooted in individualism? To answer these questions, one would do well to borrow a leaf from anthropology, which has had decades of experience in investigating different cultures. Anthropologists have interpreted other cultures in three essential ways—evolutionism, universalism, and relativism—each with its own underlying premises (Shweder and Bourne 1984). These three approaches are equally relevant to that small but increasing number of psychoanalysts and psychoanalytic anthropologists who have worked in radically different cultures, as well as to psychoanalysts working with patients from diverse cultures such as Hispanic, Mediterranean, African-American, or Eastern European ones. The theoretical dilemmas posed by each of these three approaches will become readily apparent in the psychoanalytic sphere, and will have to be resolved for a viable theoretical perspective to emerge. The advantages and pitfalls of all three approaches are most readily observable in the exploration of psychoanalytic work conducted in civilizations that are radically different from the Northern European and North American ones, such as Asian ones.

Evolutionism as applied to psychoanalysis posits definitive norms for what healthy human nature should be and how it develops. Invariably, these norms derive from a contemporary normative model of the individualized self as formulated in current psychoanalytic theory, and are assumed to be universal and superior. Others from radically different cultures who do not measure up to this universal normative model are then seen as having inferior psychological development or psychopathology.

An example of the pitfalls of such an evolutionist view of human nature is easily seen in Sudhir Kakar's psychoanalytic work on Indians (1978, 1982, 1989, 1991). Unfortunately, these undermine his many perceptive observations. Kakar well recognizes that Indian psychological makeup is modally different from Westerners', but he holds to the basic premise that the psychoanalytic theory of human nature is universally normative. By thus subscribing to these norms, he invariably assesses Indian personality as modally inferior to the individualism of Westerners. Indians in Kakar's analysis emerge as having an underdeveloped ego. They appear not to have the independent, self-reliant, self-directing ego of Western individualism; are considered to be lacking in rational, logical secondary process thinking—another hallmark value of individualism; are seen as having vague emotional boundaries between self and other, with much less of the self–other demarcation characteristic of individualism; and as having a weak conscience or superego, evident from their looking to others and using highly contextual ethical norms rather than following the categorical imperative of Western male individualism. Further, Kakar basically accepts the demystification and secularization of religion in psychoanalytic theory, which views spiritual experiences—so valued in Indian society—as regression to the early mother–infant relationship.

The second approach to assessing the universality and variability of the self in different cultural settings is essentially to search for universals only. Differences or variability is seen as only superficially colored by culture. In universalism, higher order generalities predominate and specific, culture-rich, thick descriptions of human nature are bleached out from consideration.

An example of the problems of psychological universalism is found in the work of Catherine Ewing (1991), an American psychoanalytic anthropologist who has worked in Pakistan. She avoided the pitfalls of evolutionism found in Kakar's work, with its value-laden judgments of Indians, by combining the usual cultural relativism of anthropology with the universalism of psychoanalysis—that is, by positing that everyone is essentially psychologically the same everywhere. Ewing well recognized that people behave and interact very differently in Pakistan than in the United States, but she attributed this solely to their very different cultural patterns of interpersonal engagement and interpersonal autonomy (individualism). These patterns are given equal weight, thus avoiding the implicit superiority–inferiority norms of evolutionism. Otherwise, Ewing sees Pakistanis as being no different psychologically from North Americans, their self being basically alike. In this regard, her position is similar to that of many other psychoanalytic anthropologists.

Ewing utilizes an ego psychology framework to focus on the differentiation and separateness between inner representations of the self and object. However, unlike Kakar who views Indians' degree of inner separateness of self and object representations as less than that of Westerners and therefore inferior, Ewing simply emphasizes the necessity for separation to occur in order to avoid psychopathology.

By being so completely oriented toward the universal, in this case the necessity for separation between inner images of self and object, Ewing completely ignores the different degrees of inner separation in Pakistanis as contrasted to North Americans. She therefore does not see that Pakistanis have an experiential sense of a we-self that includes inner images of others of the extended family and community as part of the self much more than the highly individualistic, more self-contained American I-self. Thus, modal differences in psychological makeup, or variabilities in the makeup of the self, are completely missing when one focuses on universals. Ewing is unable to relate how the variability in the self in either Pakistanis or Americans enables them to function in their radically different cultural and interpersonal patterns. If evolutionism seems to commit a sin of commission, then universalism's is one of omission.

The third theoretical approach for evaluating the universality and variability of the self in diverse settings is relativism. In relativism, as applied to psychological phenomena, highly differing views of human nature in different cultures are present, but these are viewed within an entirely different framework from Western individualism, each having its own internal consistency and validity related to the indigenous culture and its social patterns. The only problem here is that there are no common categories or standards for comparison or criticism across cultures.

Perhaps the best representation of relativism in the psychological realm is the seminal psychoanalytic work of Takeo Doi (1973, 1986) who elaborated various facets of dependency relationships (*amae*) and the dual self-structure of a public and a highly private self (*omote/ura*) in Japan. Doi gave up psychoanalytic theory because its norms of individualism are too Western-centric and its categories did not encompass central dimensions of the Japanese psyche. What he did maintain, however, was a psychoanalytic sensibility of exploring the inner world of the Japanese and of probing for its developmental antecedents through exploring predominant Japanese linguistic terms. He formulated a culturally variable psychology of Japanese in many of its important configurations that differs radically from the psychoanalytic self of Northern European/North American individualism.

Doi's basic theoretical approach differs greatly from the evolutionism of Kakar and the universalism of Ewing as he focused on the variabilities of the Japanese self and viewed them as being on a par with those of individualism's self. However, after elaborating this modal psychology of the Japanese, Doi searches for the universality of their kind of dependency, *amae*, in Americans. He does indeed find it to be present, but in such diminished form—because of the Northern European/North American cultural emphasis on self-reliance—that it is recognized conceptually only by Balint's psychoanalytic formulation of passive object love. Psychological variabilities hardly present in Northern European/North American psychological makeup simply do not play a salient part in psychoanalytic theory. It stands to reason that a theory without this kind of category will either completely miss this variability in others or see it as inferior or psychopathological.

A profound insight of Doi's approach is to move from the exploration of psychological variabilities in a given culture to formulating some of these variabilities, such as the *amae* dependency relationship, as universal categories that are present in all cultures, manifesting themselves in significantly different patterns and configurations that may be observed without positing any value-laden universal norms. One can see that psychoanalysis itself has actually developed this way—from the extensive investigation into the psychological variability of Northern Europeans and North Americans to a formulation of universal categories. However, unlike Doi, Western psychoanalysts, without the benefit of a comparative experience of working in different civilizations, have not realized how much of their elaboration of the contents, norms, and configurations of various psychoanalytic categories almost completely involves the particular variabilities of the highly individualistic Northern European/North American self.

What are the limitations of Doi's psychoanalytic relativism? Most salient is his wholesale jettisoning of psychoanalytic theory as too burdensome. While this was initially highly liberating, enabling Doi to formulate an indigenous psychology of the Japanese that is related to Japanese cultural and social patterns, we are left with an essentially atheoretical approach. Thus, while Doi's work contributes to our much fuller understanding of the variability of the Japanese self, and while he identifies a couple of new universal categories minimally present in Westerners, we still remain without a comprehensive theory with which to evaluate both universality and variability in human nature across cultures. The absence of such a framework becomes particularly salient when one wishes to make highly useful comparisons between, for instance, the configurations of the Japanese self and those of other Asians, who are much closer to the Japanese in psychological makeup than are Westerners, or even between this self and the Hispanic self.

It is evident then that evolutionism, universalism, and relativism all present their own particular problems related to the attempt to utilize current individualistically oriented psychoanalytic theory across cultures. Nevertheless, variability, universals, and normality—psychopathology are essential issues in assessing the self across cultures. Therefore, it is imperative to develop newer modes of resolving these issues.

TOWARD A COMPARATIVE PSYCHOANALYSIS

To evolve a comparative psychoanalysis suitable for patients across a wide variety of cultures, it is necessary to develop a new theoretical approach. A new paradigm (Roland 1988) involves using psychoanalytic categories of personality and therapy from a variety of psychoanalytic models, and treating these as universals. These categories and concepts include: super-ego and ego-ideal, ego boundaries, developmental stages, selfobject relationships, self and object representations, self-identity, internal object world, affects and drives, transference, resistance, and dream-analysis, among others. One must then decontextualize them of their current Northern European/North American content and norms—the particular variability they are accorded by psychoanalytic theory—and then proceed to recontextualize them using the clinical data of persons from significantly or radically different cultures. The new contents and norms of each category are then integrated with the cultural, social, and historical contexts of that culture. This approach would also add new universal categories, as Doi has done with *amae* dependency relationships and the *omote/ura* dual self-structure.

Most important, to capture the true variability of human nature, a further step must be taken to put these recontextualized categories into their unique configurations or organizations of the self in different cultures. We must approach this as one would a painting, in which—whether it is representational or abstract—issues of darks and lights, color harmonies and contrasts, line, texture, compositional structure, dissonances, and such must all achieve a unique balance or configuration. Artists are well aware of this, and psychoanalysts must be guided by analogous considerations in their efforts to understand the universality and variability of the self across cultures.

As a simple example of this new approach, one can take the category of ego boundaries. In a North American context, current psychoanalytic norms call for outer ego boundaries between self and object to be relatively firm so that a person can have close relationships without being involved in merger experiences, which constitute psychopathology. By contrast, inner ego boundaries should be somewhat flexible so that a person is in touch with inner feelings, fantasies, and impulses, but is not flooded by them. In cultures different from those governed by individualism, such as India and Japan, one easily observes that outer ego boundaries are far more permeable and vague than in North America. This is in keeping with Indian and Japanese close emotional enmeshment in family, group, and community—the Japanese variant having even vaguer outer boundaries than the Indian one.

But balancing this permeable outer boundary, which allows semi-merger experiences with others, is an inner boundary of a highly private, secret self—in Japanese it is more secretive than in Indians—a repository of individuality that is rarely found in North Americans, whose individuality is characteristically expressed in the social world. The innermost ego boundary varies even more between Indians and Japanese, the former usually being far more in touch with their inner world than the latter and even somewhat more so than North Americans. This is due to differing cultural norms. The Japanese have a far more perfectionistic ego-ideal and rigorous social etiquette than Indians and North Americans, and so are less in touch with their innermost wishes and fantasies. By contrast, Indian culture, while insisting on the behavioral observation of proper social etiquette in family and group hierarchical relationships, gives considerable latitude to a wide variety of personal ideas, feelings, and fantasies. Thus North Americans, Indians, and Japanese all possess the universal category of ego boundaries, but this category has to be recontextualized for Indians and Japanese from the usual norms of psychoanalysis, adding the new aspect of an inner boundary involving a highly private self. Finally, the relationship of outer to inner boundaries has dramatically different configurations for these three groups.

From the diagnostic perspective, norms vary considerably from one configuration of ego boundaries to another. Merger or semi-merger experiences that would be considered borderline if not more severe psychopathology for most North Americans are usually in the neurotic range for Japanese. By the same token, the relatively firm outer ego boundary normal for North Americans is highly maladaptive for Japanese and Indians in their emotionally enmeshed group relationships, and is therefore neurotic.

Other categories also enter into unique configurations in the overall organization of the self in a given cultural area. Modes of communication, such as verbal and nonverbal, clearly vary along with the configuration of ego boundaries. The firmer the outer ego boundary, as in North Americans, the more reliance there is on verbal communication, as if to bridge the separateness of individuals. Whereas, when there is a highly developed private self, nonverbal empathic sensing becomes more salient. The more the private self becomes highly secretive and not to be intruded upon, as in the case of the Japanese self, the more finely tuned empathic, intuitive sensing must be. Verbal expression is then used mainly to observe proper social etiquette in the hierarchical relationships.

A new paradigm would also incorporate the sociohistorical experiences of persons from a given civilization as these have become internalized within the psyche. Certainly, the psychological makeup of women in contemporary North America is profoundly related to the women's movement and feminism of the last thirty years, which incorporate and critique the values of individualism hitherto reserved for men. Over the last century or two Indians and Japanese have become increasingly exposed to the antithetical values of Western individualism, which has had profound psychological effects. When these values have been posited in the sociopolitical context of colonialism that is so denigrating to indigenous cultures, the psychological effects have been devastating, as in India.

The new paradigm must also include other psychological phenomena that have been looked askance at by psychoanalysis, with its Enlightenment philosophical heritage. Chief among these are the realm of spiritual experiences and disciplines, which, with but the rarest of exceptions, psychoanalysts from Freud on have consistently relegated to the stage of infant–mother symbiotic merger states, and the even more disparaged magic-cosmic world of personal destiny. Patients from a variety of cultures are involved in this world in a number of ways, related to, for example, astrology, palmistry, the spirit world, psychics and mediums, and rituals. This is anathema to most psychoanalysts. Psychoanalysts, coming from a tradition of the self-contained, rational individual, simply do not appreciate that patients outside of the Northern European/North American culture belt have a self that is not only far more enmeshed and embedded in an extended family/group/community context—now being referred to as sociocentric/organic societies (Markus and Kitayama 1991)—but often also in a world of invisible influences. To assume a denigrating attitude toward these psychological phenomena will be to miss a major portion of these patients' psyches.

REFERENCES

Allen, D. (1996). Indian, Marxist, and feminist critiques of the "modern" concepts of the self. In *Culture and Self: Philosophical and Religious Perspective, East and West*, ed. D. Allen and A. Malhotra. New York: Westview.

Bernstein, D. (1993). *Female Identity Conflict in Clinical Practice*, ed. N. Freedman and B. Distler. Northvale, NJ: Jason Aronson.

Deri, S. (1984). *Symbolization and Creativity*. New York: International Universities Press.

Doi, T. (1973). *The Anatomy of Dependence*. Tokyo: Kodansha International Ltd.

—— (1986). *The Anatomy of Self: The Individual versus the Society*. Tokyo: Kodansha International Ltd.

Dumont, L. (1986). *Essays on Individualism.* Chicago: University of Chicago Press.

Erikson, E. (1950). *Childhood and Society.* New York: Norton.

—— (1968). *Identity, Youth, and Crisis.* New York: Norton.

Ewing, C. (1991). Can psychoanalytic theories explain the Pakistani woman? Intrapsychic autonomy and interpersonal engagement in the extended family. *Ethos:* 19:131–160.

Gilligan, C. (1980). *In a Different Voice.* Cambridge: Harvard University Press.

Grolnick, S., and Barkin L., eds. (1978). *Between Reality and Fantasy.* New York: Jason Aronson.

Joseph, B. (1985). Transference: the total situation. *International Journal of Psycho-Analysis* 66:447–454.

Kakar, S. (1978). *The Inner World: A Psychoanalytic Study of Childhood and Society in India.* Delhi: Oxford University Press.

—— (1982). *Shamans, Mystics, and Doctors.* New York: Knopf.

—— (1989). *Intimate Relations: Exploring Indian Sexuality.* Chicago: University of Chicago Press.

—— (1991). *The Analyst and the Mystic.* New Delhi: Viking, Penguin.

Kirschner, S. R. (1992). Anglo-American values in post-Freudian psychoanalysis. In *Psychoanalytic Anthropology after Freud,* ed. D. H. Spain, pp. 162–197. New York: Psyche.

Kohut, H. (1977). *The Restoration of the Self.* New York: International Universities Press.

—— (1984). *How Does Analysis Cure?* Chicago: University of Chicago Press.

Mahler, M., Pine F., and Bergman A. (1975). *The Psychological Birth of the Human Infant.* New York: Basic Books.

Markus, H., and Kitayama, S. (1991). Culture and the self: implications for cognition, emotion, and motivation. *Psychological Review* 98:224–253.

Marriott, M. (1990). Constructing an Indian ethnosociology. In *India through Hindu Categories,* ed. M. Marriott, pp. 1–40. New Delhi, London: Sage.

Menaker, E, (1982). *Otto Rank: A Rediscovered Legacy.* New York: Columbia University Press.

Nelson, B. (1965). Self-images and systems of spiritual direction in the history of European civilization. In *The Quest for Self-control,* ed. S. Z. Klausner. New York: Free Press.

Noy, P. (1969). A revision of the psychoanalytic theory of the primary process. *International Journal of Psycho-Analysis* 50:155–178.

Roland, A. (1972). Imagery and symbolic expression in dreams and art. *International Journal of Psycho-Analysis* 53:531–539.

—— (1988). *In Search of Self in India and Japan: Toward a Cross-Cultural Psychology.* Princeton: Princeton University Press.

Rycroft, C. (1968). *Imagination and Reality.* New York: International Universities Press.

Schafer, R. (1983). *The Analytic Attitude.* New York: Basic Books.

Shweder, R. A., and Bourne, E. J. (1984). Does the concept of the person vary cross-culturally? In *Culture Theory: Essays on Mind, Self, and Emotion,* ed. R. A. Shweder and R. A. LeVine. New York: Cambridge University Press.

Spitz, R. (1959). *A Genetic Field Theory of Ego Formation.* New York: International Universities Press.

Stolorow, R., and Atwood, G. (1992). *Contexts of Being: The Intersubjective Foundations of Psychological Life*. New York: Analytic Press.

Winnicott, D. W. (1951). Transitional objects and transitional phenomena. In *Collected Papers*. New York: Basic Books.

—— (1965). *The Maturational Processes and the Facilitating Environment*. London: Hogarth.

II

The Dynamics of
Diversity in the
Treatment Process

Racial, cultural, and class differences between therapist and patient involve issues of conscious and unconscious meaning at many levels of emotional significance. The pull toward collusive denial of these issues, or, conversely, toward their exaggerated emphasis aimed at obscuring intrapsychic determinants, is finally being described in the literature. Whether patients and analysts resist their differentness, or use it as a resistance, it is becoming clear that these decisions reside within the disavowed, intersubjective communications of their transference–countertransference worlds.

In Chapter 5, Javier describes the process of his work with poor Hispanic patients in urban New York, highlighting how the therapist's own assumptions about cultural groups can either expand or limit the depth of the analytic work. Chapter 6 is Thompson's three-part consideration of how race and social minority status interface with psychic development, and the way these dynamics emerge in the treatment within the live action of the transference–countertransference matrix. In Chapter 7, Whitson elaborates on the interaction of class difference in the therapeutic situation, noting how psychoanalysis's own value presuppositions about behavioral and affective expression can collide with working-class values and modes of expression. Gorkin, in Chapter 8, discusses the countertransference issues that arise when a Jewish therapist treats an Arab patient. This situation, which arises in a social context in which antipathy and distrust between Jew and Arab is the norm, offers many parallels to black–white therapy dyads in contemporary America. Dealing with the intense feelings that arise in such treatment situations is a difficult task for both therapist and patient. That some of these treatments do achieve a satisfactory outcome is testimony to the fact that this task can be accomplished.

5

Psychodynamic Treatment with the Urban Poor[*]

Rafael Art. Javier, Ph.D.

Finding the most appropriate treatment approach to respond to the psychological needs of the poor continues to be a source of great controversy (Altman 1993, Foster 1993, Javier and Herron 1992). Depending upon one's understanding of this phenomenon and one's familiarity with individuals suffering from the consequences of socioeconomic deprivation, different treatment approaches are advanced as the most appropriate interventions. In general, psychodynamic psychotherapy has been greatly criticized as inappropriate, even by individuals whose professional activities include extensive work with this population (Costantino et al. 1986, Minuchin et al. 1967, Padilla et al. 1975). Some of the arguments advanced in support of this view focus on the psychological impact of socioeconomic deprivation in this population, suggesting that insight-oriented therapy is uneconomical and irrelevant to the context of the lives of the urban poor (Ruiz 1981, Sue and Sue 1977).

Treatment interventions, such as Minuchin's family therapy model (Minuchin et al. 1967), Cuento therapy (Costantino et al. 1985), psychiatric and psychoeducational models, and other similar treatment interventions are assumed to address directly the kinds of problems frequently confronting the poor in a concrete and expeditious manner. The underlying assumption of these interventions is that poor individuals are uninterested in exploration and/or are unable to engage in exploratory psychotherapy due to the negative impact of the "culture of poverty" (Allen 1970, Javier and Herron 1995, Lewis 1964, 1966, Malgady et al. 1987, Rogler

---

[*]Portions of this chapter appeared previously in *The American Journal of Psychoanalysis.*

et al. 1987, Sarbin 1970). This assumption may also be evident among professionals who, despite having been able to work psychoanalytically with this population, nevertheless have suggested that a relational or an interpersonal approach is more appropriate than other psychoanalytic approaches for work with these individuals (Altman 1993).

It is important to determine the possible sources of these assumptions and to assess their specific impact on theory about and treatment of this population. In this chapter, I will expand on many of the issues already advanced in the literature with the hope of encouraging further discussion. Three basic propositions are advanced: (1) It is possible to successfully apply psychoanalytic principles, including Freudian principles, to understand the psychological reality of those suffering from socioeconomic and sociopolitical deprivation. (2) These principles can be successfully utilized to provide treatment of these individuals in the context of their socioeconomic, sociopolitical, and cultural realities. And (3) the successful utilization of psychoanalytic principles for the understanding and treatment of this population depends, for the most part, on the extent to which the personal characteristics of those providing services are also part of the exploratory process. Clinical examples are introduced to illustrate concretely the issues discussed and the extent to which they influence the nature of the therapeutic process.

THE IMPACT OF POVERTY ON PSYCHOLOGICAL FUNCTION: PREVALENT ASSUMPTIONS

Poverty is a condition whose prevalence, cause, and impact on the individual continues to remain an area of great concern for social and behavioral scientists. An increasing number of individuals in many of our cities are, indeed, becoming affected by this phenomenon at a time when major social programs are being threatened with termination or at least serious curtailment (Bureau of Census 1992). The possible consequence of this development is likely to be that the mental health needs of the poor will be further neglected in favor of programs based upon negative assumptions about these individuals' motivations. Because minority groups are disproportionately represented among the poor, ethnic, cultural, and linguistic factors also become intertwined in these negative assumptions and complicate the clinical picture of these individuals (Javier and Herron

1995). I will review the source of the negative assumptions about the poor in detail as they seriously compromise our capacity to develop objective appraisals about these individuals' psychological condition.

Psychological Correlates of the "Culture of Poverty"

In reviewing the assumptions normally made about the poor, one is immediately directed to the numerous contributions made by the social anthropologist Oscar Lewis (1964, 1966). His description of the poverty condition and its psychological correlates captures the complexity and power of the basic dilemma affecting these individuals in a very real way. According to Lewis, there are three basic conditions in society that, when present, are likely to result in poverty, with its attendant socioeconomic and sociopolitical deprivation and disorganization: (1) when there is a set of values in the dominant class that stresses wealth and property, and where other values are relegated to less important roles; (2) when a high rate of unemployment exists for a protracted period of time; and, (3) when low socioeconomic status is viewed in terms of the individual's personal inadequacy or inferiority (Lewis 1966).

The continued exposure to these types of conditions could result in an individual whose basic view of him- or herself and others, and whose view of the world, are affected by what Lewis termed the "Culture of Poverty." Serious and pervasive psychological consequences are usually associated with this condition:

1. a strong feeling of marginality, inferiority, helplessness, and dependency for individuals belonging to the low socioeconomic class
2. a high incidence of maternal deprivation
3. a tendency to suffer from weak ego structure, pathological superego functions, confusion of sexual identity, and lack of impulse control
4. a strong present-time orientation and relative inability to defer gratification and to plan for the future, which dictates interactions vis-à-vis the self and others
5. a tendency to remain at the mercy of socioeconomic-political forces that are always outside of the individual's control
6. a narrow and provincial view of the world and the self
7. a strong sense of resignation and fatalism, a widespread belief in male superiority, and a high tolerance for psychological pathology of all sorts

8. a preference toward action rather than observation and awareness, and a preference toward externalization and somatization rather than introspection
9. a view of the world that is negative and maintains a general distrust of others and an impaired capacity for object relations.

If we are to accept these descriptions as representing an accurate picture of those suffering from poverty, we are forced to conclude that these individuals' psychological lives are primitive and desperate in nature, allowing time only for survival concerns. We are aware, however, that such a description does not accurately represent the lives of all the poor and that there are other psychological sequelae that could result from the psychological challenges inherent in deprived conditions and that have not been included in the listing above.

Lewis's description of the psychological consequences of poverty is remarkably similar to Kernberg's (1975) and Masterson's (1976) with regard to borderline personality organization. It suggests, then, that poverty produces severe pathology characterized by poor and persecutory internalized objects, leading to disruptive transferential manifestations. Similarly, the view that socioeconomic status is the result of the individual's personal inadequacy or inferiority places the responsibility solely and squarely on that individual. From that perspective, it advances the view of the poor as being masochistic, psychologically unsophisticated, and lacking the human quality to fare better in life. These assumptions, however, are indefensible in view both of the lack of research support for them and our own experience in treating individuals suffering from different degrees of poverty.

A frequent criticism regarding the research studies often cited in support of these dimensions is that they are of dubious quality and fraught with serious methodological deficiencies (Allen 1970, Javier 1990). Specifically, in reviewing studies investigating time perspective, delay of gratification, achievement motivation, expectancy for internal vs. external control, the role of concrete vs. abstract incentive, and the self concept among the poor, these studies failed to provide proper controls for such obviously confounding effects as the influence of social class of the examiner and the intelligence of the subject. They frequently had small and nonrepresentative samples and tended to use measuring instruments of dubious validity.

I do recognize that anyone whose immediate environment is characterized by these elements faces a tremendous struggle for psychological survival (Shen and Murray 1981). However, I think it is not always clear how, or to what extent, these elements are experienced and processed by different individuals. If an individual's sense of self is derived either solely or partially in reference to an environment with these characteristics, it is possible that he or she will develop a self-definition in which the feelings of marginality, alienation, helplessness, powerlessness, and anomia play a crucial role (Thompson 1995). According to Sarbin (1970), these influences may result in the development of a cognitive process characterized by present-time perspective, restrictive and undifferentiated linguistic codes, and beliefs in the external locus of control. It may also result in the view that verbalization of feelings and thoughts is not only difficult but also not helpful.

My experience with poor patients in a community mental health clinic, however, suggests that when the role played by these aspects of self-definition, interpersonal interactions, views of the future, nature of the transference, and the like is incorporated in the interpretative process of the treatment, their effect lessens. Similarly, when one becomes familiar with the linguistic behaviors of disadvantaged individuals, the issue of restrictive and undifferentiated linguistic codes referred to by Sarbin tends to change, suggesting that it partly reflects the professional's inability to understand the patient's specific code, and not only the patient's inability to communicate. Such is the case with so-called "black language," which could be so confusing to those unfamiliar with its meaning and so comforting and meaningful to those for whom it is intended.

An important distinction that needs to be made here has to do with the difference between a consideration of the possible psychological vulnerability associated with the continued exposure to socioeconomic and sociopolitical deprivation and the belief that these individuals are incapable of benefiting from insight-oriented psychological intervention. It is not possible to sustain negative beliefs about the poor in psychoanalytic treatment without a serious infraction of psychoanalytic principles related to the manifestation of countertransference. That is, such assumptions may serve a specific unconscious purpose for the individual who maintains them, particularly in connection to his or her self-definition. This issue has been amply discussed with regard to the development of prejudice (Herron 1995, Javier and Rendon 1995, and Thompson 1995). The perception of the poor as psychologically and intellectually inferior and deficient can only be maintained in contrast to a perception of the non-poor as superior and more psychologically sophisticated. Since most psychotherapies are practiced by therapists from a middle-class background who are usually guided by theories of mental functions based on middle-class values, it is not surprising that negative assumptions about the poor find their way into the treatment process. When that is the case, these negative assumptions may function as a convenient scapegoat for the therapist/analyst's projection of unacceptable, negative, and hostile impulses onto the patient (Brantley 1983, Comer 1969, Pinderhughes 1969). This may reflect, in part, a therapist's own anxiety in being unable fully to appreciate the psychological characteristics associated with these individuals.

Since Hispanics, blacks, and other minority groups are overrepresented among the poor in many urban cities (Bureau of Census 1992), negative projections are also frequently applied to members of these groups. In the case of the Hispanic group, such a tendency may have contributed to our difficulties in distinguishing between the cultural and ethnic characteristics of the Hispanic poor on the one hand, and the characteristics emanating from the pure socioeconomic and sociopolitical influence of the poverty condition on the other. It is not unusual to construe cultural, ethnic, and linguistic behavior on the part of poor Hispanic individuals as abnormal or pathological (Fitzpatrick and Gould 1972, Marcos et al. 1973). This kind of mentality results in those social policies aimed largely at this population—public assistance and Medicaid for example—encouraging treatment programs that predominantly emphasize concrete and immediate solutions to complex life problems. Such interventions may be both desirable and necessary for many poor individuals. However, Medicaid policies that only allow limited therapy sessions with an emphasis on medication treatment and a focus on situational immediacy do not provide these individuals with empowerment opportunities that would enable them to transcend their realities and take over their own destiny. They thus remain at the mercy of the social conditions associated with their economic status, which may have originally contributed to their pathology. A treatment intervention that emphasizes personal exploration gives this population a more powerful, respectful, lasting, and effective tool to deal with the vicissitudes of their lives.

Psychodynamic Formulations and the Poor

The psychoanalytic literature provides another source of negative assumptions about the poor's ability to utilize psychoanalytic principles productively. The strength of the ego is a sine qua non for analytic work. Freud (1937) suggested that the accumulation of frustration with regard to important basic needs tends to reinforce the strength of the instinctual drives, altering and transforming the ego, perhaps permanently, and thus weakening its capacity. The ego function is then characterized in the main by its defensive position. Freud referred to psychoses, some character pathology, physical illnesses, and other debilitating symptomatologies as conditions that are not amenable to analysis (Freud 1937). Continued exposure to the economic and sociopolitical deprivation associated with the culture of poverty has been assumed to produce a similar alteration of the ego. By extension, the appropriateness of an analytic intervention is then deemed questionable for individuals such as poor Hispanics and blacks whose ego is assumed to have been altered or transformed by conditions related to poverty (Arnson and Collins 1970, Goldberg and Kane 1974, Minuchin et al. 1967, Rogler et al. 1987, Ruiz 1981, Sue and Sue 1977).

Classical psychoanalysis in the Freudian tradition provides opportunities for change at the deepest layer of the individual's internal reality in an atmosphere of pure abstinence and neutrality on the part of the analyst (Freud 1912, 1913). It is not designed to handle and provide immediate satisfaction to concrete needs. However, psychoanalytic action does not need to be accomplished solely in this manner. It can also be accomplished in an atmosphere in which the patient's need—rather than degree of adherence to so-called analytic standards—becomes the reference point for evaluating the appropriateness of the analyst's action. From this vantage point, it is possible to appreciate how psychoanalytic principles can be productively applied even in the treatment of poor individuals whose lives are affected by the culture of poverty.

I have witnessed the growth of many of my poor patients who were able to take advantage of psychoanalytic interventions in various degrees. Many required a period of didactic approach in which they learned a new "conceptual matrix," that is, a verbal reformulation of their symptoms and the importance of their personal dynamic history (Olarte and Lenz 1984). They were, however, eventually able to appreciate the importance of insights for the modification of their conditions. Other poor patients came into the treatment situation with a great deal of curiosity about and desire for understanding their own internal world (see Javier and Herron 1992 for a clinical example).

If one maintains that psychoanalytic intervention is, in principle, totally out of reach for all poor, then there is no room for these kinds of liberating experiences to occur. Any exploration of the cause(s) and motivating forces for the present conditions affecting these people are relegated to non-issues. In the process, poor individuals are provided only with immediate solutions to specific problems, albeit immediately crucial ones.

They are not being provided with the more lasting tools, problem-solving and self-direction, that only the understanding of the cause(s) and motivations of their behavior may offer. The underlying message is that their internal world—their fantasies, dreams, thoughts, emotions, and wishes— are not only irrelevant but also unimportant and unnecessary. But are these not the very components that distinguish humans from non-humans? A treatment approach that de-emphasizes personal exploration and denies that unconscious conflicts and external stress combine to contribute to symptoms, dysfunctions, and distress is biased against the poor and ultimately minimizes the importance of these individuals' most human components (Lawrence 1982, Lerner 1974).

The challenge to the therapist/analyst, however, is to be able to evaluate the extent to which difficulty in the treatment of the poor is the result of resistance, impairment in ego functions, other psychological symptomatology, difficulties in linguistic processing (Javier 1989, 1990, Marcos and Alpert 1976), or just a failure on the therapist/analyst's part to appreciate the culturally influenced communication matrix of these patients. This is particularly the case for poor patients whose first language is not English and whose reference culture is different from the dominant American culture. For example, there are a number of elements in Spanish culture that, in various degrees, dictate the behavior of even highly acculturated Hispanic individuals (Ghali 1982, Lauria 1964). Take, for instance, the view of time and space. For many Hispanics, being on time to a meeting has less relevance than making it to the meeting. This is reflected by common reference to "Latino time," "Puerto Rican time," or "Hispanic time." Thus the importance of the human interconnectedness is stressed. Similarly, adherence to the so-called machismo trait, which emphasizes toughness and action rather than verbalization of feelings and perceives tenderness as a sign of weakness or femininity, may influence the Hispanic individual's willingness (but not his capacity) to use psychoanalytic treatment productively. Hence, underlying feelings of shame (*vergüenza*) and concerns about homosexuality associated with violating the macho code of self-reliance may be present in various degrees in Hispanic male patients. The female Hispanic patient, on the other hand, may show reluctance to reveal information with sexual content to a male therapist for fear of being viewed as a "loose woman," or she may be prone to "*ataques*" (epileptic-like seizures) as a coping mechanism for stress (Ghali 1982, Javier and Yussef 1995).

The issue of *respeto* (respect) may also play an important role in the treatment of Hispanic patients. Adherence to the cultural code of *respeto* calls for the individual to be submissive and deferential to the authority figure of the clinician, hence affecting the nature of the transference. I am reminded of a Spanish female patient whose psychotic condition was manifested, in part, by disrobing in front of other patients at the hospital where she was confined. When confronted by the ward administrator to explain her behavior, she refused to face him, her eyes remaining downcast. She finally explained her behavior that it would be a lack of respect to look up while one is being reprimanded. "I was raised never to dare to look up while a more mature person (*una persona mayor*) is giving me advice or scolding me," she explained.

I suspect that the extent to which an individual adheres to his or her cultural code will depend on social class, level of education, and degree of psychological sophistication (Marin et al. 1987). In this regard, it is important to consider that the fact that a behavior can be understood in cultural terms does not suggest that it cannot also have a psychological significance. Indeed, culture and linguistic characteristics can be used as defensive operations to deal with anxiety-laden situations (Javier 1989, Marcos 1976).

APPLICABILITY OF BASIC PSYCHOANALYTIC CONCEPTS IN THE TREATMENT OF THE POOR: CLINICAL ILLUSTRATIONS

The following clinical examples are meant to highlight some of the ways that the issues delineated above may find clinical applicability. As I discuss the complexity of the treatment of two patients, I am cognizant of the distinction between psychoanalytic principles and practice. While I support making certain adjustments in traditional psychoanalytic *approaches* when treating a more deprived and disturbed population (see Lawrence 1982 and Olarte and Lenz 1984), the application of psychoanalytic *principles* remains unaltered. The two male patients discussed represent the variety of psychoanalytic interventions that are possible even with this population (see Javier 1990, and Javier and Herron 1992 for earlier discussions of these cases). Although I recognize that the treatment of female poor patients brings its own unique challenges to the treatment process (see Javier and Yussef 1995 for a discussion), the description of the treatment of poor male Hispanics allows us to deal with the additional issue of machismo, which has been described as one of the greatest obstacles in the treatment of males in general and Hispanics in particular.

First Example

A young Hispanic man was hospitalized with a reactive schizophrenic condition, following the loss of his job as an elevator operator. This was his first and only job since he migrated from one of the Caribbean Islands to the United States. He obtained this job after several months of an arduous and frustrating search, which left him with a sense of personal vulnerability and an intense fear of failure. As a newly arrived immigrant, he lacked the necessary sophistication and skills to negotiate effectively the complexity of his new sociopolitical and economic system. In fact, his problem was further complicated by his poor knowledge of English. It was not surprising, then, that he viewed this job as his only and perhaps his last anchor to a more functional and productive life. With no immediate family in the States, he was forced to live with acquaintances, thus increasing his sense of marginality and alienation. His concern about losing his living quarters was, indeed, a real one.

The patient was given an appointment to see me at the community mental health center upon discharge from the hospital. He came to his appointment visibly shaken, apparently depressed, and with a deep sense of futility and fear in his voice. He immediately indicated to me that he could not work. He had been informed by hospital personnel that he was eligible for public assistance and Medicaid and requested my help in this regard. During his visits to my office, he worked arduously to convince me of his disability so that any attempts to explore the events leading to his hospitalization, his present condition, and his goals for the future were quickly dismissed. In fact, he would frequently miss appointments that were not directly related to getting forms signed for the Department of Disability Determination, Medicaid, or prescriptions of psychotropic medication.

It was clear that any intervention that did not include assisting this patient to secure his physical and psychiatric survival on a concrete and tangible level was doomed to failure. It was also clear that he did not see any practical benefit to exploratory intervention. Distrustful of all systems, he saw me as an advocate of the system that could make detrimental decisions about his survival (the therapist could make a negative recommendation to the Department of Disability and Medicaid, for example). Hence, he felt the need to be cautious with me and to make sure that only his weaknesses were revealed. On several occasions, he abruptly interrupted himself when he found himself talking about his strengths and things he used to do well.

I could very easily have accepted the patient's reluctance to explore personal issues as the result of his poverty or cultural background and given up on this aspect of treatment. The question here is, however, should we accept the patient's present condition and apparent decision to shy away from any personal exploration? Should we accept the patient's current expression of unconscious processes and instinctual manifestations as an intractable condition? Do we not have a responsibility as therapists or agents of change to strongly encourage and then facilitate the patient's emotional growth in an atmosphere where his basic needs are also secured?

At the initial stage of treatment, a great deal of work has to take place on changing the patient's perception of the therapist from a negative and threatening agent to a more positive, supportive, and trustworthy one. That is, with these and with all patients, a working alliance has to be developed.

In the case of this patient, such a transformation could only occur over a long period of time and only on the basis of a demonstration of the therapist's willingness to communicate in a way the patient could understand. Thus, I used home visits, phone calls, the patient's sporadic visits to the center, my own functioning as a troubleshooter for the patient with the Department of Social Services and other essential agencies in making sure that he had secure shelter and food, to communicate to the patient my willingness to work with him. These were also used as opportunities to explore the patient's feelings about these events and the ways he had historically used to deal with difficult issues in his life. The emphasis of these explorations was on evaluating his true capacity and potential for change. Joint visits to the different agencies were used to educate him on how to go about negotiating the adequate satisfaction of his concrete and basic needs. The goal was to increase the patient's personal power in this regard. In the same vein, learning basic English was also seen as an opportunity to increase his personal power and control.

An important issue that played a crucial role in this patient's behavior and that needed to be addressed from the onset had to do with the interplay of cultural background, his economic situation, and finally his pathology. His pathological manifestations, which rendered him dysfunctional, ran counter to his cultural expectations as a Hispanic male. Indeed, he found himself trapped by a very difficult dilemma. By exaggerating his illness, he felt that he could guarantee his survival in a place where he felt impotent, but by remaining sick, he found himself haunted by a deep-seated feeling of shame and embarrassment, which, in the process, validated frequently held negative assumptions about the poor Hispanic's limited capacity for self-reliance. Attempts at neutralizing the anxiety that such feelings generated resulted in the patient's further embracing and stubbornly holding on to his dysfunctional behavior. Disclaiming any responsibility for his condition, he saw it as an honorable way out of this dilemma: "It is not that I don't want to . . . it's that I can't."

This is indeed a difficult cycle to break, but one that can only be addressed in an atmosphere of respect for the patient's dilemma. Failure to address it, however, will certainly have a negative impact on the working alliance and the transference. Although this patient's visits were irregular and were normally dictated by concrete requests, he showed a mixture of discomfort, disbelief, and pleasant surprise at my exploratory stance. After a period of about six or seven months, he finally verbalized that he was "feeling listened to and understood" in one of the sessions. It was clear that some level of working alliance had been achieved.

What added to the strength of this working alliance was the constant focus of the sessions on helping the patient to differentiate between what he needed to do for his survival—secure shelter and food and confront the socioeconomic and sociopolitical limitations of his reality—and the view of himself as inadequate and degraded. His self-definition derived directly from, and reflected, the prejudicial and negative quality of his environment. However, these qualities also became a convenient occasion for the projection of his negative introjects. The beginning realization that his view of himself does not have to include these negative components was assisted by the therapist's expressed belief in his capability. In this context, the identification of the concrete manifestations of the pathological transformations of his feelings was accomplished while their more functional expressions were encouraged. Thus, the paralysis of his functioning, evident from his hospitalization, was viewed, in part, as an expression of his intense, albeit unconscious, rage, which was now being projected onto the world, and a sadomasochistic tendency. It forced recognition of his unresolved symbiotic dependency with a mother who was described as emotionally unavailable.

Although we cannot speak about complete cure for this patient—a strong tendency to psychopathological transformations remained—it was clear that some positive movement had taken place. The patient was able to obtain part-time work but was fired a few weeks later. At this time, however, we were able to look at his role more carefully, as well as to identify the feeling of well-being and personal pride he felt as a result of this experience. Other job opportunities were also short-lived, but with the continuous support from the therapist, and through self-exploration, the patient was finally able to maintain a part-time job on a more consistent and long-term basis. Perhaps the initial reorganization of his instinctual drives, along with a less anxious and stronger ego structure, was beginning to occur.

Second Example

A 24–year-old Hispanic patient is the youngest male and the sixth in a family of nine siblings. His overall history is characterized by uncertainty, inconsistency, and a lack of permanence. He grew up in a broken home in a dilapidated section of the Bronx, surrounded by drugs and alcohol, gangs, burnt-out buildings, school dropouts, and unemployed friends. He dropped out of school in the eighth grade, and fathered a daughter out of wedlock at the age of 14. He spent some of his adolescence trying out alcohol and different kinds of drugs, being part of a gang, and living a life in which only the immediate was relevant. His perception of himself and others was one of distrust, hopelessness, and helplessness. This basic view was bound not only by a great deal of anger and hostility but also by fear.

The patient's relationship with his father, mother, and some of his siblings had similar characteristics. His father dropped out of the family when the patient was very young, remaining uninvolved with the patient for most of his life. His mother was described as a manipulative, rejecting, and narcissistically preoccupied person. According to him, she frequently verbalized feelings of being bothered and overwhelmed by her children's demands, using "fake chest pain" to avoid involvement with them and as an effective leverage to control their behavior. Consequently, the patient derived most of his mothering from his oldest sister, who frequently served as a haven when things got too difficult for him to handle. He went to this sister for financial assistance in order to come for treatment since he had not been able to sustain a job for some time. At this point, he still maintained a strong wish to establish a more positive relationship with his mother, who remained physically and emotionally unavailable. His rage toward her was kept at bay by his equally strong wish to be closer to her.

The patient decided to seek treatment at this juncture as he felt "things in my life are getting out of control." He was referring to his sporadic but intense suicidal ideations, his agoraphobic and claustrophobic condition, and his general feeling of confusion. He reported being particularly confused about what kind of a commitment to make regarding a five-year relationship with his live-in girlfriend. Up to now, he had maintained that his relationship with this girlfriend did not have any romantic importance and that they lived together for financial reasons. "I could not pay the rent by myself. I did not make her any promises and what I told her is that I am here today, no guarantees about tomorrow." However, it was clear that despite the patient's verbalization, they had developed a strong interdependence on one another, not only financially but emotionally. Incidentally, this same tentativeness characterized his behavior with friends and with his various jobs. "I don't want to be tied down by anything," he would say, explaining the abruptness with which he would leave a job or stop seeing a friend.

The difficulties in treating this patient were immediately evident. He certainly presented a challenge to the traditional treatment approach. There will be an inclination to explain the nature of the difficulties treating this patient from the perspective of Lewis's description of the culture of poverty, given this patient's poor background, that someone with such a history cannot help but develop serious ego deficits, superego deficiency, and a poor capacity for object relations. However, despite his apparent lack of psychological sophistication, it was clear that he was somewhat connected with his internal pain, had an active and rich fantasy life, and demonstrated a strong wish to improve his condition. It was his decision to seek psychological help and to find out his role in perpetuating his difficulties.

There were other psychological characteristics in this individual that supported the appropriateness of using psychoanalytic intervention. In assessing his suicidal tendencies, for instance, it was clear that his ego structure had sufficient strength to withstand the pressure of his pain and self-destructive feelings, judging by his ability to wean himself off most drugs, with the exception of marijuana, and to divert three of his own suicide attempts by himself. The fact that he managed to enlist the assistance of his sister, to whom he had revealed the intensity and depth of his confusion, strongly suggests the patient's capacity to utilize verbalization as a meaningful method of communication. If we follow a traditional view of health, the fact that the patient had been able to maintain a five-year relationship, was a responsible father to his daughter, and was able to take care of his basic needs through various, albeit unstable, jobs, all spoke to the patient's capacity for object relations and his readiness for some level of commitment. His commitment to a more stable function was reflected in his effort to remain more faithful to his girlfriend despite his previous tendency to have two or three relationships simultaneously. Although it was clear these qualities were of a tenuous nature that needed to be constantly reinforced, and there were no guarantees that they would be influential factors in the treatment process, still they functioned as a continual reminder of this patient's potential.

There were many challenges to the development of the working alliance. For instance, the patient frequently missed sessions without any notification and responded with exasperation to any attempt to analyze his behavior's meaning. An active and consistent involvement by the therapist made it possible to develop a positive alliance with the healthy part of the patient. That is, the work focused on the development of a new conceptual matrix, which could then permit a new and different codification of his experience (see Olarte and Lenz 1984). It was possible in this context to demonstrate the transferential nature of the patient's behavior to him, to examine how missing sessions reflected his basic view of himself and others. This behavioral pattern was connected to his view that there was nothing permanent about a relationship, and his relationship with the therapist was no different. He reported, in this regard, that he would find himself remembering appointments with male friends, girlfriends, and the therapist days after they were supposed to occur. He made it clear that he could not guarantee appointments. "I forget and I feel bad when I remember that I stood somebody up, so I let them know ahead of time not to be surprised if I don't show up."

The patient's feelings of shame connected to missing sessions, and his fear of not being able to keep his word, behavior expected of a responsible man, needed to be explored. Similarly, his concern about the meaning of not only being in therapy but also having to rely on his sister to pay for the sessions, which reflected his sense of inadequacy and failure as a man, also had to be explored. As suggested earlier, these elements have an extreme cultural importance for the Hispanic population. The tendency of this patient to adhere to the macho code of conduct as a way of defining his current behavior could only be explored in an atmosphere where the basic sense of self as defined by this code was not directly challenged. It was with this in mind that considerable reframing of the patient's experience was made.

His willingness to come to treatment and withstand the anxiety associated with the analytic exploration was seen as a tremendous expression of personal courage and one that only a bright, sensitive, and responsible man would be able to allow. The fact that the therapist was an older male appeared to facilitate, in some way, his identification with this new expression of manhood. Similarly, the fact that the patient had the opportunity to change his language from English to Spanish and vice versa whenever the material under discussion demanded it, strengthened his positive transference and further facilitated the development of a working alliance.

The patient always verbalized his various experiences about his mother and, to a lesser extent, about his father, in Spanish. It was in his verbalization in Spanish that a more tender aspect of his mother was revealed, helping to put in perspective his intense craving for her. For instance, he could not understand her drastic change from an involved and caring mother to a detached and unavailable one. He finally said, "I guess she suffered too much and she just had it." It was in this context that an interpretation was made regarding the strong influence his conflictual relationship with his mother and father had on his relationships with different females in his life, including his sister. His agoraphobic and claustrophobic symptomatologies were also viewed in light of his strong identification with his mother, who was prone to somatization, and as reflecting his wish to be closer to her.

The turning point in the establishment of a working alliance occurred when the patient experienced the effect of the continuous exploration of his experiences and feelings associated with them. A great deal of time had to be spent on helping the patient identify more clearly his different feelings, especially his anger. While this work was being done, he frequently verbalized feelings of confusion of "not knowing what is supposed to happen here" and would miss appointments following an intense session. As the exploration continued, he began to experience a noticeable decrease in his claustrophobic and agoraphobic condition, to the point of feeling more comfortable being alone in his apartment and going out with his girlfriend to restaurants and other public places. At this time he also began to pay more frequent visits to his mother and friends and was reported to be less intense and much more relaxed and personable.

One crucial issue of the treatment was to help the patient develop some level of permanency and integration of his present with his past. Memories of his childhood, however, were vague and fragmented. He only had "a clear feeling of having been robbed of my childhood." Similarly, his tendency to pay little attention to aspects of his current experience was pronounced. Eventually his childhood memories became crystalized, albeit remaining fraught with a great deal of pain and anxiety, and his verbalizations about his current experiences became much richer in detail. Efforts were made to make direct connections about the similarities between his earlier and most recent experiences. For instance, it was shown that his inability to sustain a job or his reluctance to make a commitment to a relationship was a way of preserving his early life-style in which future plans were never part of the equation. By not sustaining a job, having neither health nor retirement insurance nor a savings or checking account, he was guaranteed a life controlled by crises and by the demands of the immediate. It provided a way to act out his dependency wishes.

During this period, the patient began to introduce dreams into the sessions and to call whenever he needed to postpone his sessions. He became particularly anxious to return to the Bronx as a counselor to provide guidance for the youngsters. "They are not bad, just confused, with nobody to guide them, so they get frustrated and hopeless." He was, of course, refer-ring to his own experience.

While this part of the treatment was unfolding, the patient continued to improve at work. He obtained a full-time job at a large company and received benefits for the first time. Additionally, he began to introduce his girlfriend to his family and to make vacation plans with her for the sum-mer, six months later. However, he also continued to question his involve-ment in the therapeutic situation. He gave the impression of someone who was constantly struggling to remain faithful to the therapeutic accomplish-ments. He remained cautiously surprised about the positive effect of the therapeutic process and was continuously prone to sabotaging it by miss-ing sessions and other acting-out behaviors.

Unfortunately, this patient's treatment was interrupted after about eight months, when he abruptly decided to leave his current job for a better one. It became difficult to establish a regular appointment, although he continued to contact me on the phone, attempting to establish one. My work with this patient may resume in the near future. However, even if treatment does not resume, the nature and quality of the therapeutic accomplishments cannot be minimized. The patient became less confused about his feelings, his symptoms were substantially reduced, and he began to use insights to organize his experience in a more meaningful way. He was able to work with the transference manifestation and to reorganize his culturally based version of a Hispanic male more psychologically and to allow psychoanalytic exploration in this context. There are many other important aspects of this case that have not yet been addressed in the treatment. I hope that future treatment will afford this patient further opportunity for self-examination and a deeper analysis of his psychic structure.

CONCLUSION

This chapter aimed to demonstrate the usefulness of psychoanalytic in-terventions with the urban poor. The nature, quantity, and quality of the problems normally confronting this population call for therapeutic inter-ventions that may deviate in various degrees from the more "traditional" approach. Despite these adjustments, psychoanalytic principles can still be productively utilized. It may be argued that the fact that the treat-ment of the patients presented here was so short in duration, rather abruptly terminated, and constantly prone to acting out, is a convincing indication of the inappropriateness and irrelevance of insight-oriented approach for this population. On the other hand, it may also be argued that the extent to which the patients were able to utilize insights, to change their views of self and others, and the extent to which these insights may have played a crucial role in improving the quality of their lives is a convincing indication of their capacity to use psychoanalytic principles productively. What is clear, is that as their internal structure became more organized through the active participation of the therapist, so their external reality became more organized and predictable.

At times it may be necessary to become more actively and directly involved with the patient's actual lived experience. At other times, it may be possible to focus on more purely intrapsychic material (see especially Javier and Herron 1992). The ultimate goal of insight-oriented therapy is the restoration of personal power, self-understanding, self-control, self-direction, and self-esteem (Lerner 1974). When the therapist attentively and respectfully listens to the depth and complexity of the poor individual's dilemma regarding a search for solutions, this patient may feel the necessary empathic affirmation and holding environment that then results in cognitive clarity, emotional strength, and personal empowerment (Winnicott 1965).

The internal personal growth that results from this experience can thus provide the necessary structure that forces and sustains other more tangible and immediately crucial changes. In turn, these changes can then be used to encourage deeper and more personal changes. Such a view is supported by a five-year study conducted by Lerner (1974) using clients' ratings, therapists' ratings, blind analysis of projective test data, and independent measures of behavioral change. Lerner found insight-oriented therapy to be highly effective with the urban black poor. Olarte and Lenz's (1984) paper on learning to do psychoanalytic therapy with the inner-city population is also relevant in this regard, as is Becnel and Gurgone's work (1987), which demonstrated that psychoanalytically informed intervention could prove beneficial even for a poor, chronic psychiatric population. Others (Bluestone and Vela 1982, Javier 1989, 1990, Maduro and Martinez 1974, Marcos 1976) found effective ways to apply psychoanalytic principles in a culturally and linguistically sensitive manner in the treatment of Hispanic patients. The degree and extent of the technical realignments that may be required is a function of the nature and urgency of the problem(s) at hand and the nature and quality of the psychological sophistication of the individuals involved.

REFERENCES

Allen, V. L. (1970). Personality correlates of poverty. In *Psychological Factors in Poverty*, pp. 242–266. New York: Academic Press.

Altman, N. (1993). Psychoanalysis and the urban poor. *Psychoanalytic Dialogues* 3(1): 29–50.

Aponte, H. J. (1986). If I don't get simple, I cry. *Family Process* 25: 531–548.

Arnson, A. N., and Collins, R. (1970). Treating low-income patients in a neighborhood center. *Hospital and Community Psychiatry* 21: 111–113.

Becnel, A., and Gurgone, D. (1987). Personal growth in chronic psychiatric patients: a new look at an old problem. *International Journal of Partial Hospitalization* 4: 291–301.

Bluestone, H., and Vela, R. (1982). Transcultural aspects in the psychotherapy of the Puerto Rican poor in New York City. *Journal of the American Academy of Psychoanalysis* 10: 269–283.

Brantley, T. (1983). Racism and its impact on psychotherapy. *American Journal of Psychotherapy* 140: 1605–1608.

Bureau of Census. (1992). Poverty in the United States. Washington, DC: U.S. Department of Commerce, Economics, and Statistics Administration, Bureau of Census, September, 1993.

Comer, J. P. (1969). White racism: its roots, form and function. *American Journal of Psychiatry* 126: 802–806.

Costantino, G., Malgady, R., and Rogler, L. (1985). *Cuento therapy: folktales as a culturally sensitive psychotherapy for Puerto Rican children*. Hispanic Research Center, Monograph No. 12. Maplewood, NJ: Waterfront Press.

—— (1986). Cuento therapy: a culturally sensitive modality for Puerto Rican children. *Journal of Consulting and Clinical Psychology* 54: 639–645.

Fitzpatrick, J., and Gould, R. (1972). Mental illness among Puerto Ricans in New York: Cultural condition or intercultural misunderstanding? In *On the Urban Scene*, ed. N. Levitt and B. Rubenstein. Detroit, MI: Wayne State University Press.

Foster, R. M. (1993). The social politics of psychoanalysis: commentary on Neil Altman's "Psychoanalysis and the Urban Poor." *Psychoanalytic Dialogues* 3: 69–83.

Freud, S. (1912). Recommendations to physicians practicing psychoanalysis *Standard Edition* 12.

—— (1913). On beginning the treatment (further recommendations of the technique of psychoanalysis I) *Standard Edition* 12.

—— (1937). Analysis terminable and interminable *Standard Edition* 23.

Ghali, S. B. (1982). Understanding Puerto Rican traditions. *Social Work*, January, 98–102.

Goldberg, C., and Kane, J. (1974). A missing component in mental health services to the urban poor: services in-kind to others. In *Mental Health Issues and the Urban Poor*, ed. D. A. Evans and W. L. Clairborn, pp. 91–110. New York: Pergamon.

Herron, W. G. (1995). The development of the ethnic unconscious. *Psychoanalytic Psychology* 12(4): 521–532.

Javier, R. A. (1989). Linguistic consideration in the treatment of bilinguals. *Psychoanalytic Psychology* 6: 87–96.

—— (1990). The suitability of insight-oriented therapy for the Hispanic poor. *American Journal of Psychoanalysis* 50: 305–318.

Javier, R. A., and Herron, W. G. (1992). Psychoanalysis, the Hispanic poor, and the disadvantaged: application and conceptualization. *Journal of the American Academy of Psychoanalysis* 20: 455–476.

—— (1995). Urban poverty, ethnicity, and personality development. *Journal of Social Distress and the Homeless* 4(3): 219–235.

Javier, R. A., and Rendon, M. (1995). The ethnic unconscious and its role in transference, resistance, and countertransference: an introduction. *Psychoanalytic Psychology* 12(4): 513–520.

Javier, R. A., and Yussef, M. (1995). A Latino perspective on the role of ethnicity in the development of moral values: implication for psychoanalytic theory and practice. *Journal of the American Academy of Psychoanalysis* 23(1): 79–97.

Kernberg, O. (1975). *Borderline Conditions and Pathological Narcissism*. New York: Jason Aronson.

Lauria, A. (1964). "Respeto," "Relajo" and interpersonal relations in Puerto Rico. *Anthropological Quarterly* 38: 53–66.

Lawrence, M. M. (1982). Psychoanalytic psychotherapy among poverty populations and the therapist's use of the self. *Journal of the American Academy of Psychoanalysis* 10: 241–255.

Lerner, B. (1974). Is psychotherapy relevant to the needs of the urban poor? In *Mental Health Issues and the Urban Poor*, ed. D. A. Evans and W. L. Clairborn, pp. 49–54. New York: Pergamon.

Lewis, O. (1964). The culture of poverty. In *Explosive Forces in Latin America*, ed. J. J. Tepaske and S. N. Fisher, pp. 149–174. Columbus, OH: Ohio State University Press.

—— (1966). *La Vida: A Puerto Rican family in the culture of poverty–San Juan and New York*. New York: Random House.

Maduro, R., and Martinez, C. (1974). Latino dream analysis: opportunity for confrontation. *Social Case Work* 55: 461–469.

Malgady, R. G., Rogler, L. H., and Costantino, G. (1987). Ethnocultural and linguistic bias in mental health evaluation of Hispanics. *American Psychologist* 42: 228–234.

Marcos, L. R. (1976). Bilinguals in psychotherapy–language as an emotional barrier. *American Journal of Psychotherapy* 30: 552–560.

Marcos, L. R., and Alpert, M. (1976). Strategies and risks in psychotherapy with bilingual patients: the phenomenon of language independence. *American Journal of Psychiatry* 133: 1275–1278.

Marcos, L. R., Alpert, M., Urcuyo, L., and Kesselman. M. (1973). The effect of interview language on the evaluation of psychopathology in Spanish-American schizophrenic patients. *American Journal of Psychiatry* 130: 540–553.

Marin, G., Sabogal, F., Marin, B., et al. (1987). Development of a short acculturation scale for Hispanics. *Hispanic Journal of Behavior Sciences* 9: 183–205.

Masterson, J. F. (1976). *Psychotherapy of the Borderline Adult: A Developmental Approach.* New York: Brunner/Mazel.

Minuchin, S., Montalvo, B., Guerney, B., et al. (1967). *Families of the Slums.* New York: Basic Books.

Olarte, S., and Lenz, R. (1984). Learning to do psychoanalytic therapy with inner city population. *Journal of the American Academy of Psychoanalysis* 12: 89–99.

Padilla, A., Ruiz, R., and Alvarez, R. (1975). Community mental health services for the Spanish-speaking, surnamed populations. *American Psychologist* 30: 892–905.

Pinderhughes, C. A. (1969). The origin of racism. *International Journal of Psychiatry* 8: 914–928.

Rogler, L. H., Malgady, R. G., Costantino, G., and Blumenthal, R. (1987). What do culturally sensitive mental health services mean? The case of Hispanics. *American Psychologist* 42: 565–570.

Ruiz, R. (1981). Cultural and historical perspectives. In *Counseling the Culturally Different,* ed. D. Sue, pp. 186–215. New York: Wiley.

Sarbin, T. R. (1970). The culture of poverty, social identity, and cognitive outcomes. In *Psychological Factors in Poverty,* ed. V. L. Allen, pp. 29–46. New York: Academic Press.

Shen, J., and Murray, J. (1981). Psychotherapy with the disadvantaged. *American Journal of Psychotherapy* 35: 268–275.

Sue, D. W., and Sue, D. (1977). Barriers to effective cross-cultural counseling. *Journal of Counseling Psychology* 24: 420–429.

Thompson, S. (1995). Self-definition by opposition: a consequence of minority status. *Psychoanalytic Psychology* 12(4): 533–545.

Winnicott, D. W. (1965). *The Maturational Processes and the Facilitating Environment.* New York: International Universities Press.

6

The African-American Patient in Psychodynamic Treatment

Cheryl L. Thompson, Ph.D.

THE CHANGING VIEW OF BLACK ISSUES IN PSYCHOANALYTIC WORK

Black people are not well represented in the psychoanalytic movement. In part this appears to be a result of the sometimes clear, sometimes vague references to blacks as primitive, base, and representative of all the wishes and urges that society ambivalently denies, such as sexuality or emotionality. Further, there are implications as well as statements about the analyzability of many black patients (Cohen 1974, Kardiner and Ovesy 1951). The black experience in psychoanalytic research and thought is not unlike the female experience. Women were seen as castrated men. Supposedly, they could not develop the same level of superego integration as men because they had no fear of the loss of body integrity. Women had already been damaged. They were seen as creatures who want to be men and who satisfy this need by giving birth to males. In reality, it is the rare woman who truly envies a man for his penis. We need only to look at the work of Gilligan (1982), Klein (1975), Chodorow (1978) and a host of others to see that women have no universal belief in castration nor do they possess less well-developed superegos.

Women surely do want power, acknowledgment, the freedom to succeed, to define themselves, and to be whatever they can be without external inhibition. These wishes are the same as those of any oppressed person. However, the wish to be free and live life to the fullest is frequently misunderstood or distorted when one group has the opportunity to do so and another is deprived. This is the reality for most black people. This means that for the oppressed group, movement toward autonomy, the opportunity to be productive, to experience self-control and, most important, to contribute to the society in a manner chosen by the individual are frequently misinterpreted as the defensive strivings of those who feel inferior and basically hate themselves. In my view, the negative ways in which black patients have been understood in psychoanalytic writing has actively discouraged greater clinical and academic exploration of black psychology. One might say that an unconscious frame of reference has been created that blames the voiceless victim. However, if we care about how we are understood and defined, we must become a clear voice in psychoanalytic thought. Black people have much to contribute to psychoanalysis as theorists, therapists, and patients. It is time that blacks are seen in the full complexity of their humanness rather than in the projected images of the privileged group.

It should be noted that the small number of us who are black psychoanalysts have noted an interesting byproduct inherent to our situation. Because black people are so seriously underrepresented in psychoanalytic training and treatment, the experience of the few participants is much like that of the early psychoanalysts. This is especially true when the issue of anonymity is considered. As a black psychologist/psychoanalyst, I am frequently known of by my patients because they travel in my social circle or have friends who do. I cannot, by virtue of being who I am, slide into obscurity even if I so wanted. This inability unalterably impacts on my treatment approach. In fact, it has taken years for me to understand this. Only in reading about the relationships Freud had with his early students-patients can one begin to understand the similarities involved in treating black patients. This results in some basic differences between being an analyst who can move freely into the majority culture with greater anonymity, and being someone like myself, who cannot. The smallness of the current black psychoanalytic community takes away any possibility of anonymity. In essence, the reality of the social situation pushes toward an inevitable inclusion of the analyst's real self in the dyadic relationship, therefore involving a much wider spectrum of psychological data in the analytic frame.

In this chapter, I will selectively review the important psychoanalytic literature trends on treatment with the black patient, then offer case material from my own work. The issues involved in treating black patients are varied and complex. The literature reflects both growing participation of black patients in psychoanalytic treatment and changes in the social situation of blacks. The earliest research focused on the psychological effects of discriminatory laws and practices (Butts 1964, Comer 1969, Kardiner and Ovesy 1951, Pinderhughes 1969). Most of the research was written at the height of the civil rights movement. At that time, psychological work focused on the external distress of patients in treatment and most of the problems described were seen as the obvious result of discriminatory laws and practices (Jones 1974).

However, with changes in society, there were parallel changes in the focal issues of psychological treatment as reported in the analytic literature. Babcock and Hunter (1967) discussed the impact of minority status on the development of intrapsychic structures and how this was manifested in formal learning processes and work functioning. Schacter and Butts (1968) described interpersonal relationships and the development of transference when psychoanalyst and patient are of different racial groups. Calnek (1972) described countertransference feelings that were evoked in psychotherapeutic treatment when both patient and therapist were black. Cohen (1974) explored questions about transference, countertransference, and psychoanalytic technique when the patient is of minority status and low income. A crucial issue in the literature at the time these papers appeared was whether a psychoanalytic treatment could take place in an interracial dyad. These writers all discussed certain aspects of transference development in interracial dyads that did not occur in same-race psychoanalytic treatment. The data reported usually reflected some aspect of cultural stereotypes of minority people.

Over the last decade, the ranks of minority mental health professionals have increased together with the general rise of minorities in professional occupations. The issues reported in the literature have interestingly shifted with the larger numbers of black mental health professionals and black patients involved in the therapeutic enterprise. Griffin (1977) reported that a major theme emerging in psychotherapy when the therapist is white and the patient is black is trust. When both the patient and the therapist are black, identity emerges as a major theme. It would be for psychoanalysis to explore the transferential–countertransferential processes that probably drive these phenomena. My own clinical observations support Griffin's research, and I will describe relevant case material later in this chapter.

In a 1983 paper, Brantley highlighted the enmeshment of psychodynamic issues with racism for the black patient. However, his case descriptions were more focused on the side of racism as a variable than on the side of psychodynamic exploration. It is evident throughout the limited literature of this period that therapists have had a consistent problem maintaining a balanced view when working with minority patients (Carter and Haizlip 1979, Flowers 1972, Jones 1974, Krantz 1973, Mayo 1974). This difficulty is probably indicative of the intensity and uncertainty of racial feelings in the intimacy of a psychotherapeutic relationship, where these factors are both reflected and enacted in the transference–countertransference interaction. Myers (1984) has noted the strong influence of the therapist's countertransference when working with racial issues.

It is important to be aware of key social and potential clinical differences in the black patient who enters treatment in the post- vs. pre-civil rights era. The young black person in treatment today is part of the first generation of blacks to have lived with overt discrimination being illegal and to have had the opportunity for legal protection in cases of overt and covert discrimination. (The terms racism and discrimination are used as equivalents here and are understood to mean an external limitation or inhibition on the basis of one's ethnic background or gender.) Technically, the ability to have greater recourse to action empowers any individual to cope differently with environmental situations. Legal recourse carries with it a greater repertoire of coping actions. This is especially true of educated, upwardly mobile blacks. However, people of minority status continue to report both overt and covert forms of discrimination as major impasses to the progress of their daily lives. These experiences deserve careful analytic exploration. What has become apparent in my own work is that these experiences are often overdetermined. That is, the particularly painful aspects of the reported discrimination often have complex genetic correlates. As the social balance slowly tilts toward decreasing external limitations for people of color, the data that emerges from psychoanalytic inquiry will represent new levels of exploration of the black individual.

Case One

This case demonstrates some of the intertwining of social issues and internal conflicts that are frequently part of the black middle-class experience.

When Juanita entered treatment she was a 31-year-old schoolteacher with extremely limited interpersonal contacts outside her family. She attributed her isolation at work to discrimination by her colleagues. She worked in a school with three other black teachers, but their schedules and work locations did not allow for interaction during the school day. Juanita ate her lunch in her classroom, explaining that she did not feel welcome in the teachers' cafeteria. She described her attempts at interaction with colleagues as too painful to endure. When she tried to participate in lunchtime conversations, she felt ignored. When she began treatment she had not had lunch with others in over a year. Juanita's major interpersonal contact was with her mother and was characterized by her mother's delivery of diatribes of hurt and rejection directed toward her. She felt that her mother only accepted her when her siblings were not around. When they were together as a family she felt ignored.

As the oldest of three children, Juanita lived most of her childhood with her divorced mother, her grandmother, her aunt, and two siblings. She came from an essentially middle-class family where skin color was part of the attribution of middle-class status. Juanita initially experienced herself as favored by her aunt and her grandmother. However, she described herself as falling from grace once she began to make friends with the neighborhood children. The following two vignettes helped us disentangle and begin to understand the patient's morass of rejection and isolation. At about age 7, Juanita was playing with a neighborhood child when her aunt came outside and sent the child away, yelling at the patient that she was not to play with that child because she was too dark-skinned. The patient needed to deny the perception that the child rejected by her caretakers was more like her mother in appearance than anyone else in the family. To protect herself, and to preserve the idealization of her mother, she accepted the rejection to be of herself, rather than her mother. Self-rejection further served to shield her from her mother's pain. When the patient became angry with her mother and devalued her, she raged at her for not protecting her from the aunt and grandmother. She was unable to see that her mother could not protect her because she too was a victim of the same rejection.

When she was 20, Juanita spent the summer in a theater company where she became friends with a young white man. She invited him to her home to meet her family. After the family visit, she stopped being friendly with him because she felt the young man did not accept her more obviously black mother.

These vignettes allowed the patient to understand the reversal and ambivalence that characterized her relationship with her mother. She began to feel the deeply denied pain of her mother's existence. During this process, Juanita also came to understand her mother's idealization of her, and that her light skin was seen by her mother as a means for gaining acceptance within her mother's own family. With the development of some empathy, the patient was able to talk with her mother and allow her to share information that, up until then, Juanita had not known. Her mother had been adopted and had never felt accepted by the aunt or grandmother. The adoption had not been a legal one—she was delivered to the grandmother in early childhood. Juanita's mother could not explain why she had been adopted. It was a family secret, but she hypothesized that she was the product of some extended family member's indiscretion.

Later in treatment we began to understand that this family used skin color as a vehicle for expression of unacceptable libidinous urges. The pain carried to the next generation and was experienced by my patient as her being unacceptable. However, her feelings were not without a basis in reality. She could not serve as her mother's wished-for vehicle of reunion with the family not because of her black friends but because she enjoyed dancing, acting, and boys. In this family, gratification of pleasure was unacceptable because it meant that they could become perceived as "lazy, childlike Negroes."

It appears Juanita's interest in boys was thoroughly discouraged. She would occasionally date. If the man was white, she quickly rejected him because interracial dating attracted too much attention. If the man was black, he was unacceptable because he was presumed to be too interested in sex. These perceptions allowed Juanita to avoid any possibility of an intimate relationship. The real danger appeared to be the expression of sexuality.

As Juanita began to understand some of the sources of her feelings of rejection, she tentatively began interacting with colleagues. She was able to eat lunch in the cafeteria, to go to faculty social functions, and, most important, to begin dating. At present she has a social life and has joined a group of other black teachers who are working toward removing some barriers to quality education. Juanita is a talented teacher who enjoys her occupation. She is becoming increasingly creative as an educator now that she feels less tentative about herself.

The transference in the treatment has remained an idealizing one. She sees me as the "doctor" who can protect her and guide her and treats the relationship with reverence, fearful that I could reject her. Not until the fourth year of treatment was she able to acknowledge that any rejection might come from her. This becomes an issue for Juanita when she feels that I misunderstand her. This is an area for further work and exploration, as Juanita will still only reluctantly discuss any disappointment she experiences with me or her treatment.

Juanita demonstrates some of the specific issues about middle class status, skin color, and family secrets that are often ubiquitous factors in the psychodynamic treatment of black patients. As each of these issues appears in the treatment, it is important to explore its significance for the particular patient. The next two cases demonstrate some of the particular struggles black patients experience when they come from less economically secure or stable families. For these patients issues of identity and autonomy are pivotal factors in the work.

Case Two

Charles began treatment when he was 32 years old. We have had many interruptions in the work. He is currently a 42-year-old single black man. He is usually seen at the rate of one session per week and his fee is very reduced. In 1989, despite his college education, Charles was working as a bellman in a New York City hotel. He had tremendous difficulty maintaining employment despite many very decent job opportunities. When Charles initially presented for treatment he was an undergraduate working toward a B.A. in a local university and having a difficult time completing his courses. He was afraid because he had already dropped out of an Ivy League school. Charles was a Vietnam veteran who had already finished a two-year degree with honors. He began having academic difficulty only after arriving at the Ivy League school. He had no girlfriends and wasn't sure of his sexual preference. When he was discharged from the military, he returned to his neighborhood and began to use heroin. After 18 months of heroin abuse he withdrew on his own.

Charles had three prior therapists before me. A recurrent dream had to do with his conviction that he did not deserve to succeed because everyone in his family was doing poorly. He was one of three siblings, all with different fathers, and had spent his entire childhood in foster care. His mother was described by him as a "hooker" who even wanted to have sex with him. Other recurrent dreams were of being rejected on college campuses because of his past. He felt anyone who looked at him would know he was a junkie.

My first focus with this patient was on reality testing. This was to help him appreciate that people could not judge others' pasts simply by looking at them. We even experimented with his telling about the past as he would have liked it to be. He began to feel more secure, but a recurrent dream of being swallowed in a ghetto remained. Eventually, we were able to move deeper into the internalized split between his good and bad self, the latter of which he experienced as his ever lurking "evil" past. During the course of his treatment Charles was able to complete college and because he has no real family, I attended his college graduation. The acquisition of a degree did help his self-esteem.

The work with Charles's object relationships continues to be central in his treatment. He is afraid of black women, but feels he would be hurt physically for dating white women. He is especially afraid that I would reject him because of his dislike (fear) of black women. We have explored this from the vantage point of his very painful past. The rejection and seduction he experienced from his mother had become organized in a racial schism in which black women are bad and white women are good. As Charles began to understand that I would not reject him and that I was not hurt by this object choice, he was able to focus his pain more specifically. It took six years before he could really assess his mother and determine that she had been unable, not unwilling, to parent him. As he began to understand her inability, he could appreciate some of the very hurtful things he himself had done to women.

Charles continued to experience problems with work. He was always underpaid and never able to find a position that offered him work satisfaction. Living quarters was another area of serious concern. He lived mostly in dormitory arrangements, which frequently resulted in serious physical altercations with roommates. He often put himself in positions of great physical danger. Over the last three years he has come to assess his own need for creating enemies. As we have moved through this phase of the work, Charles has finally come to live and work with people without fighting. He has also acquired a stable job, which pays the tuition for a Master's degree, and a small apartment in New York City.

For the first time in his life, Charles has a real home of his own. He has furnished it, and now invites some newfound friends to enjoy the space with him. This phase in his development has followed a period of work focused on understanding his deep sense of isolation and deprivation. Currently, he feels this pain most acutely at holiday time, when he is most aware of his isolation. Charles is now working on the establishment of reliable relationships so that he is not always so painfully alone.

Broadly speaking, Charles needs improved self-esteem, expanded autonomy, greater resolution of the splits in ego functioning, a capacity to tolerate ambivalence, and a reduction in the engulfment–abandonment conflict. He understands that we have a long way to go and is willing to work very hard in his therapy because he can vividly remember the enormity of his pain when we started. However, a significant factor addressed in Charles's treatment, which appears to be crucial for his future adaptation, is that he had made the transition from a lower-class life to a more middle-class experience. Charles no longer exists simply from day to day or paycheck to paycheck. We have defined this experience in the treatment as a shift from a survival mode of existence to a greater opportunity to live.

Juanita and Charles reflect many of the issues reported by earlier psychoanalytic clinicians. Conflict about identity and self-definition and the ability to trust others were focal areas of distress in these patients' lives, and prominent issues in the unfolding transference–countertransference. Juanita's and Charles's negative internal experiences found external validation in the way they experienced their ethnicity in the external environment. The often corrective experience of finding confirmation for achievement did not occur for either of these patients until they could link and acknowledge reactions to discriminatory interactions in the real world, with experiences of family rejections from a more vulnerable time in their lives.

SELF-DEFINITION BY OPPOSITION: BLACKNESS AND THE SENSE OF SELF

Being an African American entails identification with an ethnic group that has more negative variables attributed to it than most other ethnic groups (Gibbs et al. 1990). Even attributes that could be seen as positive have a high negative valence in connection with this group (Hacker 1992). For example, when African Americans are congratulated for the success they experience in athletics, the unspoken element is that sports are mindless activities; thus, achievement in this area confirms people's underlying views regarding their limited cognitive ability. It is the very enormity of the negative valence that makes many well-meaning black and white people overlook areas of true concern, fearing that the very acknowledgment of an issue would result in justification for practices that either maintain the status quo or seek reversals of prior accomplishments. An example of this is seen in the Jensen controversy (1969), which resulted in the dismantling of most of the Headstart programs before their usefulness could be accurately evaluated. This left the very real problem of the disparity between the African-American and white performance on standardized measures of intelligence without a cohesive avenue for redress or real continued dialogue.

Many of these large and sometimes painful social issues impact on African-American patients in varied ways. There is some aspect of this massive negative valence that affects every black patient. Some patients have only vague anxieties that are experienced as related to their ethnicity, while others are directly and deeply impacted by it. It is the process of assisting patients in the development of their own lives, separate from the race-related attributes many patients feel impaired by, that is the specific challenge in working with black patients. Somehow a sense of self must emerge that reflects acknowledgment of the negative issues without being limited by their implied constrictions.

Blackness permeates all aspects of being. It seems most accurate to think of being black as a grid upon which every aspect of psychic development is constructed. This kind of formulation helps visualize the possibility of some areas being more affected by race than other areas. The range of impairment can be minimal to very severe, depending on the perception of race as an explanation for the kinds of difficulties patients experience.

One of the striking differences between black and white people is in the very perception of blackness. For most white people, black is simply defined—black is black. For black America, blackness is a continuum that has multiple variables: education, income, geographic location, skin color, language, and so on. The blend of these variables contributes to the process of identification with blackness as self-description. It is in the space between the simple white definition and the complex black definition where many of my patients struggle with identity. The black continuum is further complicated by the experience of the 1960s when it was politically wise to come together as a mass group for civil action. One unfortunate paradoxical consequence of this process is that many black people have idealized the most disenfranchised in the group as the "true black person" (Steele 1990). Clinically this social image of the "true black person" does not resonate with all blacks, given wide differences in individual psychic development. However, a black image has been constructed that potentially subsumes the operations and expressions of drives, adaptive functions, and object relations within a distorted and victimized black ego ideal. One way this cultural definition interferes with self-development is that various aspects of personality or behavior come to be defined as black and/or white when in reality they are neither. The following are some brief clinical examples.

A 40-year-old professional black woman was describing her boss in one session. The boss was also a black woman whom the patient admired. The patient stated that some of the other black co-workers did not perceive this boss as supportive of them because she did not join them in the corridors speaking loudly and cracking jokes. The boss had been described as outside the group because she did not "act black." When questioned about the "blackness of this behavior," the patient stated emphatically that to not gather and speak loudly was to accept the white demand of black invisibility through silence. While this exchange suggests many possible assessments, self and object aspects of it are focused upon here because this patient seemed to experience the most pain in the areas of self psychology and object relations. Rather than feel free to assess the reality of her own perceptions of her boss, the patient found herself judging the woman on a basis that was not helpful to her own sense of self or her need in relation to her boss.

Another patient, a 43-year-old black professional man finds himself unable to date black women because he experiences them as too sexually demanding. He has not really noticed that he also complains just as intensely about white women being sexually demanding. He has used black and white as a defensive split in order to avoid addressing a bisexual conflict. Race has become a shield to help him avoid the pain of his early abandonment by his mother. It is this abandonment and a confused sexual identification that are central to his current sexual inhibitions.

Recently, a 26-year-old successful black woman sought consultation with me, complaining that her white therapist did not understand the intricacies of her relationship with her boyfriend. This patient was dating a married man with a young baby. She gave him gifts of large sums of money. Her explanation for the gifts was that black women were not supportive of their black men, and these donations were proof of her willingness to be helpful to them. It was explained to this patient that her problem was that she was too willing to personalize a large social myth rather than protect herself. Her involvement with a married man was not a racial issue, but rather a reflection of some worry about having a relationship of her own. This patient was told that her therapist did not misunderstand her difficulty but was genuinely trying to help her come to terms with a difficult relationship in which her desire to be seen as a good person was probably being manipulated. The patient seemed able to see the formulation presented and returned to her therapist.

In treating many black patients, the initial clarification of their struggles requires what I call a type of "racial surgery," which involves helping them discern the differences between those struggles that would be theirs regardless of ethnicity, and those that might be complicated specifically because of their race.

For many people of color, the factor of skin color itself is deeply intertwined with the sense of self-value.

A 42-year-old professional woman entered my office immaculately groomed, her hair styled in a classic French twist. Her face and features reflected the stunning beauty of a multi-ethnic Caribbean. In this first session, the woman talked about her fear that a new relationship would be doomed to failure because of her unattractiveness. When I commented that she would have to be seen as very attractive by almost anyone, this woman broke into tears saying her mother had convinced her that she was ugly. She was the darkest child in a family of three and was the only one with kinky hair. In reality, this woman has a physical beauty that one would describe as universal. Rather than focusing on her distortion of reality, I asked who in her family looked the most like the mother. The patient confirmed my suspicion that she did, and therefore was burdened with many expectations and pain passed from generation to generation—a dynamic strikingly similar to the one noted in the case of Juanita. The approach with this patient has been to explore the family relationships in great detail. The patient is the most successful person in her family in terms of career. However, she has not resolved her quest for her mother's approval enough to feel free to have a relationship with a man.

When presented in the treatment situation, skin color can serve various aspects of psychic organization. A case that represents my most obvious treatment failure centered around the use of skin color as a transference resistance.

A 40-year-old black single woman who was an elementary school teacher entered treatment with me because I was a provider available to her through her insurance company. She quickly used skin color as a mode of defending against her inner fears. This woman was moderately paranoid, a condition that I had had previous success with. When I attempted to support her ideas and added the possibility that multiple conclusions could be drawn from the initial data, I was met with a rageful attack about my being jealous of her light skin and hazel eyes. This attack reverberated with years-old distress in my own family of origin where skin color has been the only recognized form of achievement. My family openly disliked brown skin. I often felt disregarded around my achievements because I thought that the family would have preferred to see success in my lighter-skinned relatives. I had no distance from this confrontation and felt reduced to a pile of rubble. I understood the patient's behavior to reflect her defensiveness. Most specifically, I felt the patient was worried about being seen as crazy. This patient left with her pain and left me with the realization that I had an area that had to be analyzed so that I could maintain better therapeutic neutrality.

Another patient, a 44-year-old divorced professional woman with very light skin, began talking about her disappointment with her 17-year-old son's selection of a date for his prom. She described her son as very pro-black but when looking for a prom date, he only sought out light-skinned women with long hair. My patient seemed ashamed of her son's object choice. When questioned about her feelings, she apologetically stated that she thought his pro-blackness would result in his interest in darker women. It was pointed out that something that could have been seen as a wonderful compliment to her as a parent—in fact, her son was interested in women like his mother—was being overlooked because of race. This patient's ambivalence about her sense of self is reflected in her distress that her son would have an object preference reflective of her. It also reflected feelings that were not conscious at the time, such as guilt about her ability to transcend social classes with relative ease assisted by her light skin.

My own struggle with skin color and that of my patients has helped me appreciate the complexity of this issue for black people. Skin color is seen as a vehicle that can promote or defeat achievement in the wider society. The reality remains that in the United States, lighter-skinned black people are able to achieve greater success regardless of education, occupation, and family background. In many families of color a new birth is frequently met with the question, "What color is the child?" This question often precedes that of the child's sex. Initially, I simply understood this as a form of self-hatred. While this may be an aspect of the question, it is also a reflection of hope. Skin color becomes the variable around which hope or despair for the next generation is aroused. While a child may or may not consciously understand the affects involved, he or she clearly understands the experience of acceptance or rejection.

The significance of color is surely not unidirectional. While light skin may be valued in many families, in some it is dark skin that is prized. In yet other families, color is truly irrelevant. The affective valence of this issue appears most related to the level of acceptance and nurturance that each person feels in the family of origin. Thus, skin color becomes a factor that either impedes or enhances the specific caretakers' mirroring function. For many black people in treatment, such as the cases described above, a goal of the therapeutic work must be to establish a self-definition that is devoid of color as its marker.

The workplace is a charged sphere of functioning for many blacks where conflicts of self-definition can become manifest. Work is experienced by some as a tension-laden dialectic between achievement and isolation. Around this issue, inner and outer reality become entangled in a web that makes clarification of issues extremely difficult. As soon as external achievements become a viable activity for some black patients, there is a concurrent inner concern about acceptance in the family, school, and community. For many black people of poor socioeconomic backgrounds, achievement is not an ordinary expectation of living, but rather a statement that the achiever is rejecting his or her station in life. Thus, achievement becomes an aspect of racial identity. It becomes color laden. Doing well in school or speaking standard English becomes "being white" rather than being oneself. The position that many black patients take on this continuum varies, based often on the level of expectation for achievement and/or the nature of the separation achieved from the family of origin.

Adding further to this dilemma is tokenism as a social factor. Many patients find the reality experience of tokenism in the marketplace an exacerbation of an internal conflict between race-related grandiosity and worthlessness. Being the sole black person in a particular job position can be a double-edged experience—it leaves some patients assured at times of their specialness and at other times convinced that they have no real value at all. Thus minor failures and successes can result in dramatic shifts in self-esteem.

The 44-year-old professional woman spoken of earlier has moved away from any contact with her family of origin. Family dynamics have served to allow her vocational success, but in an oppositional way. The price that she has paid for this severance of contact is a limited ability to connect with anyone except her children. This patient does not feel torn by her achievement, and experiences her work-related isolation as quite acceptable. The isolation and specialness serve to redress some of the early experiences of insignificance she felt in the family of origin. Tokenism has become a fragile narcissistic gratification. The patient is currently seeking employment in a company where she would be the only professional of her discipline and the only black woman. She desires such a position because it would allow her to be appreciated for her uniqueness.

A 41-year-old professional black woman addresses the charged issue of her achievement by keeping each aspect of her life completely separated. She is the first person in her family to complete a college education. She describes her work personality as "cutthroat," seeing herself as a "pit bull."

She feels that as the only black person in her department, it is her responsibility to take every challenge presented to her and attack it head on. She has no contact with anyone from her job when she is not at work. Her social life consists of hanging out in a series of neighborhood bars. Her bar friends know her to be fun-loving and hard-drinking. She has not allowed any of them to visit her home or know where she works or what type of work she does. Her family is aware of her job, but they likewise have no idea how successful she really is. The family frequently seeks her out when there is a need for money or a need to negotiate a social situation such as banking, job seeking, or consumer complaints; however, the patient feels that to tell them of her accomplishments would be to lose the relationship with them. She feels that all she can do is pay her relatives, fight at work, and not ever have an intimate relationship, because to be known would be to risk rejection. Her isolated style serves as a defense against her overwhelming fears of punishment for having transcended her family's level of achievement.

A third patient, a 43-year-old man, experiences every success as an opportunity to be revealed as a "Street Nigger." This patient comes from very humble beginnings. He is a foster child who in his twenties had a period of being an active IV drug user. During that time of his life, he was homeless and had been arrested for drug use and loitering. Since that time he has been ever-vigilant lest his true identity be discovered and he will be banished again to the streets. He has now completed a Master's degree. At each stage of achievement, this patient has dreams of being chased by drug addicts and held in a dirty place so that he cannot go where he wants to go. This dream is recurrent and becomes intensely repetitive just before the end of each semester, before graduation, a new job, any new purchases, a new apartment, or a new date. Achievement for this patient is a split between black and white; however, black for him is a very constricted idea. Black is homeless, drug addicted, and hopeless. He experiences himself as rejecting his "true self" whenever he rejects those negative constructs and tries to take care of himself. Race becomes a major source of inhibitions for him. The reality of his psychopathology is that there are many areas of defect. Each exploration is initially met with the rage he feels reflects his blackness. His ethnicity helps to consolidate a sense of self because he can use aspects of his racial experiences to defend against his deep anxieties about his personhood. Not even real achievements are exempt from this conflict.

In the area of adult object relations, race can likewise impact on the sense of self with the other. For some patients, there is difficulty even beginning to think about self and others in a non-racial context.

The 41-year-old woman with the completely compartmentalized life finds herself unable to become involved with any man who is on her professional level. She is convinced that she will be rejected if she is not the person with the best job and the highest income. She has not yet become able to work through her early abandonment by her mother. This woman did not know until about age 7 that the person she believed to be her mother was her aunt. The patient has developed an intellectual acceptance of her mother's reality limitations but up to this point has avoided the real pain that is a consequence of that reality. Her chronic fear of abandonment has resulted in seeking men who make her feel superior. She has the notion that these men would be so grateful to have her that they would not abandon her. While her actions have proved nonadaptive, she has developed a moral rationale in which it is her social responsibility to seek out less educated black men. It is difficult for her to separate her deep internal fears from her sense of race-related social responsibility.

Another patient, a 42-year-old black male civil servant who has only been involved with black women feels outraged whenever his current girlfriend disagrees with any of his ideas about how one should conduct life. The patient's awareness of racial issues is narrowly skewed. He feels that as a black man he should be venerated because he maintains consistent employment. However, his girlfriend finds his peculiar relationship to financial obligations problematic. He feels that it is better to pay one bill in full rather than to make regular payments on all bills. His girlfriend has a difficult time dealing with telephone calls from bill collectors because of nonpayment. This patient experiences his girlfriend's concern as inappropriate and reflective of the negative social opinion that black women have of black men. Helping this patient come to terms with his internal difficulties with women, as well as the demands of external reality, is complicated by his use of the racial variable in interpersonal interactions.

For many black people in the United States, the struggle for the true sense of self is complicated by factors unique to this society and its expectations. Blacks must define a self without being the salvation of the family or acceptable to the larger society. Neither the black community with its current maintenance of a victim idealization nor the wider white community can serve as an effective means of identification because both contain unreasonable expectations. It seems that all black patients must come to terms with aspects of being—love, work, and play—in a manner that allows them to feel comfortable with being what they are. In reality, every black patient faces some genuine impediments to full participation in living. However, the person who holds racism responsible for every experience in life is as out of touch with reality as the person who does not experience the consequences of racism at all. Each patient will raise this issue at a different time in treatment and within his or her own individualized context, which reflects the severity of psychopathology and the experience that patient had with his or her family of origin.

What remains as a countertransferential issue for me is the question of how much of an activist a black patient must become in order to demonstrate mental health. Sometimes I see this issue as a reflection of the tokenism that black professionals experience while at other times it seems clear that without activism there is no progression of black achievement. Helping black patients come to terms with this is a particularly difficult problem because of the social injunction that every black person must reach back and help someone who has achieved less. For many patients who already feel depleted from life's demands, this can serve as a source of inhibition. The wish to give up for fear of further deprivation is sometimes complicated by the irrational belief that failure is deserved because one does not hold noble ideals regarding the relationship to one's community. It is not clear why this burden has become part of the black middle class, but it seems that this requirement makes achievement much less a pleasure of the self and the ego than it could be. In fact, this unrealistic expectation often results in failures that are not based on intellectual inefficiency but on a deeper fear that achievement is not a fitting part of the black experience. To achieve is often equated with the rejection of being black. Helping patients come to terms with their individual wishes and needs despite their ethnic group's social expectations continues to be a most troublesome issue.

Neither the patient nor the therapist has seen any consistent societal confirmation that achievement is all right for black Americans. Finding a way to support black patients' efforts to strive to achieve without guilt, and to expect that their accomplishments will be acknowledged and accepted remains elusive. Additionally, many patients continue to struggle with self-definitions that are more readily determined on the basis of what they are not, rather than what they are. These difficulties reflect the coalescence of conflicted intrapsychic, interpersonal, and societal demands. The negative valences attached to both success and failure leave many blacks torn by their various life choices. While living a thoughtful and committed life is difficult enough, the burden of defining oneself in light of conflicting and sometimes impossible social demands continues to underscore the particular life experience of many blacks in a white-dominated culture.

AFRICAN-AMERICAN WOMEN IN TREATMENT

Women of color present with many of the same problems that other women do. Essentially, they need to learn how to maintain significant relationships where they can achieve some balance between the needs of others and the need to care for themselves (Gilligan 1982). Most women who enter psychotherapy do so primarily because they feel thwarted in their relationships. Notwithstanding clear neurotic symptoms or the experience of work-related difficulties, their focus remains primarily on their intimate connections and how these either impede or foster personal growth and development.

Women of color, however, present with the additional issue of the minority experience and its implications. Many minority women do not define their self in terms of the autonomous entity that is the Anglo-American ego ideal. Their notion of self is often seen as a part of an extended family network such that self-perception is blurred by the needs and demands of others. In health, this self-perception can be seen as a mature dependency (Fairbairn 1954). That is, the woman sees herself in relationships with others and addresses the issues of her life in harmony with competing demands. She operates with a clear sense of self as the center of many complex interactions. However, for many patients the maintenance of balanced caring between the self and others is often skewed. In the psychoanalytic treatment of African-American women the issues of color, appearance, social class, family support, adult interpersonal relationships, and adaptation to urban environments are often intertwined.

In my view, black female patients often struggle with basic ideas about dependency and femininity. Because race has played such a powerful role in the development of black American identity, many black women think of their gender only secondarily. The relative weights attached to race and gender were most obvious during the height of the civil rights movement, when a large group of black Americans came together for civil action. The movement was dominated by men, and while women actively participated they saw their roles primarily as black persons and/or as supports for the men. When the women's movement began, there was much resistance to participation by minority women. Many felt that women of color did not require liberation. For many of my black patients the ideal of femininity is tied to a southern white model. This is essentially a pre-civil war fantasy ideal of a dependent and pampered woman who is taken care of by a man. The internalization of this ego-ideal has left many patients involved in an internal dialogue that makes them reject the idea of femininity. The level of dependency and passivity evoked by this type of femininity proves much too limiting and anxiety-producing for many. Thus, their self-definition contains a formulation of the self as nonfeminine. At the base of this perception, however, is an unresolved conflict between passive dependency and anger at not being responded to as women with strengths. The wishes to be taken care of and to experience adult mutuality become divided along the internal split between white and black.

Because race has presented such a powerful polarity in this country, many psychological issues have become internally defined in terms of the opposition between black and white. For black women, the issue of the intertwining of race and gender further complicates their self understanding. I have selected the following cases to point out the complex blending of racial, gender, and psychopathological factors in the psychological world of some African-American women today.

Case One: Louise

The patient is a 50-year-old African American who is now employed as a medical social worker. Her transition from a small southern town to an urban center has contributed to her struggle for self-identity. Louise was the first person in her family to complete a college education. She is a divorced mother of two adult children. She has a long-term relationship with a man with whom she is quite content. She entered treatment four years ago with a presenting problem of poorly regulated self-esteem. Louise felt particularly pained because she experienced herself as unattractive, unfeminine, and essentially unlovable. Louise had done so much introspective work alone that during the early phase of her treatment I felt I was watching a bottle of champagne pop its cork. Ideas, wishes, fears, and self-experiences were shared with speed and intensity. She experienced herself as strong and independent. To those around her, she appeared self-sufficient and un-needy. She could not bring herself to talk with her family about her needs for affection.

Race immediately presented itself as a significant source of her conflict. Louise is an extremely light-skinned African-American woman. She has found herself having to defend her blackness in interaction with blacks as well as whites. Louise spent her childhood in a small southern town in which her family had much status as a result of her father's position, size, and biracial heritage. Louise migrated to the Northeast thirty years ago. She came at a time when industrial work was available and has spent about half of her life in manufacturing jobs. With the demise of the industrial base in the area, Louise acquired a college education. She has viewed this achievement as a source of separation from her family. As a result, Louise has been hesitant to allow herself to achieve to an extent commensurate with her ability. She has experienced herself as rejected by her siblings and her mother because of her "book knowledge." As a result, Louise has limited her achievement and her income. Some of her resistance to embracing a middle-class lifestyle has been derived from an unconscious fear of loss of black identity and a greater loss of family. Louise has made a conscious effort to maintain a working-class identification even though her family values are middle-class. Her strong identification with the underprivileged has helped her performance at work where she has successfully articulated the needs of her poorest clients.

Louise's fear of success, which would bring family alienation, is coupled with another longstanding source of family rejection. She had been told from early childhood that she was unattractive. This issue remains as yet unresolved because it has deep and complex derivatives from many sources. A constant source of distress for her is an ego ideal of black attractiveness, which consists of almond-colored skin, European features, and straight or wavy hair. Louise has two siblings who meet these criteria. Further, this model of black attractiveness finds almost universal acceptance. The initial premise for her exclusion from the circle of attractive daughters was her kinky hair, more African features, and lighter skin. However, as we have worked together, it has become clear that race serves primarily as a veneer to cover other family dynamics.

Louise was determined to be quite intelligent early in her life. A second child, she had become an astute observer of family mythology. Louise has a quick wit and acerbic tongue, and she is outspoken about her observations. She sees these qualities as products of a lifelong adaptation. She became the bearer of realities the family wanted to deny. Louise often sided with her father, who was quite a charmer. This appears to have deeply disappointed her mother, who often faced the burden of financial responsibility for the family. Louise's open adoration of the father appears to have been associated with her mother's declaring her unattractive.

While Louise grew up in the segregated South, she never experienced the dehumanizing impact of discrimination until she arrived in the Northeast. The confrontation with discrimination has served to exacerbate her familiar experience of rejection. She has approached each situation with an aggressive verbal defense. The strategy is somewhat adaptive. However, her guilt about her outspokenness does not allow transfer of ability to other aspects of functioning. Louise readily defends the rights of others, but still has a difficult time asking to have her own needs met.

Louise's basic resistance to defining herself as an educated, self-sufficient, and socially mobile black woman is multi-determined. First, she fears that achieving more than her family would leave her even more alienated. Second, true self-sufficiency would eliminate the minimal feelings she has about her femininity. Finally, her capacity to speak for and identify with the underprivileged is tied to her maintenance of an identity within the group. These issues remain the most significant foci of Louise's continued treatment and serve as graphic examples of the complex interaction of racial, gender, class, and interpersonal factors that can be involved in the self-definition of many women of color.

Case Two: Keira

The following case of an African-American woman demonstrates some of the pathological issues that can ensue from multi-generational caretaking and life in a non-supportive extended family.

Keira is a 37-year-old black single woman who selected her pseudonym for this presentation. She is substantially overweight, dresses very stylishly, and uses makeup attractively. Keira completed two years of college while in treatment. She currently works as a secretary. This has been her primary form of employment for the last ten years. Keira lives in one of New York City's high drug use communities because she cannot afford housing in a safer area. Her housing has served as a source of inhibition. She has often been wary of leaving her apartment or befriending any of the neighbors for fear of being robbed. As an avocation, Keira sings back-up with several lead singers. However, she resists socializing because she fears being taken advantage of. Because of her anxieties, Keira, who has a beautiful singing voice, misses many good opportunities to sing. When challenged about going to more tryouts, she says that her grandmother would be outraged.

Keira presented for treatment five years ago, stating that she felt empty inside. She was unable to complete her college education and she hated working as a secretary. She also complained of her inability to establish long-term relationships with women or men. Her initial presentation was that of a witty, humorous, personable young woman dealing with the problems of isolation that are so common to the urban life experience. However, as we got to know each other, what unfolded was a long developmental history of isolation, abandonment, and victimization. Keira was reared by her grandmother in another state. She has always been separated from her mother and other siblings. The relationship between mother and grandmother was always estranged.

Keira experienced her grandmother as cold because of the limited physical contact and harsh treatment she received from her. The grandmother was a deeply religious woman who lived with rigid behavioral expectations. When Keira was a young teenager she and her grandmother resided in a Pentecostal religious community. This community was essentially a cult—it was suspicious of all strangers, allowing no contact with outsiders. The community had specific behavioral and dress codes. No contact between the sexes was allowed, including conversation. Women were not allowed in public unless covered from head to foot. Dancing, singing that was non-religious, and any playful interaction were not allowed. Further, the community had specific financial demands of its members that had to be met on a daily basis. A basic premise of the cult was that through prayer and sacrifice black people would be uplifted.

When Keira became interested in boys, at about age 17, she ran away from the community. After she arrived in a strange new city, she was befriended by an older black man who impregnated her. She surrendered that child for adoption. Her reasoning was that the child should have a "real" family. Keira now realizes that in her family there is an intergenerational pattern of not rearing the firstborn child. After her infant daughter was given away, Keira found her way to New York and has remained there ever since.

Keira and her mother have never been able to establish a warm relationship. Keira has always wanted her mother to explain why she was given to the grandmother. The mother saw the adult Keira as a successful peer who would be able to provide financial support for other family members. Keira so desperately wanted to feel connected to her mother that she provided financial support at the expense of her well-being and her education. Keira felt that as a good daughter and a good person she should give her mother her student loan money to help with family expenses. The money was never repaid and Keira was unable to continue her schooling. Keira felt that as a black person she was obligated to help her family. It took a long time for her to realize that her family members were basically strangers who were now exploiting her.

Keira continues to feel desperately lonely. She has had several short-lived, intense relationships with men, which sometimes involved abuse. When she dates now, she does not allow men to pick her up at her home or return her to her home. Her fear is that since she lives alone no one will be there to protect her. Keira has used several different names, sometimes as a reflection of her current feeling state, sometimes as a way of acquiring needed social services. Her chosen names often reflect hope or despair about her ability to take care of herself. She has used different names to socialize, to work, or to seek help. At times she has been homeless or on public assistance. I see this as a reflection of her deep fragmentation, as well as the psychopathy that can be an aspect of poverty.

In the treatment we focused initially on the patient's name because it seemed so crucially tied to her identity, her expectations, and her estranged family. Keira never liked her given name or herself. Her wit and humor were defensive, a way of entertaining people, because she believed no one would want to be with her if she didn't make them laugh. This humorous aspect of herself was defined by Keira as her "Aunt Jemima." She experienced her capacity for humor as denigrating. She found herself behaving most like "Aunt Jemima" at work. Over time, this facade would wear thin, resulting in a mood change and so much discomfort that she would end up leaving her job. Her explanation for this was that white people only accepted her as "Aunt Jemima." As we explored this aspect of her person, she curtailed her humor, no longer needing to entertain indiscriminately. She began to discover that people liked her even when she wasn't funny. She did not have to play the part of a jolly, fat, black person.

An essential part of Keira's treatment has been a quest to learn as much as possible about her biological mother and grandmother. This was considered crucial because Keira felt disconnected from all the significant people in her life and was unable to sustain new connections. While there remain many serious deficits in the factual data, she has been able to extrapolate from her mother's present life situation that her mother is in fact a fragile woman. Keira now understands that her mother has never been able to take care of herself. Keira has also come to see that her grandmother was able to provide a better start in life than her mother ever could have.

Over the course of treatment, both Keira's mother and grandmother died. Mother's death meant the end of a childhood hope that she might someday have a "real mother." As Keira has elaborated and worked through issues in her treatment, she no longer feels torn by the two women in her life. She has come to feel a connection to each of them—something that soothes the loneliness that is so much a part of her inner experience. In turn, she has begun to form friendly relationships with women in her current life. Another significant shift in Keira's understanding of her history came about with the knowledge of her grandmother's painful loneliness. It was this loneliness that probably precipitated her membership in the religious community. Keira now understands that her grandmother was preparing her for a world that she saw as having little concern or affection for either of them.

Recently, Keira has begun to sing more actively. She now remembers how much her grandmother encouraged her singing. Her voice has become an additional vehicle for rekindling a more loving internal representation. The reorganization of her internal object world has allowed Keira to form warmer relationships in the real world. Keira is now open to self-discovery. Her expanded awareness of her early experiences has given her a greater sense of meaning, much more freedom of expression, and greater self-acceptance. Keira had a fixed world view that as a black woman, she had no right to expect to be treated fairly, to be respected, or to be cared about. She believed that pleasure and success had to be denied in order to be seen as a good person. Each aspect of exploration was initially met with race as a primary explanation for her ideas and behavior. This was a factor that would eventually come to be understood within the larger context of her multi-faceted personality.

These cases demonstrate the need for keen racial sensitivity and a willingness on the part of the therapist to help isolate as well as synthesize the issues of race and gender as markers and organizers for the vicissitudes of being. The painful affects and utter helplessness often experienced around the issues of race can result in a treatment in which race is essentially avoided by both therapist and patient. Minority status profoundly impacts upon self-definition. We noted how basic human conflict areas such as passivity versus aggression and masculinity versus femininity were dynamically intertwined with ethnoracial valences. For many women of color, the very perception of femininity as helpless, passive, and dependent is so onerous that these affects are often rejected in their entirety, leaving no avenue for the experience of mutuality or mature dependency. This leaves them conflicted about what it means to be a woman, and how as women of color they can satisfyingly establish, balance, and maintain deep interpersonal relationships.

All patients enter psychoanalytic treatment with a knowledge that something is impeding their ability to function freely within their social, family, work, or private milieus. For adults in psychoanalysis the sources of inhibition and humiliation usually rest in their histories. That is, pain exists in unmetabolized memories. In the process of life review and active reworking through the transference and countertransference, the patient finds less inhibiting ways of integrating and understanding disturbing early experiences.

Work with the African-American patient can frequently result in heightened treatment tensions because of the ongoing painful experience of discrimination that is such an integral part of the patient's daily life. In a biracial treatment, discrimination issues may emerge early because of obvious differences between patient and analyst. As noted earlier in the literature review, racial issues in biracial dyads often present within the context of trust in the therapeutic relationship. Same-race treatment is not devoid of race-related impasses; in these situations race's reverberating impact is often approached through the exploration of self-identity.

In the treatment dyad, the affective components of race usually unfold around issues of power, privilege, deprivation, and rejection. Given race's powerful impact on life in this country, and the heavy charge that it can carry in the treatment situation, it is striking that most psychoanalysts are so poorly trained in addressing racial transference and countertransference. I, in fact, view the racial factor as a unique treatment variable because of the sheer enormity of its ongoing impact on the reality of African-American patients. However, we know that patients and therapists, both black and white, allow many racial issues to go undiscussed between them. This silence often results in truncated treatment, loss of the opportunity to explore both the real and intrapsychic determinants of discriminatory experiences, and the splitting off of race-related affect from both the interpersonal and intrapsychic interaction of therapist and patient. It is the psychoanalytic task to explore this painful and complex issue with the same degree of intensity and clarity that is applied to other aspects of personality in the analytic work. Race is a legitimate and necessary aspect of psychoanalytic exploration for most patients in this culture, but it is so especially for those whose ethnic groups define race as an integral aspect of self-identity.

REFERENCES

Babcock, C., and Hunter, D. (1967). Some aspects of the intrapsychic structure of certain American Negroes as viewed in the intercultural dynamic. *Journal of the American Psychoanalytic Association* 4:124–169.

Boyd-Franklin, N. (1989). *Black Families in Therapy: A Multi-systems Approach.* New York: Guilford.

Brantley, T. (1983). Racism and its impact on psychotherapy. *American Journal of Psychiatry* 140:1605–1608.

Butts, H. (1964). White racism: its origins, institutions and the implications for professional practice in mental health. *International Journal of Psychiatry* 8:914–928.

Calnek, M. (1972). Racial factors in the countertransference: the black therapist and the black client. *American Journal of Orthopsychiatry* 42:865–871.

Carter, J. H., and Haizlip, T. M. (1979). Frequent mistakes made with black patients in psychotherapy. *Journal of the National Medical Association* 71:1007–1009.

Chodorow, N. (1978). *The Reproduction of Mothering.* Berkeley: University of California Press.

Cohen, A. I. (1974). Treating the black patient: transference questions. *American Journal of Psychiatry* 28:137–143.

Comer, J. P. (1969). White racism: its root, form and function. *American Journal of Psychiatry* 128:802–806.

Davis, G., and Watson, C. (1982). *Black Life in Corporate America.* New York: Anchor/ Doubleday.

Eissler, K. (1953). The effect of the ego on psychoanalytic technique. In *Classics in Psychoanalytic Technique*, ed. R. Langs. New York: Jason Aronson, 1981.

Erikson, E. (1980). *Identity and the Life Cycle.* New York: Norton.

Fairbairn, W. (1954). *An Object-Relations Theory of the Personality.* New York: Basic Books.

Flowers, L. K. (1972). Psychotherapy: black and white. *Journal of the National Medical Association* 64:19–22.

Gibbs, J., Huang, L., and associates. (1990). *Children of Color.* San Francisco: Jossey-Bass.

Gilligan, C. (1982). *In a Different Voice.* Cambridge: Harvard University Press.

Greenberg, J., and Mitchell, S. (1983). *Object Relations in Psychoanalytic Theory.* Cambridge: Harvard University Press.

Griffin, M. S. (1977). The influence of race on the psychotherapeutic relationship. *Psychiatry* 40:27–40.

Hacker, A. (1992). *Two Nations, Black and White, Separate, Hostile, Unequal.* New York: Charles Scribner's Sons.

Hartmann, H. (1958). *Ego Psychology and the Problem of Adaptation.* New York: International Universities Press.

Holmes, D. (1992). Race and transference in psychoanalysis and psychotherapy. *International Journal of Psycho-Analysis* 73:1–11.

Jenkins, A. (1990). Dynamics of the relationship in clinical work with African-American clients. *Group* 14:36–43.

Jensen, A. R. (1969). How much can we boost IQ and scholastic achievement? *Harvard Educational Review* 39:1–123.

Jones, A., and Seagull, A. (1977). Dimensions of the relationship between the black client and the white therapist. *American Psychologist*, October, pp. 850–855.

Jones, B. E., and Gray, B. A. (1984). Similarities and differences in black men and women in psychotherapy. *Journal of the National Medical Association* 76(1): 21–27.

Jones, E. (1974). Social class and psychotherapy: a critical review of research. *Psychiatry* 37:307–320.

Jones, N. (1990). Black/white issues in psychotherapy: a framework for clinical practice. *Journal of Social Behavior and Personality* 5: 305–322.

Kardiner, A., and Ovesey, L. (1951). *The Mark of Oppression.* New York: World Publishing.

Klein, M. (1975). *Love, Guilt and Reparation and Other Works, vol. 1–1921–1945.* London: Hogarth.

Kohut, H. (1977). *The Restoration of the Self.* New York: International Universities Press.

Krantz, P. L. (1973). Toward achieving more meaningful encounters with minority group clients. *Hospital and Community Psychiatry* 24:343–344.

Lee, C. (1990). Psychology and African Americans: new perspectives for the 1990s. *The Journal of Training and Practice in Professional Psychology* 4: 36–44.

Lightfoot, S. (1988). *Balm in Gilead.* New York: Addison–Wesley.

Mahler, M. (1975). *The Psychological Birth of the Human Infant.* New York: Basic Books.

Mayo, J. A. (1974). The significance of sociocultural variables in the psychiatric treatment of black outpatients. *Psychiatry* 15:471–482.

McKiney, C. K. (1970). The upward mobile Negro family in therapy. *Diseases of the Nervous System* 31: 710–715.

Meers, D. (1992). Sexual identity in the ghetto. *Child and Adolescent Social Work Journal* 9:99–116.

Miller, A. (1981). *Prisoners of Childhood.* New York: Basic Books.

Myers, W. A. (1984). Therapeutic neutrality and racial issues in treatment. *American Journal of Psychiatry* 141:918–919.

Neal, A., and Wilson, M. (1989). The role of skin color and features in the black community: implications for black women in therapy. *Clinical Psychology Review* 9:323–333.

Parson, E. (1985). The black Vietnam veteran: his representational world in post-traumatic stress disorder. In *Post-Traumatic Stress Disorder and the War Veteran Patient,* ed. W. Kelly. New York: Brunner/Mazel.

—— (1990). Post-traumatic psychocultural therapy (PTpsyCT): integration of trauma and shattering social labels of the self. *Journal of Contemporary Psychotherapy* 20: 237–259.

Phillips, F. (1990). NTU psychotherapy: an Afrocentric approach. *The Journal of Black Psychology* 17:55–74.

Pinderhughes, C. (1969). The origins of racism. *International Journal of Psychiatry* 8:929–933.

Pine, F. (1990). *Drive, Ego, Object, & Self.* New York: Basic Books.

Ridley, C. R. (1984). Clinical treatment of the nondisclosing black client: a therapeutic paradox. *American Psychologist* 39: 1234–1244.

Robinson, T., and Ward, J. (1991). "A Belief in Self Far Greater Than Anyone's Disbelief": cultivating resistance among African-American female adolescents. *Women and Therapy* 11: 87–103.

Sachs, W. (1947). *Black Hamlet.* Boston: Little Brown.

Sager, C. J. (1972). Black patient–white therapist. *American Journal of Orthopsychiatry* 42:415–423.

Schacter, J. S., and Butts, H. F. (1968). Transference and countertransference in inter-racial analysis. *Journal of the American Psychoanalytic Association* 16:792–808.

Smith, B. (1991). Raising a resister. *Women and Therapy* 11: 137–148.

Solomon, A. (1992). Clinical diagnosis among diverse populations: a multicultural per-spective. *Families in Society: The Journal of Contemporary Human Service* 73: 371–377.

Steele, S. (1990). *The Content of Our Character*. New York: Harper Collins.

Stern, D. (1985). *The Interpersonal World of the Human Infant*. New York: Basic Books.

Sue, D. (1991). A diversity perspective on contextualism. *Journal of Counseling and Development* 70:300–301.

Sue, D., Arredondo, P., and McDavis, R. (1992). Multicultural counseling competencies and standards: a call·to the profession. *Journal of Counseling and Development* 70:477–486.

Swartz, L. (1987). Transcultural psychiatry in South Africa. *Transcultural Psychiatric Research Review* 24: 5–30.

Thomas, A., and Sillen, S. (1974). *Racism and Psychiatry*. Secaucus, NJ: Citadel.

Thompson, C. (1987). Racism or neuroticism: an entangled dilemma for the black middle-class patient. *Journal of the American Academy of Psychoanalysis*. 15(3):395–405.

—— (1989). Psychoanalytic psychotherapy with inner city patients. *Journal of Contem-porary Psychotherapy* 19(2): 137–148.

Watkins-Duncan, B. (1992). Principles for formulating treatment with black patients. *Psychotherapy* 29: 452–457.

Willis, J. (1990). Some destructive elements in African-American male–female relation-ships. *Family Therapy* 17: 139–147.

Winnicott, D. (1965). The *Maturational Processes and the Facilitating Environment*. London: Hogarth.

7

Working-Class Issues

George Whitson, Ph.D.

Contemporary psychoanalysis increasingly embraces a more pluralistic view of both theory and the nature of clinical practice. This broadening view can be seen in the articulation of the social constructionist position (Hoffman 1992) as well as the growth of acceptance of a two-person rather than a one-person psychology (Aron 1990). This metamorphosis parallels an increased appreciation for the multicultural world in which we live and practice. Davidson (1987) notes that psychoanalysis still resists the full impact of these profound cultural changes. Given the changing nature of our patient population, if the role of culture is not addressed, psychoanalytic thought may become more and more narrow in its range of applicability.

This chapter is an attempt to illuminate some of these issues, particularly the powerful effect the therapist's embeddedness in a psychoanalytic culture has on his or her effectiveness with the wide spectrum of patients seen today. We work from within an established analytic culture that is central to our identities. For reasons both situational and unconscious we cannot see the restrictions our analytic culture places on our clinical work. Given the growth of the number of patients from multicultural backgrounds often different from most analysts', the consequences of remaining unaware of the impact of our own cultural biases are considerable. I believe this is related to the phenomenon that while an increasing number of individuals from different socioeconomic classes and cultures seek therapy, fewer are seeking analysis.

I will develop the concept of a psychoanalytic culture, trace its development, and illustrate its effects on both theory and practice.

THE NATURE OF CULTURE

Culture is viewed in various ways depending on the context of study. For purposes of this discussion a society's culture is defined as consisting of "whatever it is that one has to know or believe in, in order to operate in a manner acceptable to its members" (Baker 1976, p. 814).

The anthropological concept of ethnocentricity posits that all individuals view their own culture as superior to others. In a seminal series of articles, Geertz (1973) notes that every culture attempts to shape a worldview for its members so that they will experience the nature of the world within the symbols of that culture. Attending only to those aspects of experience that validate the cultural system leads to an "aura of factuality" (Geertz 1973) in which the members view their beliefs not as representative of their particular cultural system but as a definitive reality. Relevant to psychoanalysis is Rhodes's (1990) application of these concepts to medicine in Western society. He states that medicine is viewed as operating within the world of facts, rather than beliefs; therefore illness is fallaciously seen as free from the social and political context within which it arises. An account of this position as it pertains to psychology is offered by Szapoczik and Kurtines (1993) and Howard (1991), who note the increased appreciation in mainstream psychology for contexualism by which an individual cannot be viewed as independent of the multifactored environment in which he or she lives.

THE FORMATION OF THE ANALYTIC CULTURE

Some cultural influences, such as socioeconomic class and race, are circumstances of birth. In contrast, we choose to join the psychoanalytic culture. It is sought, pursued for many years with considerable expenditures of time and money. Training in psychoanalysis extends beyond expertise in a particular model of psychotherapy. It is also a process of initiation into a desired group, with all the markings of a culture: rites of entry, specific rituals, and traditions, such as the use of the couch and August vacations.

Candidates begin training with many shared cultural characteristics. They are often white, urban, and middle class, with upwardly mobile aspirations. Their capacity to tolerate frustration, delay gratification, and submit to authority and ritual is well-established before they apply to an institute. The very acts of completing graduate school, writing a thesis (a rite of passage in itself), and incurring significant financial expense are forms of preselection. The rigors of graduate school ferret out those with less capacity or desire to engage in such an arduous process. In short, beginning analytic candidates are generally highly intellectualized, disciplined, and capable of responding to extensive authoritarian requirements. Ben-Avi (personal communication 1983) notes that those who choose to complete this long apprenticeship, with its delays of gratification and required compliance, tend not to be an adventurous group. Ironically this quality has become romanticized as intellectual superiority, a form of specialness. I will return to this idea later in this chapter.

These preselected candidates begin the development of their analytic identity through a series of powerful interpersonal experiences. While classroom and supervisory experiences are profound, the training analysis is truly unique and is the single most important factor in developing a capacity to work analytically. It is also necessary for admission to the culture. Various authors have noted how both analysands and their analysts are affected in unique ways by training analyses. Analysands must cope not just with the turmoil of their analysis but also the added burden of knowing that their analysts are senior members of the field to which they are applying for admission. Analytic candidates' anxiety about being too "crazy" may result in an overemphasis of their intellectual understanding of their dynamics and moderation of their actual affective experience.

The training analyst, after working with a candidate for a period of time, may feel that the analysand's performance reflects the level of his or her competence. This may lead to an overemphasis on certain aspects of the analysand's character or, conversely, to attempts to inhibit certain personality traits from being displayed at the institute. Lesser (1983) notes that issues of competition and self-esteem may unconsciously enter an analysis not only through interactions in the treatment but also through contaminations introduced by the analysand's supervisors. Epstein (1979) reports that some analysts attempt to disguise the intensity of their countertransference experiences toward their analysand, especially strong affective responses such as hate. The potential for stifled responses on the part of both the analysand and the analyst may lead to aspects of the patient's experience reamining unanalyzed and an overvaluing of intellectual understanding and self-control by both parties. Szalita (1972) reports that many reanalyses are with graduates of analytic institutes who felt their training analyses were compromised by anxiety arising from having their first analysis while they were in training.

Our training shapes not just our conception of how a therapist is supposed to act but also how a patient is supposed to be. Fromm's (1941) thoughts on social character are relevant here on two points. According to Fromm, social character serves as a dynamic force molding one's whole zeitgeist to perpetuate the culture involved without the participant being consciously aware of this process. The function of the social character is to shape the energies of the members of societies in such a way that their behavior is not a matter of conscious decision to follow the social pattern, but one of wanting to act as they have to act and at the same time finding gratifications in action according to the requirements of the culture (1941).

The analytic treatment of working-class patients, and in particular the interaction between the working-class patient and his or her therapist, allows for an appreciation of the subtle ways in which cultural bias can be enacted. The cultural differences between the working-class patient and the analyst incorporate not just socioeconomic class differences, but also divergent experiences of the same phenomena within their shared cultural perspective. My contention is that the particular values, beliefs, and relational styles of the working-class patient generate considerable anxiety for therapists. Such values are often misunderstood, or they are presented as a limitation of the patient.

THE WORKING-CLASS PATIENT

Any attempt to define a class as broad and heterogeneous as the working class is bound to rely too heavily on stereotypes and simplifications. The "working-class patient" has been defined by qualities as varied as behavioral traits, socioeconomic class, academic achievement, or degrees of psychological mindedness. Here I am referring particularly to a population that doesn't share the middle- and upper-middle-class biases toward the analytic culture.

There have been many reasons given for the ineffectiveness of analytic therapy with working-class patients, usually focusing on the deficiencies of the patients' personality or attitudes. Grey (1966), reviewing the historical analytic perspective on working-class patients, suggested that they are believed to be action oriented rather than verbal, and extrospective rather than introspective. They are often considered to be relatively unimaginative and less given to fantasy than middle-class patients. These perceived limitations are used to support the pessimism of utilizing analytic psychotherapy with the working-class patient due to its emphasis on introspection, fantasy, and dream material. Therefore, we speak of being forced to modify technique. Our ethnocentricity leads us selectively to ignore two facts—that we are as fixed in our own cultural symbols as much as any other culture, and that when we attend to differences in this manner we condescendingly speak of adjusting pure technique to accommodate those who need special work.

The analytic community has been reluctant to look to itself as the source of its limited success in working with such patients and rarely considers its own cultural boundedness as the main interference. However, as Hirsch (1984) notes, it is unclear to what extent analyzability is a patient variable, a therapist variable, or an interactional one.

Some therapists have obfuscated this issue by couching their recommendations in political terms. They argue that the problems of working-class patients stem from external realities; therefore these patients would most benefit from help that emphasizes practical considerations. While presented as politically sensitive, this perspective runs the risk of denying the existence of an inner life for working-class patients. Singer (1970) points to the presumptuousness accompanying the belief that patients from lower economic classes are not interested in understanding the nature of their experience or that they lack the capacity to develop emotional insight. As Espin (1993) notes, traditional psychology is unable to "hear" central experiences of individuals who deviate from the therapist's class, ethnicity, or political experiences. Therefore, many differences are often perceived as pathological.

THE TOOLS AND TOTEMS
OF ANALYTIC CULTURE

As is true with all cultures, the analytic culture contains rituals and totems that are expressed in the form of tools and techniques. This presents difficulties for some analysts because the tools are often experienced as extensions of metapsychological truth with its aura of factuality. Prescriptions for analytic neutrality and frequency of sessions are just two such examples. More subtle are technical considerations such as the answering of questions and the responses to demands for direct services.

Technique is particularly vulnerable to being culturally institutionalized. Even when culture and class differences are addressed, technical questions are often viewed in terms of modifications of pure technique, psychotherapy rather than analysis, or the necessity of preparing a patient to be ready (read good enough), for analysis. We have confused the traditions, rituals, and totems of our cultural perspective with the actual work of analysis. As Espin (1993) notes, this process amounts to "asking people to catch only the illness we know how to cure, rather than developing the cure needed for the illness" (p. 409).

The following clinical vignette illustrates one such technical issue—physical contact with one's patients. A therapist reports that a patient he sees in psychoanalytic therapy gives him a "roundhouse handshake" before and after every session. The therapist had given considerable thought to his possible responses, and while unclear about the patient's motivation, he felt certain that to avoid shaking the patient's hand or to try to talk to him about it would be disruptive to the work. He felt that shaking hands, in greeting and departure, was a basic cultural idiom for this patient. This therapist had maintained an uneasy peace with this conceptualization until one session, when, to his total surprise, he found himself swinging back his arm and initiating the shake. This created considerable anxiety for the therapist, temporarily obscuring the productive work he had accomplished with the patient and leaving him with a sense of having done something wrong. Only with an appreciation of the importance of ritual within the analytic culture can this therapist's anxiety be fully appreciated. Has the analytic treatment been compromised? What contamination did this handshake bring to the work?

To answer these questions I believe we must sort out issues truly central to our work from those that are central mainly to our identity as analysts. When technical considerations become central to one's definition of self-as-analyst, their meaning is no longer based on their efficacy but is contaminated by their ritualistic meaning and therefore more resistant to modification.

Approaches that go beyond traditional notions of good techniques tend to reflect specific theoretical stances. What would be de rigueur for a Freudian analyst may be unacceptable to an interpersonalist. One's position on issues as varied as visiting patients in their homes, talking to other family members, or sessions held on the telephone is typically determined by one's theoretical affiliation. Discriminating good technique from cultural prescriptions is at the heart of the matter.

ELITISM

The connection between the kinds of patients an analyst has and his or her feelings of self-worth is reflected in the literature's discussion of "good" and "bad" analytic patients. These conceptualizations are often presented as theoretical discussions with no acknowledgment of their cultural bias.

Spiegel (1970) attempted to further our appreciation of the complications raised by therapists' needs to attain self-esteem and a sense of personal specialness through their patients. Szalita (1968) has commented that "Analysis is an aristocratic method. It is meant for few by few" (p. 89). This upper-class view of both the analyst and his or her patient highlights that one's sense of specialness is not derived only from the position of being an analyst but also from the quality of the patients one treats. To feel like analysts, we depend not just on what we do but on whom we do it with. Regardless of the intensity of the work, many of our patients do not fit the idealized image of an analysand—an image of ourselves—who attends three or four times a week sessions, lies on the couch, and free associates, concerned with the core of his or her inner experience.

The patient's class can reflect on the desirability and therefore the self-esteem of the analyst. This can even be seen in the referral process. A colleague noted that when she received a referral of a seemingly unsophisticated patient she was told, "I'm not sure this is a great case, but she can pay full fee." Why should a referral of this type generate such an apologetic tone? Do we risk being viewed as unsophisticated by our peers if we (as referrers) do not distance ourselves from these patients?

Spiegel (1970) points out that in our rather small world of peers and colleagues, our private craving for recognition and acceptance can influence our perceptions and actions both consciously and unconsciously. Having to cope with unrealized idealized selves as well as fears of rejection by colleagues may leave us vulnerable to worries concerning our worthiness as members of the analytic culture. Given this anxiety, any population that challenges our ability to work analytically may trigger strong counterresistances. Spiegel underlines this anxiety by noting that the consideration of a patient for a "real analysis" is like the evaluation of a candidate for a membership in an exclusive club.

THE CLINICAL IMPACT

The therapist's behaviors and assumptions may unconsciously disturb working-class patients in unintended ways, but the reverse is also true. Certain aspects of working-class culture exacerbate the defenses of many therapists. I believe that this series of mutual transformations (Levenson 1972), while inevitable, would be more accessible to exploration if we attend to the unconscious factors expressed in the cultural exchange.

A colleague reported that a patient brought her a gift each year at the holiday season. This therapist's sense was that the giving of the gift had considerable dynamic meaning and she chose to accept the gift, thank the patient, and not comment. She decided to wait for the meaning of this gift giving to emerge from the patient. She felt this choice was not defensive or evidence of counterresistance, but appropriate to her understanding of her patient's needs. Despite this, the therapist still felt a nagging fear that she was not behaving in an analytic manner. The force of this internal pressure, while subtle, became clear during the fourth year of their therapy when the patient, while giving the therapist the annual gift, said, "Here we go again." The therapist, with a mixture of relief and urgency, began to question the meaning of the gift in such a way that it disturbed the patient. Startled, the patient realized that she had committed a social gaffe. She had done something inappropriate within the analytic culture. Even worse, she realized her therapist had known this all along and hadn't told her. She experienced her therapist as having been deceitful by accepting the gift graciously the past three years.

While this created a difficult time therapeutically, it is important to note that it also presented an opportunity for the therapist to become aware of her own parallel anxiety about committing an analytic gaffe. Her discussion with the patient led to an increased sense of understanding that they both felt the need to fit in and to not feel like a fool.

This example leads to a general consideration of the concept of acting out. Unfortunately, this theoretical construct often takes the form of critical judgment, suggesting wrongdoing on the part of either the analyst or the patient. This may be a function of the analytic preference for verbalization over other forms of expression. The analyst may overlook other possible meanings of the patient's behavior. To illustrate, utilizing the example of the "roundhouse handshake" described earlier, one could hypothesize that the use of the handshake may be a way to defuse some of the class differentiation between doctor and patient that is often a limiting factor in treating so-called working-class patients. Or, equally possible, the use of the handshake to open and close each session might have been a symbolic expression for this patient of leaving the security of his social self and entering into an exploration of his preconscious self. This willingness to explore his inner life is a courageous act for someone brought up to devalue any examination or expression of feelings.

It is important not to oversimplify these issues. Clearly in each example multiple meanings—some unrelated to cultural factors—could be assigned to both the patient's and the analyst's behavior. Not all interactions can be viewed as reflecting only culturally determined factors. Zaphiropoulous (1987) cautions us against these blind alleys in his work on ethnocentricity. I am suggesting that therapists strive to be aware of the effect that their cultural attitudes have on how they view and respond to the patient's deviation from analytic norms.

In this regard, it is equally important to avoid setting up technique as a straw man to be knocked down repeatedly with a prescription to "loosen up." There is the potential that the analyst's anxiety may lead to modifying technique, not in reaction to cultural differences but rather to avoid difficult situations in the work. Attributing these decisions to cultural sensitivity could lead to inappropriate acting out on the part of the analyst. Siassi and Messer (1976) note that analysts sometimes become overly identified with their working-class patients based on the analysts' belief that the working-class patient is more instinctually free and less inhibited.

THE NATURE OF COMMUNICATION

Therapists' primary relatedness is expressed through verbal exchange. In this realm of verbal interaction an overly intellectualized analyst may feel discomfort with working-class patients who appear to be bluntly direct. Working-class patients' emotional directness often threatens the therapist into pressured decisions about answering questions. It may also lead to more self-exposure than many therapists desire for both theoretical and personal reasons. I will compare two patient–therapist inter-actions to underscore this point.

A female attorney said in response to questions concerning sexual activity, "You know, I never thought I'd be able to discuss any of these feelings with anyone, especially a man. But sometimes I get frightened by this, I don't know what you feel . . . I worry that you might be affected by all my talk of sex. Is this a worry or a wish? I don't know. Sometimes I'd like to know how you feel when I talk about my sex life."

This is in sharp contrast to a secretary who in response to similar ques-tioning said: "Dr. Whitson! You're a pisser! Is this turning you on?"

The second patient made her observation, asked her question, and then waited for a response. We can assume that my reaction, regardless of whether I chose to respond verbally, was probably exposed. As Benedek stated in 1958—and this has been echoed by others such as Racker (1968), Singer (1970), and Hoffman (1983)—the patient is capable of perceiving the preconscious of the analyst and developing an awareness of the analyst's personality, problems, and strengths.

Both women in this example were communicating honestly within their own class idiom. Both conveyed their perception of what might be my motivation for the inquiry. The primary difference was the comparative bluntness of their comments. The secretary's directness startled and embarrassed me and my reaction was apparent as I blushed. To deny or avoid her observation and my reaction would not further the work. In fact, it might serve solely as confirmation of my voyeurism, rather than point out my own discomfort with an exchange that was turned back on me. This exchange, while uncomfortable in the moment, proved to be a significant referent for a variety of themes including, but not limited to, her provocative use of sexual confrontation when she became anxious.

THE IMPACT OF THE WORKING-CLASS PATIENT'S CULTURAL IDIOM

The image of the silent analyst is a stereotype in our society. One patient related reading a story of an analyst who had died in his office. It took two days until a patient noticed, and when he did it was only because the analyst's corpse fell off the chair during a session. When speaking with people from the working class one often hears statements that they had tried therapy but it didn't help because their therapist never spoke. Analysts also report working-class patients saying "you talk to me" as a sign of satisfaction with the work. We limit our understanding if we take this too literally. It is possible that the patient is conveying a sense of the therapist's attunement to his or her experience. I think this evolves not just from our verbalizations, but from the nature of our inquiry, which can convey to the patient our understanding of the struggle that he or she is facing. The working-class patient is most familiar with the stereotypic doctor–patient relationship wherein the patient presents the symptoms and waits passively while the physician diagnoses and recommends a course of treatment. Communications from the patient are often in response to direct questions from the physician. Silence on the physician's part is something these patients may never have experienced.

As analysts we tend to think of our nonintrusive silence as a means of allowing patients to stay focused on their experience and to deepen it. However, with working-class patients, especially early in treatment, the analyst's silence is often experienced as confusing and embarrassing. As anxiety increases, the patient may think the therapist is silent because he or she is doubting the veracity of his or her comments, or perhaps because the patient is boring or missing the therapist's point. Other patients feel it as a test. Whatever the specific feeling, it can often generate anger, frustration, or humiliation, and evoke either angry noncompliance, passive resistance, or anxious compliance in the service of their attempt to please us.

We have to ask ourselves if our remaining silent is in the service of furthering the work or an attempt to coerce our patients into being the kind of patients we need them to be in order for us to feel sufficiently analytic. Unfortunately, when patients comply, the therapist may experience them as more psychologically minded, which increases the therapist's affection for the patients and reaffirms for these patients the value of attempts to attend to the needs of the analyst. This runs the risk of creating a successful false-self analysis. This is often the case with anxious patients who feel a need to please their analysts, creating an ongoing cycle where the patient is valued for those exchanges that least reflect their core self.

THE INTERPLAY BETWEEN CULTURES

In discussing the cross-cultural therapeutic dyad, Davidson (1987) cautions that we must remain aware of dissociated devalued aspects of our patients' heritage. While Davidson's examples were patients from mixed ethnic backgrounds where the traits associated with one parent's background were viewed as less desirable, the concept applies equally well to working-class patients. These patients often have a sense of class-related inferiority, fostered by our society in which simply being middle-class is viewed as a sign of health. This is also true for analysts whose heritage may be squarely rooted in working-class families. Status and self-esteem needs may lead analysts to distance themselves from the experiences of their working-class patients.

I became aware of this phenomenon recently, when a colleague who had referred his barber to me as a patient offhandedly mentioned that during his last haircut his barber said that his sessions were going well. The word "sessions" surprised my colleague, given the barber's usual vocabulary. He offered it to me as a compliment. While it initially pleased me, soon I became troubled. Subsequent sessions helped me see that my concerns had been justified—our sessions contained previously unattended to transferential issues. I became aware that my patient was reporting incidents in particular ways that made him appear more thoughtful and introspective. While he was indeed becoming more introspective, the more central issue was that this man, whose father was sent to prison for ten years when the patient was 9, felt I would care more for him if he were more like me. In a way he was right. I had heard his reports of thinking more about his experiences only on the manifest level. I believe that while I was secretly pleased at having had an effect on my gruff patient I underestimated his vulnerability and his desire that I care for him.

Caution is indicated whenever our working-class patients begin to look more and more like us. This case serves to draw our attention to the issue of working in the transference—countertransference matrix with working-class patients. It is a common experience that these patients often resist discussing the therapeutic relationship because they fail to see how such a discussion could help them with their presenting problems. However, this skepticism has little to do with what they may actually observe about their therapist's personality. Unfortunately, this reluctance on the part of patients allows therapists the freedom to avoid addressing their own countertransference and its impact on negative therapeutic reactions. Transference observations that are made without the counterbalancing perspective of the other participant allow therapists to pathologize the patients' observations or avoid them altogether, especially when they are often poorly articulated. There may be a temptation to minimize these patients' perception of us. This is made easier since we often have to help them formulate and articulate their experience. A recent supervisory session provided an example of this. A candidate felt threatened by a patient's accurate transference observation. This led the candidate to correctly identify the patient's felt experience but to attribute the origins to displaced historical feelings rather than considering the patient's observation to have any validity concerning the personality of the supervisee.

Recently other analysts have attempted to transcend this bias. In his provocative paper Altman (1993) encourages analysts to rethink the practical responsibilities that providing treatment in a public agency demands. He views the issues presented in such situations as opportunities to enter the experiential world of the patient rather than considering them a deviation from the ideal. Using an object relations model he presents many creative ways to conceptualize the experience of the other. Javier's work with the Hispanic poor (1990) (see Chapter 5) and Foster's (1992, 1993) conceptualizations of analysis with bilingual patients also offer us a way to hear the central experiences of the other.

The rarely acknowledged effects of the analytic culture on theory and practice are major inhibitors to our work with culturally diverse populations. The ethnocentricity of psychoanalytic thinking, with its emphasis on the individual, the need to experience itself as factually correct, and the unacknowledged prejudices toward those who have distinctly different life experiences have hindered our ability to work effectively. We should remember that the current theoretical and technical advances have come as a result of our acknowledgment of the impact of the therapist's personality on the work. Let us consider the issues addressed here as forms of cultural countertransference. If we can free ourselves to acknowledge and explore this cultural dimension, there is considerable potential to vitalize and expand the applicability of our theories and our treatment methods to the diverse populations seeking treatment today.

REFERENCES

Altman, N. (1993). Psychoanalysis and the urban poor. *Psychoanalytic Dialogues* 3:29–49.
Aron, L. (1990). One-person and two-person psychologies and the method of psychoanalysis. *Psychoanalytic Psychology* 7:475–485.
Baker, G. T. (1976). Anthropology in the American diaspora as quoted in W. LaBarre (1978) *Freudian Biology, Magic, and Religion. Journal of the American Psychoanalytic Association* 26:813–830.

Ben-Avi, A. (1983). Personal communication.

Benedek, T. (1958). Dynamics of the countertransference. *Bulletin of the Menninger Clinic* 17: 201–208.

Caligor, L., Zaphiropoulos, M. L., Grey, A., and Ortmeyer, D. (1971). The Union Therapy Project of the William Alanson White Institute of Psychiatry, Psychoanalysis and Psychology: A psychoanalytic venture in treating the blue-collar patient. In *Psychoanalytic Contributions to Community Psychology*, ed. D. Milman and G. Goldman, pp. 173–200. Springfield, IL: Charles C Thomas.

Davidson, L.(1980). Ethnic roots, transcultural methodology and psychoanalysis. *Journal of the American Academy of Psychoanalysis* 8:272–278.

—— (1987). The cross-cultural therapeutic dyad. *Contemporary Psychoanalysis* 23:659–675.

Epstein, L. (1983). The therapeutic function of hate in the countertransference. In *The Therapist's Contribution to the Therapeutic Situation*, ed. L. Epstein and A. H. Feiner, pp. 213–234. New York: Jason Aronson.

Espin, O. (1993). Giving voice to silence: the psychologist as witness. *American Psychologist* 48:408–414.

Foster, R. P. (1992). Psychoanalysis and the bilingual patient: some observations on the influence of language choice on the transference. *Psychoanalytic Psychology* 9: 61–76.

—— (1993). The social politics of psychoanalysis. *Psychoanalytic Dialogues* 3: 69–83.

Fromm, E. (1941). *Escape from Freedom*. New York: Rinehart.

Geertz, C. (1973). *The Interpretation of Culture*. New York: Basic Books.

Grey, A. (1966). Social class and the psychiatric patient. *Contemporary Psychology* 2: 87–121.

—— (1988). The problem of cross-cultural analysis. *Contemporary Psychoanalysis* 24: 169–173.

Hirsch, I. (1984). Toward a more subjective view of analyzability. *American Journal of Psychoanalysis* 44:169–182.

Hoffman, I. Z. (1983). The patient as interpreter of the analyst's experience. *Contemporary Psychoanalysis* 19:389–422.

—— (1992). Discussion: toward a social-constructionist view of the psychoanalytic solution. *Psychoanalytic Dialogues* 3:74–105.

Howard, G. (1991). Culture tales: a narrative approach to thinking, cross-cultural psychology and psychotherapy. *American Psychologist* 46:187–197.

Javier, R. (1990). The suitability of insight oriented therapy for the Hispanic poor. *American Journal of Psychoanalysis* 50: 305–318.

Lesser, R. (1983). Supervision: illusions, anxieties and questions. *Contemporary Psychoanalysis* 19: 120–129.

Levenson, E. (1972). *The Fallacy of Understanding: An Inquiry into the Changing Structure of Psychoanalysis*. New York: Basic Books.

Racker, H. (1968). *Transference and Countertransference*. New York: International Universities Press.

Rhodes, L. (1990). Studying biomedicine as a cultural system. In *Medical Anthropology: Contemporary Theory and Method*, ed. T. Johnson and C. Sargent, pp. 159–173. New York: Praeger.

Siassi, I., and Messer, S., (1976). Psychotherapy with patients from lower socioeconomic groups. *American Journal of Psychotherapy* 30: 29–39.

Singer, E. (1970). *Key Concepts in Psychotherapy*, 2nd ed. New York: Basic Books.

Spiegel, R. (1970). Psychoanalysis—for an elite? *Contemorary Psychoanalysis* 7: 48–63.

Szalita, A. (1968). Reanalysis. *Contemporary Psychoanalysis* 14:88–103.

—— (1972). Further thoughts on reanalysis. *Contemporary Psychoanalysis* 18:327–348.

Szapoczik, J., and Kurtines, W. (1993). Family psychology and cultural diversity: opportunities for theory, research, and application. *American Psychologist* 48:400–407.

Zaphiropoulos, M. L. (1982). Transcultural parameters in the transference and countertransference. *Journal of the American Academy of Psychoanalysis* 10:571–584.

—— (1987). Ethnocentricity in psychoanalysis: blind spots and blind alleys. *Contemporary Psychoanalysis* 33:446–461.

Zaphiropoulos, M. L., and Caligor, L. (1986). Providing limited income groups with mental health services: problems and possibilities. In *Proceedings of the 1966 Conference of Psychiatric Outpatient Centers of America*. Oil City, PA.

8

Countertransference in Cross-Cultural Psychotherapy

Michael Gorkin, Ph.D.

In the past the cultural background of the therapist vis-à-vis the patient seldom emerged as a potential barrier to psychotherapeutic treatment. This was so for the simple reason that both participants usually shared similar backgrounds. When this is not the case, however, divergent cultural values and assumptions may invade the treatment, sometimes undermining it altogether. This chapter will focus on some of the countertransference issues in cross-cultural psychotherapy, with reference to one specific, and in some ways unique, therapist–patient dyad: the Jewish (Israeli) therapist and the Arab patient.

The Jewish therapist–Arab patient dyad has received no attention in the literature, largely because Arab patients in Israel have only recently begun to seek modern forms of outpatient psychotherapy. Today, Arab Israeli patients are increasingly appearing at outpatient clinics, especially in areas with large Arab populations. They are also appearing at the university-based psychological services and they are beginning to turn to private psychotherapy.

These patients are usually treated by Jewish therapists, inasmuch as there are only a few trained Arab therapists in Israel. During a two-year stint as a psychotherapy supervisor at the Student Counselling Services of the Hebrew University in Jerusalem, I supervised several Jewish therapists who were treating Arab patients. In addition, I consulted with therapists who worked in other facilities. Their struggles, and those of their patients, provide the data on which this chapter is based.

A number of researchers have delineated some of the more frequent countertransference problems that arise when the therapist is treating patients from a different culture (Abel and Métraux 1974, Basch-Kahre 1984, Devereux 1953, Ticho 1971, Tseng and McDermott 1972). In the last two decades, countertransference issues in interracial psychotherapy have received particular attention (Griffith 1977, Jackson 1983, Schachter and Butts 1968, Wohlberg 1975). Some of their findings are germane to this study, but rather than outline them here, I have chosen to discuss them by way of comparison with some of my observations. Suffice it to say at this point that while the countertransference issues that arise in the Jewish therapist–Arab patient dyad are similar to those in other cross-cultural psychotherapies, the extreme nature of the ongoing political struggle between these two peoples tends to exacerbate the countertransferential difficulties—sometimes to the extent that the therapist can no longer continue to work with the patient. But this is not usually the case. Most treatments do go on—to the enormous credit of both participants.

A point that needs to be made explicit from the outset, especially in discussing cross-cultural psychotherapy, is that the therapist may at times respond inappropriately for reasons that are not due to his internal conflicts, but rather are due to a lack of knowledge about the patient's culture. Perhaps an example will elucidate this distinction.

P., an unmarried Arab woman with masochistic features, informed her therapist that she had just discovered she was pregnant. She knew that she must have an abortion and was thinking of asking her sister and a friend from her village about where she might go for the procedure. The therapist, a Jewish male, encouraged P. to go right ahead and consult with her sister and friend. He completely overlooked the fact that his patient might be in danger if her parents, particularly her father, were to discover her mishap, which in their village would be regarded as an unpardonable disgrace for the family.

The therapist failed to recognize that a course of action that would be sensible in his culture was for his patient probably a hazardous expression of her masochism. This oversight did not issue from any countertransferential sadism. It was simply, though dangerously, an initial failure to grasp the cultural meaning of the patient's intended action. Fortunately, the therapist was able to undo his error in time and to follow up with a useful exploration of the patient's masochism.

There is, however, a category of misunderstandings or misreadings that generally do reflect the therapist's underlying subjective countertransference—namely, those global misreadings known as "stereotypes" and "prejudices." As Ticho (1971) has stated, both stereotypes and prejudices are "projections of ambivalence toward various cultural values and ideals" (p. 314). They provide a framework in which countertransferential problems are expressed. Some contamination by stereotypical or prejudicial perceptions is probably unavoidable in the *initial* phase of cross-cultural psychotherapy. It is the failure to reevaluate these prejudicial and stereotypical perceptions over the course of treatment that alerts us to the likelihood of underlying countertransference issues.

An example of an especially harmful stereotype sometimes held by Jewish therapists is the perception that Arab patients are not sophisticated or psychologically minded enough to benefit from insight-oriented psychotherapy. Some therapists pointedly told me that they believed it was "impossible" to do insight-oriented treatment with Arabs. It is true that many Arab patients enter treatment with expectations of receiving advice, directives, and concrete forms of help, but it is patently untrue that these expectations are rigid and impervious to change—and it is just as inaccurate to portray Arab patients as incapable of introspection or psychological mindedness. These stereotypes obviously undermine the possibility of carrying out insight-oriented treatment. Interestingly, they are the same misconceptions and stereotypes that are occasionally held by white therapists with regard to black patients (Jackson 1983, Wohlberg 1975).

COMMON TYPES OF COUNTERTRANSFERENCE

Several of the more common countertransference issues for Jewish therapists working with Arab patients will be delineated next. The aim is not to be exhaustive but rather to focus on some of the more typical and troublesome issues. Examples from several cases will be introduced for illustrative purposes.

Excessive and Ambivalent
Curiosity about the Patient's Culture

One of the typical areas of countertransference difficulty is the therapist's pervasive, and occasionally hovering, curiosity about the patient's cultural background. The therapist seizes upon the opportunity to meet a representative of this intriguing foreign culture, and in the process loses sight of the therapeutic task. Cultural material is explored more for its intrinsic interest than for its immediate relevance to the patient.

This type of countertransference problem has been discussed by other researchers (Abel and Métraux 1974, Devereux 1953). Devereux, a psychoanalyst with an avid interest in American Indian cultures, reveals his occasional difficulty in restraining his curiosity when dealing with Indian patients. He points out that the patient may come to resent the impersonal nature of the therapist's interest; or the patient may feed into this interest, plying the therapist with cultural data in lieu of exploring more personal areas of difficulty. Devereux suggests that perhaps the only way to avoid the pitfalls of excessive curiosity is to familiarize oneself with the patient's culture before beginning the treatment.

In the psychotherapy of Arab patients, Jewish therapists also occasionally fall prey to the countertransferential problem of hypercuriosity. Most of the Jewish therapists with whom I had contact were not widely familiar with Arab culture. None of these therapists had ever had an Arab as a close friend, most had never paid a social visit to an Arab village, and only one had a fluent knowledge of Arabic. Yet most of these therapists had the desire to know more about Arab culture. The opportunity to treat an Arab patient was thus sometimes regarded as an opportunity to learn first-hand about Arab culture. A few Jewish therapists openly acknowledged choosing to work with Arab patients for this reason.

Not surprisingly, this type of curiosity sometimes led to sidetracking of the therapy. There was, for example, an occasional rambling exploration of the Arab extended family or of village life in general, or in one instance, a rather prolonged examination of sexual taboos in Arab culture. For the most part, however, these bouts of excessive curiosity, mingled as they were with an appropriate wish to understand the patient's cultural background, did not seem to cause great or enduring harm to the treatment.

What did greatly interfere with the treatment was the therapist's vacillation between a wish to understand the meaning of the patient's Arabness and an intense aversion to this Arabness—that is, curiosity interwoven with ambivalence. The matter of countertransference aggression will be discussed more fully later in this chapter. The point here is that in some instances, the therapist's curiosity seemed to be suddenly impeded by a wish (usually unconscious) to distance himself from all that was Arab in the patient.

As can readily be imagined, this countertransference problem is enhanced by the longstanding political antagonism between Jews and Arabs. This dilemma does not emerge with such poignancy in Devereux's examples of white therapist and Indian patient, nor even in the many reported cases of black–white interracial psychotherapy. Yet it seemed to be a troubling countertransference reaction for some Jewish therapists treating Arab patients. On occasion, when I had a chance to explore this issue with a therapist, what seemed to emerge was a vague but deep-seated fear about close contact with "the enemy," in spite of consciously held liberal and egalitarian political notions. This approach–avoidance seesawing had deleterious effects on the treatment, and unless it was addressed (usually in supervision), the therapy faltered.

Making an "Island" of the Treatment Situation

Sometimes allied with the above countertransference difficulty is another issue, which can be categorized as making an "island" of the treatment situation. In light of the political antagonism between Jews and Arabs, it is understandable that at times both therapist and patient may attempt to avoid discussion of their cultural differences. What happens in this instance is that each of the participants cues the other that matters of cultural difference are extraneous or, in any event, beyond the pale of exploration.

Therapists who participate in this type of obfuscation may do so under the guiding philosophy that, as Sullivan (1953) stated, "everyone is much more simply human than otherwise" (p. 32). Few would quarrel with this view. But it is also true that therapists may foster and cling to this philosophy as a resistance. Occasionally, for example, I consulted with therapists who had been treating Arab patients for periods of a year or more and who reported that cultural differences never emerged as a topic for discussion. When asked about this, a common response was, as one therapist phrased it, "For me, the Arab patient is just another person."

In discussing interracial psychotherapy, researchers have pointed to the importance of neither over- nor under-emphasizing the matter of race (Bernard 1953, Griffith 1977, Jackson 1983). If the patient attempts to avoid the topic, the therapist is advised to explore this avoidance. Failure to do so is viewed as countertransference resistance. Similarly, the Jewish therapist needs to recognize the meaning of the patient's Arabness for him, and the meaning of his Jewishness for the Arab patient. Any avoidance of this disquieting material by the therapist, in an effort to make an island of the treatment situation, is indicative of countertransference difficulties.

Some therapists attempt to make an island of the treatment situation in a narcissistic manner. They attempt to portray themselves as somehow above the cultural and political influences of their own society. They present themselves as exceptions. They may also subtly attempt to induce their Arab patients to behave as exceptions. The patients, of course, need not be passive recipients in this cover-up; they may initiate and try to evoke a response of "exceptionalism" in their therapists, who may in turn fail to confront it.

In two cases with which I am most familiar, it was the Jewish therapists (one man, one woman) who attempted to present themselves as free of cultural and political antagonisms and prejudices. Both therapists were actually something of outsiders within their society, and both held anti-Zionist views. In attempting rather early in treatment to cue their patients that they were exceptions within Jewish society, however, they aroused suspicion and rejection. Their patients wanted no part of this rapid intimacy; it was the therapist's need, not theirs. Moreover, the patients seemed to understand intuitively that creating this type of island would foreclose any possibility of discussing in a genuine way culturally and politically related conflicts.

Regrettably, only the woman therapist was able to manage her countertransference satisfactorily. She was able to see that she had allowed herself (as a woman and therefore, in her view, a second-class citizen) to overidentify with her Arab patient. She had sought to make an island with a fellow "victim"—a misalliance from which she eventually was able to disentangle herself. No such disentangling took place for the male therapist, who as a lower-class Sephardic Jew was similarly overidentified with his patient. He could grasp intellectually what was happening to him, but he could not avoid the undertow of his countertransference. The patient predictably did not last long in treatment.

Manifestations of Guilt

One of the most important and recurrent areas of countertransference difficulty for Jewish therapists treating Arab patients involves the intrusion of guilt into the treatment arena. Consciously or (more often) unconsciously, guilt reactions to the Arab patient seemed to enter, at some time or another, into nearly all cases that I witnessed. It is well beyond the aim of this chapter to discuss the "realities" of Israeli–Arab politics. What is important, though, is that most of the therapists who treated Arab patients did believe that Israel had—knowingly or not—caused some harm to its Arab citizens, and beyond that, to the larger entity referred to as "Palestinians," with whom many Arab Israelis identify. As a consequence, guilt reactions (or defenses against them) were easily triggered by the treatment situation.

For instance, all the Jewish male therapists served in army reserve units. Depending on the unit in which they served, they might have to absent themselves from treatment once to three times a year, for periods of several weeks. Since this was the era of the Lebanon War, a few of these men were serving there. When it came to informing their Arab patients that they would be absent, some of these men experienced considerable guilt. They might state that they would be absent but, in contrast to their behavior with their Jewish patients, they did not state the reason, and they found themselves hoping that the Arab patients would not inquire. Or occasionally they would forget to mention the impending absence at all.

> One therapist neglected to tell his Arab patient of his impending reserve duty until the last moment. The patient, in treatment only three months, had been working quite effectively, having established an idealizing transference to the Jewish therapist as a father figure (his own father had died when the patient was a young boy). For his part, the therapist was concerned—perhaps overconcerned—about "disappointing" the patient. Consequently, when he was called for reserve duty, he was most hesitant to inform the patient. When he finally did so at the session before his departure, the patient responded with an extended silence. Then, several minutes later, the patient's associations turned to Israeli–Arab politics, and specifically to his admiration of the Palestine Liberation Organization and its leader, Yassir Arafat, whom he described as the "father of the Palestinians." The Jewish therapist became immediately and intensely uncomfortable, but he was unable to sort out his feelings sufficiently to formulate a response. He left for reserve duty feeling guilty, not at all confident that he would still have a patient when he returned in three weeks.

The Arab patient generally senses the Jewish therapist's guilt. The patient's response to this countertransference will depend upon the nature of his character and pathology. Not uncommonly, the patient will evoke the therapist's guilt, in part as a means of camouflaging his personal difficulties.

A highly intelligent university student with a narcissistic disorder used treatment for a long while as a place to vent his frustrations with Israel society. He recounted episode after episode of his mistreatment at the hands of Jews. His female Jewish therapist sensed that even if the episodes were true—and she tended to believe they were—the patient was nonetheless hypersensitive to injury and insult; he expected tribute from others and was easily wounded when it was not forthcoming. But the therapist found herself unable to intervene or in any manner address the patient's narcissistic vulnerability. She believed that the patient would respond with political flagwaving should she confront the repetitious nature of his recitations. Beyond this, she was unable to intervene because the patient's recountings and semidisguised accusations had evoked within her a sense of irritation and, above all, a paralyzing sense of guilt. She could not bear being perceived by her Arab patient as "an unfeeling Jew," as she put it.

It is perhaps worth noting that part of what fostered the therapist's difficulty was her temporary inability to evaluate the "subjective" and "objective" elements of her countertransference. She understood that the patient was at least unconsciously aware of inducing uneasiness in her by citing episodes of Jewish injustices. Yet she had great difficulty using the informational content of her predictable (objective) countertransference to formulate all appropriate response because she also sensed that her reaction was exaggerated and unremittingly intense; that is, there were significant subjective elements. She was not only reacting but overreacting, and not only identifying but overidentifying (above all, as a victim). It look her quite some time to work through her intense reaction, at which point she was finally able to address—without feeling guilty—the patient's hypersensitivity and his need to make others feel as uncomfortable and ashamed as he himself inwardly felt.

Occasionally, when the therapist is beset by guilt, he acts out by attempting to compensate the patient. This may be done in specific ways: the therapist may allow the sessions to run overtime or be lax in setting and collecting fees. More globally, the therapist may find himself becoming—as did the aforementioned female therapist—uncharacteristically and hollowly supportive. It is as if the therapist took on personal responsibility for undoing the wrongs perpetrated upon the patient. This attempt to engineer a "corrective emotional experience" is sooner or later likely to misfire and lead to further difficulties.

One of these difficulties is that the therapist feels under pressure to avoid any confrontation or negatively tinged interaction with the patient; such interactions would only make the therapist feel more guilt. But, of course, the therapist cannot avoid negative feelings toward this patient who is repeatedly arousing guilt. A vicious circle thus evolves: guilt leading to aggression, leading in turn to more guilt and further attempts to compensate the patient.

Manifestations of Aggression

Guilt and aggression are often intertwined in countertransference reactions. Each fosters the other. Accordingly, in the various manifestations of aggression that will be described next, guilt is a common accompaniment.

One example of this aggression- and guilt-tinged countertransference reaction is when the Jewish therapist finds himself experiencing, in spite of his egalitarian ideology, persistent feelings of superiority toward the Arab patient. The therapist wants to regard the patient as an equal, and yet consciously or unconsciously he feels that the patient is from an "inferior" culture. This kind of demeaning stereotype frequently intrudes when the therapist comes from the dominant or majority culture and the patient is from a minority culture. Several studies on interracial psychotherapy point to this prejudicial attitude in the white therapist (Griffith 1977, Jackson 1983, Thomas 1962). Furthermore, such prejudice is sometimes shared by the black patient (Griffith 1977).

In the Jewish therapist–Arab patient dyad there is the additional factor of the ongoing war, in which the Jews have been winners and the Arabs losers. Both Jews and Arabs tend to attribute this political result, in part, to the supposedly superior qualities of Jewish society; the Jewish society is seen as more advanced or progressive. The mere fact that Hebrew is the spoken language in virtually all Jewish therapist–Arab patient psychotherapy further enhances this sense of social dominance and superiority.

These prejudices are sometimes brought into the treatment by *both* participants. For the Arab patient, seeking psychotherapy may represent a wish to participate in the benefits of this "progressive" society. The Jewish therapist is then idealized as a representative of that society. For the Jewish therapist who aspires to an egalitarian outlook, such idealization and all that it implies may well cause him discomfort, evoking a melange of guilt and vaguely felt triumph.

The political dominance of Jews vis-à-vis Arabs in Israel is conducive to another form of countertransference aggression. Until a sturdy therapeutic alliance is formed, the Arab patient is generally quite passive with the Jewish therapist. He hesitates to assert himself in any manner. His aggression usually takes the form of passive-aggressive maneuvers, such as noncompliance with the treatment framework (lateness and absences are examples) or vague complaints about treatment. A frequent consequence of this behavior is that it engenders an over-assertive and negatively tinged countertransference.

> One female Jewish therapist reported in supervision that she found herself becoming unusually active and confrontive with a male Arab patient. The therapist was not as a rule disposed toward therapeutic activism, nor did she have a confrontive style. As we examined the case material, which spanned several months, it became apparent that the patient was extremely passive with her, and beneath his seeming uncooperativeness was a pervasive mistrust. While the patient never said so explicitly, the therapist had the sense that she was regarded, as she put it, "as the Grand Inquisitor"— a role which she felt she had enacted at times by doggedly probing her evasive patient for more information. It thus became apparent that in his passivity, which at times bordered on passive aggression, he had evoked countertransferential hyperactivity, even aggression, from the therapist. This countertransference had both objective and subjective elements. In brief, the therapist not only was reacting to the patient's provocative passivity but also was influenced by her negative feelings about passive and unavailable men. Once the therapist was able to contain and manage her countertransference aggression, she began to explore in a nonconfrontive manner some of the patient's mistrust. It was almost a relief for her when he blurted out dramatically, "You see what is happening to the Palestinians in Lebanon; next thing you Israelis will be coming after us in Israel!"

A final type of countertransference aggression that deserves mention is one that arises out of deeply held differences of belief between therapist and patient. To be sure, this can happen in any kind of psychotherapy, but the extreme nature of the political conflict between Jews and Arabs makes this pernicious development all the more likely. The Arab patient may hold political beliefs that are anathema to the Jewish therapist. Or the patient may be directly or indirectly involved in political activity that is felt as threatening by the therapist. In either case, the therapist winds up struggling with negative feelings, even hatred, toward the patient. In extreme cases, the therapy simply cannot go on.

In one poignant example, the therapist was a concentration camp survivor whose political views generally tended toward liberalism and dovishness on Israeli–Arab questions. She had already treated three Arab patients when she was presented with the case of a young Arab intellectual with avowedly pro-PLO sympathies. She had little difficulty empathizing with the patient and his personal difficulties during the initial months of treatment. One morning, however, as she arrived at her office at the Hebrew University, she noticed a demonstration on campus by a group of Arab students protesting Israeli government policies toward Arabs. Her immediate thought was "I wonder if my patient is demonstrating there." And then, "Why in hell am I helping an Arab when one day he may turn against me?"

She realized that she was in countertransferential difficulty but was not sure how to address the issue with the patient. Much to her relief, when her patient arrived for his appointment that afternoon, *he* raised the issue. He was openly sympathetic to the demonstrators but had not personally demonstrated. The therapist, sensing that the patient wanted to explore their cultural and political differences, acknowledged that the demonstration had made her uncomfortable. This led to a candid discussion of their different political sympathies. They reached no resolution, yet each felt there had been some clearing of the air. In retrospect, the therapist felt certain that if she had attempted to avoid the issue and had not been somewhat self-disclosing, the patient would have dropped out of treatment. As it was, the patient stayed on, and the therapy continued to a satisfactory conclusion some two years later.

This case raises the issue of how the therapist can most effectively use countertransference in the service of treatment. What should be told to the patient? How much self-disclosure is useful? And what is the correct timing for such interventions? In the final section of this chapter, these technical issues will be further explored.

THE MANAGEMENT AND USE OF COUNTERTRANSFERENCE

In treating a patient from a very different background, the therapist is prone to countertransferential errors that reflect his cultural assumptions and values. He is also likely to err at times in understanding or construing the meaning of some of the patient's statements and behavior. There is no way of completely avoiding these problems. Yet, the therapist has open to him some ways of minimizing the difficulties.

One of these, as indicated by several researchers, is that before treating a patient from another culture, the therapist should attempt to familiarize himself with that culture (Bernard 1953, Devereux 1953, Griffith 1977, Jackson 1983, Ticho 1971). Realistically the therapist cannot expect to develop a thorough expertise, but he can hope to gain some access and awareness through reading and discussion with others. I have noticed that in those instances in which the therapist has made this kind of preparatory effort, the patient often seems to sense it, and it appears to strengthen the treatment alliance.

An additional facet of the therapist's preparation for working with patients of another culture is the need to examine candidly his motives for choosing to do so, especially those motives that may interfere with treatment. In short, the therapist is wise to examine the extent to which he might be bringing to the treatment situation countertransference predispositions: excessive curiosity, or aggression, or the wish to prove himself above prejudices, or the need to expiate feelings of guilt. The therapist may discover that his countertransference predispositions are of such magnitude that he would be ill-advised to begin a particular cross-cultural psychotherapy. More often, he is likely to discover what Racker (1957) has called a "personal equation"—namely those areas of countertransferential difficulty that potentially are most likely to emerge, albeit in manageable form, once the treatment is underway. These are the areas that the therapist will need to scrutinize throughout the course of therapy.

An important technical problem in cross-cultural psychotherapy is whether and when the therapist needs to initiate with the patient an exploration of their cultural differences. Is the therapist wise to wait until the patient alludes to their differences, or until obvious transference or countertransference problems arising out of their cultural differences impinge upon the treatment? Or should the therapist take up the matter at the outset of treatment, thereby alerting the patient that he believes cultural issues are likely to bear on the treatment? In this connection, several researchers on interracial psychotherapy have indicated that early discussion is advisable, even necessary (Griffith 1977, Schachter and Butts 1968, Tseng and McDermott 1972). In recommending early discussion of racial issues in interracial psychotherapy, Griffith states: "It sets the stage for openness in the therapeutic interaction and conveys the message that this crucial issue is not taboo" (p. 38).

These considerations also apply to the Jewish therapist–Arab patient dyad. Yet, in my observation, early discussion, especially in the initial session or two, was seldom initiated by the therapist. There is little question that the reluctance of the therapist to do so was fraught with countertransferential meaning in many instances. On occasion, however, it did seem that the therapist was reluctant to immediately confront the issue of cultural differences primarily out of a tactful awareness that these matters were too threatening for the patient and that, rather than setting the stage for openness, early discussion would have engendered only paranoid-like resistance. Thus it sometimes did seem more constructive for the therapist to wait for the patient's transferential allusions to the therapist's Jewishness.

Although it is clear that sooner or later (and usually sooner) it is important for the patient to explore the meaning for him of the therapist's cultural differences. it is less clear just how self-disclosing the therapist needs to be in this regard. Should the therapist's self-exploration be a silent one, or should he share some of this exploration with the patient? I am inclined to believe that in the initial phase of treatment, the therapist's self-exploration probably needs to be carried out silently. Having decided to raise the issue of cultural differences in the intake session or shortly thereafter, the therapist should then focus on the patient's thoughts and feelings. In my view, the therapist need do nothing more *at this point* than acknowledge the possibility of occasional misunderstandings due to cultural differences and *if asked*, acknowledge whether or not he has treated other patients from that culture. But the focus must be on the patient's concerns. The questions of the therapist's countertransferential predispositions and his general motives for working with the patient are a matter for his silent review; open discussion of them at this early stage would likely prove burdensome to the patient.

Once the treatment is underway, countertransference difficulties arising out of cultural differences often occur. Sometimes the therapist becomes aware of these difficulties before he acts them out; more often, however, he has already begun to act out. Indeed, it is usually his acting out that first alerts the therapist to the existence of countertransference problems. The question is then one of what should be said to the patient.

There is no absolute answer to this question. So much depends on the relationship of a particular therapist to a particular patient, as well as the nature of the countertransference problems and just how and when they arise. In general, though, it has seemed to me that therapists have erred on the side of ignoring or attempting to deal "silently" with counter-transferential impingements, rather than on the side of excessive self-disclosure. I am not suggesting that the therapist ought to engage in an exaggerated mea culpa. But it does seem that once the countertrans-ferential impingement has become obvious to the patient, or once the patient indicates an unconscious awareness of it (such as in dreams or transference allusions), the therapist needs to acknowledge, and up to a point discuss, the impingement, with a focus on its meaning for the patient.

The only valid evidence of the value of such technical suggestions comes from the examination of specific cases. Let me illustrate, then, from some of the case material already presented, what I take to be correct or incorrect handling of countertransference impingements.

The male therapist who forgot until the last moment to tell his patient that he was leaving for reserve duty mismanaged the countertransference. The therapist realized that his guilt had interfered with making the an-nouncement, as well as with his responding to the patient's veiled hostil-ity (and disappointment) once the announcement was belatedly made. The therapist left for reserve duty without having addressed these mat-ters. Even when he returned he failed to address them, although the patient immediately made transparent references to the therapist's sudden departure and supposed military activities. The therapist encouraged the patient's exploration of these "fantasies" about the departure, but he did not allude to his own countertransferential difficulty. He chose to deal "silently" with his countertransference.

In my view, the therapist's silence was in this instance neither helpful nor advisable. The therapist needed not only to focus on the patient's fantasies about the departure but also to acknowledge his own difficulty in announcing the absence. I believe that had the therapist acknowledged his own difficulty, it could have led to a fruitful exploration of transfer-ence and reality elements in the patient's perceptions, and it might have enhanced the treatment alliance between patient and therapist. Unfor-tunately, we will never know. What did happen is that the patient slowly veered away from the subject. Then, several weeks later he suddenly, and irrevocably, announced that he would be discontinuing treatment.

This case can be contrasted with the example of the woman concen-tration camp survivor who found herself overwhelmed by aggression toward her Arab patient as she contemplated a political demonstration of Arab students. She realized that she had to manage these feelings in order to go on working with her patient. When the patient came to his session the same day and mentioned the demonstration, he was obviously concerned about not only his feelings but hers as well. She could have chosen simply to explore his feelings and fantasies. She, after all, had not sufficiently worked through her countertransferential aggression. (I suspect that the patient may have sensed this.) Yet she chose to talk about her discomfort and her fantasy of the patient's participation in the demonstration. This was a bold thing to do, but she believed in retrospect that refusal to explore her countertransference would have proved deleterious to her relationship with the patient and to the treatment. I am inclined to agree with her. But again, we will never know. All we do know is that her intervention seemed to lead to a clearing of the air, and not to any signs of resistance on the patient's part.

These two examples are presented to demonstrate how some countertransferential difficulties might be technically dealt with by the therapist. While they are suggestive of the occasional usefulness of the therapist's self-disclosure, each case must be examined on its own terms. The question of just when, how, or if to openly explore countertransference issues is not one that lends itself to facile generalizations.

In summary, one more point should be emphasized: In cross-cultural psychotherapy, the management of countertransference is a technical matter of special meaning. In such therapy, the usual problems of trust and empathy are often sharply accentuated. This is all the more true in the milieu of modern-day Israel, where antipathy and distrust between Arab and Jew are the norm. Countertransference problems arising out of cultural and political differences are almost certain to occur in this situation. The therapist's adequate management of these problems—including, if necessary, self-disclosures—often seems to make the difference between successful and failed treatment. All of this is a difficult task for the Jewish therapist and imposes great demands on him—and on the Arab patient, too. But the fact that some treatments do reach a most satisfactory outcome is quiet, and perhaps even edifying, testimony that such a task can be accomplished.

ADDENDUM

I have gratefully accepted the editors' offer to add a few words to this chapter, which was written some ten years ago. At the time I had spent two years in Israel supervising the clinical work of Jewish therapists who were treating Arab patients. Since then, I have continued to live in Israel, and as part of my work here I have continued, at times, to do such supervisions. I have also done some clinical work with Arab patients.

While the main thrust of this chapter still seems accurate to me, there is one major source of countertransference difficulties that, in retrospect, I believe was insufficiently addressed. To be specific, I think that I did not pay enough attention to the problems caused by differences in cultural values (not just political views), which crop up when Jewish therapists treat Arab patients in insight-oriented psychotherapy.

The Jewish therapist's views regarding the benefits of personal autonomy, and the therapist's views concerning the value of introspection and the capacity for doubt, very often are not shared—at least not to the same extent—by his or her Arab patient. The Arab patient typically—though *not* always—considers himself or herself tied to the wishes and needs of his or her nuclear family. These ties provide the Arab patient with his or her core sense of identity, and though sometimes exasperating to the patient, he or she seldom wants to be free, autonomous, from them. In short, the autonomy that the Jewish therapist considers intrinsic to healthy psychological functioning is not an altogether appealing prospect to the Arab patient, This difference in values, if not understood and worked through by the therapist, can provide a quagmire of misunderstandings and countertransferential difficulties for the therapist.

Or take another example: the matter of introspection and capacity for doubt. As products of the Western Enlightenment—and more specifically, our therapeutic training—we Jewish therapists value introspection and find meaning, if not pleasure, in our capacity for doubt. Some Arab patients, college-educated and/or exposed to Western cultural and intellectual values, share these notions. Most, however, do not, or at least not to the same extent. Raised in a more authoritarian family environment, the majority of Arab patients learn to be keenly extrospective; that is, they are highly attuned to the feelings of others, especially the feelings of more powerful others. These patients are less accustomed than, say, Western patients to searching within for their own innermost feelings and attitudes, particularly when this search may turn up material that is in contrast to that of the group. In a word, they are less prone to introspection. And closely linked to this, Arab patients generally are less convinced of the value of doubt. They do not revel in the mists of ambiguity. The "truth" for them comes in black and white, not gray. Thus, the kind of personal search that is inherent in insight-oriented psychotherapy, the search that often leaves more questions than answers, is a process the Arab patient is relatively unaccustomed to, and one that conflicts with a penchant for absolutes.

There are other examples where differences in cultural values between Jewish therapists and Arab patients impinge on the course of the therapy process—for instance, a range of issues surrounding the therapeutic frame—but the above-mentioned differences are most critical because they go to the heart of the process of insight-oriented psychotherapy. In my experience these problems almost always arise, to some degree, in the therapies of Arab patients by Jewish therapists. Ten years ago I was less aware of these·difficulties, and I notice that my discussion of these matters was limited to a remark or two about Jewish therapists' "prejudices." Now, I am inclined to think that the issue is more complicated, a clash of cultural values and perspectives as I have here adumbrated.

Yet, despite all this, I am no less sanguine today than I was ten years ago about the prospects of Jewish therapists treating Arab patients, or— as has begun to happen—Arab therapists treating Jewish patients. The work can be done, and is being done. And one of the reasons this is so is that the therapists involved, Jews and Arabs, are increasingly aware of the full gamut of countertransferential problems that they are likely to encounter along the way.

REFERENCES

Abel, T., and Metraux, R. (1974). *Culture and Psychotherapy*. New Haven: New Haven College and University Press.

Basch-Kahre, E. (1984). On difficulties arising in transference and countertransference when analyst and analysand have different sociocultural backgrounds. *International Review of Psycho-Analysis* 11:61–67.

Bernard, V. W. (1953). Psychoanalysis and members of minority groups. *Journal of the American Psychoanalytic Association* 1:256–267.

Devereux, G., ed. (1953). *Psychoanalysis and the Occult*. New York: International Universities Press.

Griffith, M. (1977). The influence of race on the psychotherapeutic relationship. *Psychiatry* 40:27–40.

Jackson, A. (1983). Treatment issues for black patients. *Psychotherapy: Theory, Research, Practice* 20:143–151.

Racker, H. (1957). The meanings and uses of countertransference. *Psychoanalytic Quarterly* 26:303–357.

Schachter, J. S., and Butts, H. F. (1968). Transference and countertransference in interracial analyses. *Journal of the American Psychoanalytic Association* 16:792–808.

Sullivan, H. S. (1953). *The Interpersonal Theory of Psychiatry*. New York: Norton.

Thomas, A. (1962). Pseudo-transference reactions due to cultural stereotyping. *American Journal of Orthopsychiatry* 32:894–900.

Ticho, G. (1971). Cultural aspects of transference and countertransference. *Bulletin of the Menninger Clinic* 35:313–334.

Tseng, W., and McDermott, J. (1972). *Culture, Mind and Therapy: An Introduction to Cultural Psychiatry*. New York: Brunner/Mazel.

Wohlberg, G. (1975). A black patient with a white therapist. *International Journal of Psychoanalytic Psychotherapy* 4:540–562.

III

Language and Other Clinical Considerations

Having acknowledged the presence of indigenous Western values within the body of psychoanalytic thought, and understood the presence of cultural variations in the meanings that people place on experience, we are now left with the challenge of how to use the analytic method of inquiry with an ever-expanding and diverse patient population. Are we comfortable with the traditional approach of simply instituting so-called parameters in the dynamic work? Or can our own critical self-examination move us toward more valiant questioning of methodologies that inadvertently foreclose rather than expand the field of psychological inquiry?

For example, the question of analyzability or amenability to psychodynamic treatment has been traditionally viewed mainly in terms of the patients' aptitude. However, contemporary analytic writers have alerted us to the idea that this assessment is made on the basis of clinical judgments formed within the unique interaction of the patient–therapist dyad. Thus at either conscious or unconscious levels, the therapist's own psychodynamic issues and countertransference must carry formidable weight in her or his determination of any patient's ability to work psychodynamically. Moskowitz examines this problem in Chapter 9, and explores the interactional anxiety so often present in diverse dyads that may cloud the therapist's clinical judgment. In Chapter 10, Altman pursues the vein of interactional phenomena in the cross-cultural dyad, suggesting contemporary relational approaches to analyzing the transference–countertransference matrix that integrate the analyst's own subjectivity as a vital aspect of the analytic work. (Perez Foster and Moskowitz have also offered their respective views on these contemporary approaches in Chapters 1 and 2.)

Skin color can evoke powerful and painful feelings in black patients that strike at the core of their identity and self-esteem. In Chapter 11 Williams discusses how this topic is brought into the therapeutic relationship and how to deal with its transference and countertransference implications. Finally, Chapters 12 and 13 explore a poorly addressed but increasingly important technical issue in the treatment of culturally diverse patients by English-speaking clinicians. Patients whose treatments are conducted in a second language present a formidable challenge. Clinicians, besides needing to integrate the influential factors of immigration and acculturation with their patients' presenting complaint, must also consider that bilingualism per se impacts on how patients narrate their life story in the treatment process. Both Javier and Perez Foster highlight the role of bilingualism in the reconstruction and working through of early memory in treatment, the development of transference, the organization of self-experience, the introjection of early object experiences, and the formation of psychic defenses.

9

The End of Analyzability

Michael Moskowitz, Ph.D.

The question of analyzability, which occupied so much paper and hours of class discussion in the heyday of American psychoanalysis, has, for the most part, faded from the scene. There is a practical reason: there are so many psychotherapists wanting to practice analysis and so many of them trained in how to do it, that any patient who enters the office of a psychoanalyst becomes a candidate for psychoanalysis. This is not necessarily a bad thing. Praxis and theory are inextricably bound and necessity is the mother of invention. The need to analyze and the expansion of approaches to analysis have interacted to lead to the development of analytic treatments that can help almost anyone.

The pendulum has swung so far that recently Arnold Rothstein, a prominent psychoanalyst of the American Psychoanalytic Association, wrote that analysis is really the treatment of choice for everyone. Rothstein's (1994) paper is worthy of attention because it marks a sea change in official psychoanalysis: analyzability is no longer an issue. Diagnostic classification is seen as not only irrelevant but also potentially harmful to a full consideration of the patient's sensitivities. Negative feelings about patients, including negative assessments of analyzability, should be viewed as potential signals of countertransferential interference. Rothstein concludes, "Prospective analysands are analyzable until they prove they are unanalyzable in a trial analysis" (p. 694).

If analyzability is no longer an issue, why bother devoting a chapter to it? There are two reasons. First, even though the issue is dead, its ghost remains an immortal presence, with almost every analyst at some point during almost every analysis asking the question, "Can I help this patient?" Second, and more pertinent to this book, is the fact that although most analysts in private practice are willing to accept most patients who seek analysis, clinics and training institutes are still anecdotally reported to use discarded criteria to weed out patients, many of whom are poor and oppressed.

Rothstein's position is not a new one. Ferenczi (1931) felt that every patient is potentially analyzable and wrote that his analytic failures were due to his own lack of skill rather than to the patient's unanalyzability. (See Aron and Harris 1993 for a full discussion of Ferenczi's contributions.) Searles (1965), from an interpersonalist perspective, and Boyer and Giovacchini (1967), from a Freudian one, take the analyzability of the most severely disturbed patients for granted. Bergman (1985, 1993) describes the psychoanalytic treatment of initially nonverbal, psychotic children. Abend and colleagues (1983, 1988), writing from the classical Freudian position, proposed that many patients diagnosed as borderline could be treated in a relatively unmodified analysis. Ellman (1991) traced how Freud's particular countertransference difficulties led to his definition of analyzability. André Green, a French psychoanalyst (1972), wrote, "I personally do not think that all patients are analyzable, but I prefer to think that the patient about whom I have doubts is not analyzable by me" (p. 35). Rothstein's paper is noteworthy because of his position at the center of classical orthodoxy and his willingness to admit to the economic motivation for the reassessment of the idea of analyzability. He is frank in stating that the "decline in the number of such ideal potential analysands, even in the consultation rooms of respected established analysts, has contributed to the interest in questioning some of these pedagogic assumptions concerning assessment of prospective analysands" (p. 682).

Rothstein cites Abrams (1992) as representing what he (Rothstein) says "remains a majority point of view" (p. 682). " The patient brings—among other things—psychological mindedness, a capacity for controlled regression, competent integrating and organizing functions, the potential to observe at a distance, and experience with immediacy, often at the same time, and a reasonably intact psychological foundation arising from a more or less successful oedipal-age organization" (pp. 76–77).

Yet, in reality, almost no one sticks to these criteria in deciding whom to accept for analysis. That Rothstein terms Abrams's perspective the majority position reveals an interesting misrepresentation. Abrams, in fact, represents a minority view, even among Freudians. What he does represent is a sort of ideal: he describes in general terms the kind of patient many analysts would like to have, and against whom they can compare their patient if the analysis fails. Abrams offers not one clinical example of the kind of patient who is analyzable or unanalyzable. For example, he writes, "The synthesizing and integrating functions necessary to convert maturational potential into developmental organization may be defective. This creates a variety of worrisome chaotic disorders that are not treatable psychoanalytically" (p. 72). What does this mean? We can all imagine what it means, but it approaches a projective test in its vagueness. In the name of diminishing ambiguity (his paper is entitled "Ambiguity in Excess: An Obstacle to Common Ground"), Abrams (1992) makes definitive statements that are empty of definable content.

> When the maturational clock calls the next step forward, features of the unsettled conflict remain entrapped within earlier organizations and cannot be influenced by the transformational actions of the later ones. This may lead to deformations or symptoms; or to a continuous shaping of reality offerings by unconscious fantasies: or it may encumber self- and object representations; or it may compromise the newly emerging adaptive repertoire. Some of these disorders may be responsive to psychoanalytic treatment. [p. 73]

Even the conclusion is ambiguous.

I would imagine that Abrams has a sense of what he means, as do his colleagues with whom he shares clinical data. He probably knows whom he can help and whom he can't, but his assertions are uninterpretable by those outside of his particular intellectual community. Abrams continues in the unfortunate psychoanalytic tradition of pseudo-operationalism: stating something definitively, using terms that are undefined and that have marginally shared meaning, and then equivocating. Perhaps his statements are potentially operationalizable, perhaps his hypothesis potentially testable, but as they stand they provide no useful information.

WHY ANALYZABILITY DECONSTRUCTS

In a paper still used in courses on analyzability, Waldhorn (1960) examined many factors that may contraindicate psychoanalysis, including poor frustration tolerance, hyperactivity, a history of aggressiveness, a history of poor object relationships, intolerance of passivity, rebelliousness, intolerance of anxiety, defects in reality testing, the erotization of speech, the presence of malignant identifications, an inability to enjoy success, the defeating influence of a disturbed spouse or parent. Yet this paper, like all thoughtful papers on the subject, ends up deconstructing itself. Waldhorn writes:

> It will be seen at once that the practical task of summarizing evaluations made about such a roster of functions and considerations would require an awareness of the interrelatedness of many of these phenomena, of their potentiating and mitigating effects when coexisting and of their fluctuations in intensity, stability, and duration in response to a wide variety of influences. We are inevitably handicapped in any attempt to systematize such a technique of evaluation by the difficulty inherent in measuring such subtle, abstract, and evanescent clinical phenomena, and by the impropriety of fixing allegedly significant limits in regard to complex functions which exist only in a complex and ever-changing context. [p. 503]

In other words, Waldhorn says that these factors are too complex to make any useful generalization.

In a major review of the literature on analyzability Bachrach and Leaff (1978) concluded that "the majority of studies fail to indicate the evidence for their conclusions and the data upon which they are based," (p. 900) and that the findings, "are cast largely in abstract, metapsychological terms lacking empirical specification" (p. 901). They called for systematic empirical research. Some years later, Bachrach and colleagues (1991), in reviewing such research, came to the unfortunate conclusion that analyzability and therapeutic benefit were unpredictable from the perspective of the initial evaluation of seemingly suitable cases. Similarly Erle and Goldberg (1984) studied 160 patients treated by sixteen experienced analysts over a five-year period. Foreshadowing Rothstein, they concluded that the assessment of analyzability could only be made at the end of treatment.

The search for a way of determining who will benefit from analytic treatment has haunted the field from its beginnings. Freud (1905) wrote:

> One should look beyond the patient's illness and form an estimate of his whole personality; those patients who do not possess a reasonable degree of education and a fairly reliable character should be refused. It must not be forgotten that there are healthy people as well as unhealthy ones who are good for nothing in life, and that there is a temptation to ascribe to their illness everything that incapacitates them. . . . Nor is the method applicable to people who are not driven to seek treatment by their own

suffering. . . . It is gratifying that precisely the most valuable and highly developed persons are best suited for this procedure; and one may safely claim that in cases where analytic psychotherapy has been able to achieve but little, any other therapy would certainly not have been able to effect anything at all. [pp. 263–265]

Yet, Strachey, in his introduction, undermines Freud's position. "The nature of the psycho-analytic method involves indications and contra-indications with respect to the person to be treated as well as with respect to the clinical picture" (p. 253). Hysteria and the obsessional neurosis are treatable; nervous exhaustion may not be, because analysis requires effort. Anorexia is treatable unless the patient is in dire physical shape and requires immediate removal of symptoms. Then, echoing Freud, Strachey states that various other "qualifications" are necessary if the person is to be treated. "He must be capable of a psychically normal condition . . . a certain measure of natural intelligence and ethical development are to be required of him; if the physician has to deal with a worthless character, *he soon loses the interest which makes it possible for him to enter profoundly into the patient's mental life;*" (p. 254, emphasis added). He then states the inescapable reality—"Owing to various circumstances which can easily be guessed, [Freud] has for the most part been in a position to try his treatment only on very severe cases: patients have come to him after many years of illness, completely incapacitated for life, and, after being disappointed by all kinds of treatments, have had recourse as a last resort to a method which is novel and has been greeted with many doubts" (p. 254).

From the beginning, practitioners were confronted by this dilemma: the patients who showed up at their door were often not the patients that they felt most eager and able to help. Yet there seemed to be little alternative but to try, since all else had failed.

It is interesting that Strachey said Freud had only tried his method on the most severe cases. If this is so, from where did the idea of the ideal case derive? The answer would seem to be from the analytic student, people like Strachey himself, and from Freud's view of himself in his own self-analysis. There is no doubt that many of Freud's cases, and almost all of those after World War I, were some version of a training analysis (Ellman 1991). Not that there was always a clear line in degree of disturbance between some candidates and the "severe cases," to which Strachey refers, but it's probably safe to assume that most of those who came to see Freud, many from as far away as America, came prepared to love and venerate him.

As Ellman (1991) well documents, Freud had a particular difficulty with narcissistic patients. He felt that only transference neurotics could be analyzed, that patients were only accessible to the extent that they were capable of object love and thereby able to form a positive transference. This is probably what Freud meant by being of good character, that the patient had an interest in something separate from himself. For Freud, transference was primarily a libidinal phenomenon, and he was most comfortable with patients who in some way could love him, and in whom he could remain interested. Abraham and Ferenczi during Freud's time and many others since have defined transference more broadly and have identified different forms of stable and analyzable transference relationships in patients with narcissistic (e.g., Kohut), borderline (e.g., Kernberg), and psychotic (e.g. Searles) disorders.

To throw one more factor into the mix, analysts practice in remarkably diverse ways. Glover (1955) in 1938 sent a detailed questionnaire to twenty-nine members of the British Society. Twenty-four responded. Of the sixty-three points raised in the questionnaire, on only one significant point was there complete agreement: the necessity of analyzing the transference. Glover found that "the technique of interpretation was a much more individual matter than had previously been assumed," (p. 348) and that the assumption that analysts used the same criteria for selection and followed similar technical procedures was completely unwarranted. Even though the British Society at that time already was home to Kleinian, Freudian, and independent perspectives, Glover did not tie the disparities in technique to theoretical differences (Wallerstein 1992).

Psychoanalytic practice since 1938 has undoubtedly become even more heterogeneous. There is a much greater diversity of theoretical positions, and although there may still be only a loose relationship between theory and technique, there is unquestionably a wider range of technical approaches. Some theorists such as Gray (1994) have made concerted efforts to link technique to theory. It is clear that his technique differs markedly from others such as Brenner (1976) even within the same ego-psychological Freudian tradition.

If, as Rothstein (1994) and others claim, analyzability can only be determined by how a person responds to the analytic situation, then how the analyst defines the analytic situation is a critical factor in determining analyzability (Ellman 1991). To take an extreme example: by Brenner's (1976) criteria, a patient who cannot or will not use the couch is unanalyzable. Similarly, a patient who will not accept Gray's close process attention technique is not analyzable by that approach. More generically, patients who are narcissistically mortified by interpretations before an atmosphere of trust has developed are not analyzable by therapists who insist on early interpretations. It is our view (the editors) that analyzability should not be determined by the technical approach of the analyst but that the analyst should be flexible enough to vary her approach to meet the needs of the patient. Or if the analyst is committed to a particular approach to which a patient does not respond, then the analyst should explain alternative approaches that the patient might try. We believe that the most important issue is to provide an approach that the patient can use and that the particular variety of analysis, analytic psychotherapy, or analytically informed therapy, is of secondary importance to the attainment of the analytic result of insight leading to greater emotional freedom and freedom of action. At least since the time of Ferenczi there have been analysts who have argued that analysis should be defined in terms of these goals rather than by any particular technical procedure. Gedo has championed this view for more than thirty years (Gedo and Gehrie 1993). This is not to say that all analytic experiences are equivalent. It is my belief that an approach like Gray's offers the potential for greater autonomy than one that relies on the internalization of selfobject relationships. But this is just a belief, unsupported so far by empirical data. It is also my view that a four- or five-times-a-week analysis provides a much more intense and potentially life-changing experience than once-a-week psychotherapy. The issue of intensity can hardly be argued. The question of its being a better treatment can be (Josephs 1996). We are now at a point in the history of analysis where we need to ask not whether a particular patient is analyzable, but rather what approaches might be useful and what approaches the patient might be interested in pursuing.

Thus far analyzability as a patient variable has been deconstructed. There is no evidence that some people are more amenable to analysis than others. Some may be more interesting to some analysts than others. Some may be more responsive to particular approaches than others. Unfortunately we are now in the realm of conjecture, which, however unsatisfying, is a better place than false certainty.

ANALYZING ACROSS CULTURE AND CLASS

The conjectures just stated place the clinic patient at an obvious disadvantage. Rarely does a clinic patient have the opportunity to choose a therapist. The likelihood of being assigned one who is interested, whose countertransference interferences are minimal, and who offers an amenable approach are clearly lower than if the patient can seek out a therapist of her own choosing. Seligman (1995) suggests that an important variable in the success of a therapy is the patient's active participation in choosing his therapist:

> Active shoppers and active clients did better in treatment than passive recipients (determined by responses to: Was it mostly your idea to seek therapy? When choosing this therapist, did you discuss qualifications, therapist's experience, discuss frequency, duration and cost, speak to someone who was treated by this therapist, check out other therapists? During therapy, did you try to be as open as possible, ask for explanation of diagnosis and unclear terms, do homework, not cancel sessions often, discuss negative feelings toward therapist?) ... Respondents whose choice of therapist or duration of care was limited by their insurance coverage did worse. [p. 969]

This is less of an issue for the intellectual, middle-class patient, who has made up the bulk of the patients seeking low-fee treatment at psychoanalytic institutes and clinics, ever since the later days of the Berlin Clinic of the thirties (Jacoby 1983, Rendon, Chapter 3, this volume). These patients know what to expect. They may belong to the same culture as psychoanalysts. Many have shopped, in a sense, before applying for treatment. They may have decided consciously or unconsciously that the approach of a particular institution meets their needs. Outside the confines of a clinic many intellectual middle-class patients have a greater sense of entitlement in choosing their therapist, thus maximizing the chances of a good match. At least among the economically and psychically empowered, the question of analyzability has been reversed. The analyst does not choose her patient. The patient chooses her analyst. Often the choice is based on a friend's recommendation which is packed with information about the analyst's style and capabilities. Under these conditions the patient may start an analysis knowing more about the analyst than the analyst knows about the patient. Almost no therapist enjoys being shopped. But we must at least confront the possibility that such shopping increases the likelihood of a workable relationship. Undoubtedly some people choose badly. It can only be hoped that with the option of leaving, these patients will eventually find a therapist who will help them understand their history of bad choices.

From Freud to the present day much of the psychoanalytic literature is based on training analyses and other analyses in which both patient and analyst belong to the same community or subculture. Those of us who feel part of a community take a certain sense of safety for granted. We also know the signposts and danger signals. We in the psychoanalytic community may tolerate or even expect an analyst who is either relatively silent or relatively confrontational. We may be able to tolerate the oddness of the analytic situation in part because we understand why the analyst does what she or he does, and because we feel safe within a community that includes the two of us.

Literature from the seventies reported inferior therapy being offered to minority and ethnic clients in counseling and psychotherapy clinics (see Mays 1985 for an overview). Sue and colleagues (1976) found that clients who are members of minority ethnic groups are more often seen by paraprofessional staff and terminate quickly at community mental health facilities. They are also more likely to be seen in supportive psychotherapy. In 1977 Sue concluded that "minority clients receive unequal and poor mental health services" (p. 116). These studies and others have led to a plethora of papers recommending that the therapist be immersed in, or be a part of, the culture of the patient, and that different cultural groups require different approaches (See Patterson and Hidore, 1996 for a review and critique). Yet Sue (1988) concludes that research findings do not support either the assertion that ethnic minorities do worse in therapy or that patient–therapist racial matching is desirable. Patterson and Hidore (1996) conclude there is no basis for culturally specific psychotherapies.

Therapists need to be knowledgeable and sensitive to the cultural and daily realities of their patients' lives, but there is no reason to believe such knowledge and sensitivity are difficult to learn unless there are severe characterological or countertransference inhibitions. But the requisite knowledge cannot be gained from empathy in the clinical setting alone. Gedo and Gehrie (1993) write:

> The deck is stacked against an analyst's treating someone from an entirely different cultural background with no knowledge of that background. An

analyst relies heavily on shared cultural meanings in any analysis, as in any sort of intimate communication. Possibilities for misunderstanding are so broad as to be endless and not correctable solely by reliance on empathy; an empathic position requires some context for shared experiences in the absence of which others will of necessity be substituted, experiences that may or may not have anything to do with the experience of the patient. [pp. 5–6]

Interestingly, the example that Gedo cites is that of Margaret Mahler, who was a Hungarian Jewish immigrant, and her inability to understand the cultural context of an upper-class American woman.

There is every reason to believe that cultural consciousness has been raised over the past two decades. Twenty-five years ago it was not unusual to see a Vietnam veteran who had been treated in a previous psycho-therapy without the topic of Vietnam ever being raised by the therapist, or the child of a concentration camp survivor treated without the issue of the Holocaust being discussed. Issues of cultural sensitivity are now part of almost every therapist's training and the situation is much im-proved. Given the willingness to be open to issues of class and culture, there is no evidence that cultural differences cannot become part of the matrix of fantasy and understanding that constitute analytic work. Michael Gorkin, in Chapter 8, shows that even in an atmosphere of initial mutual suspicion, political antagonism, and guilt, analytic work can occur with Jews treating Arabs in Israel and now Arabs treating Jews as well. In Vietnam Veterans' Centers around the country, in the late seventies, white middle-class therapists were able to work successfully with poor African-American patients who, with every reason, were deeply distrustful of the institution that funded the treatment setting. This work required an acknowledgement both of the trauma of the war and the trauma of the daily narcissistic assault of living in a racist society.

From its beginnings psychoanalysis has been a deeply multicultural endeavor, with analysts and patients belonging to a diverse collection of European and American classes and cultures. Today, analysts and patients come from a much greater range of cultures and there is no sign that theory and technique cannot respond to and accommodate this increas-ing diversity. (See Moskowitz 1995 for a fuller discussion.) Analysts rep-resented in this volume and many others such as Ainslie (1995), Holmes (1992), Fanon, (1967), Schachter and Butts (1968), White (1987), and others have continued to use psychoanalysis to disentangle the meanings of race and ethnicity.

Still there is anecdotal evidence and much hallway discussion to indicate that now-discarded criteria of analyzability are used to exclude immigrant and minority patients from analytic treatment. With the exception of Sue and colleagues' (1976) study showing that ethnic patients were more likely to be seen in supportive psychotherapy, this topic is rarely openly discussed. Colleagues working in low-fee clinics report that in some discussions patients are still viewed as being or not being "good analytic patients" or "amenable to insight oriented therapy." Unsuited patients are more often referred for medication, support groups, behavioral interventions, and the like. Unlike therapists in private practice, therapists working in clinics still can and need to decide how to allocate resources. They can still choose their patients. Given the overwhelming nature of the reality problems poor patients have to face, it is understandable that therapists working in clinics would use criteria that make intimate connection with such painful realities less likely.

I think this process most often operates unconsciously. At the clinic of one analytic institute with which I am familiar, it was noticed that African-American patients were less likely to be found analyzable and assigned to an analyst than white patients. On consideration, it appeared that African-American applicants were more likely to report drug problems and were thus ruled out, using the now-discarded idea that drug users are less likely to be analyzable. Still, while many analysts, Rothstein (1994) included, will not work with addicted persons, there is increasing consensus that such work is possible (Richards 1993). Further, there is anecdotal evidence that white patients come to clinics better prepared to fill out "acceptable applications" and are less likely to list drug use as a presenting problem.

At other times I think more subtle countertransference difficulties latch on to cultural differences to lead the therapist to decide that he cannot work with a particular patient. In a recent presentation Kirkland Vaughans (1994) noted that analysts do not devote enough attention to their own ethnicity. As he put it, from the analytic perspective, the world seems to be made up of blacks, Latinos, and psychoanalysts. Analysts rarely consider how their subjectively experienced ethnicity enters into the analytic interaction. The same, I think, is true of issues of language, often the most concrete representation of ethnicity. Most of us use English well enough. Few of us descend from the Mayflower. We are mostly immigrants or children or grandchildren of immigrants, rarely great-grandchildren of immigrants. Many of us, I suspect, have heard other languages spoken by parents or grandparents. But, in part because we live in a rigidly monolingual culture, we may not fully recognize the impact of this experience.

One of the first patients I saw when I was working in a college counseling office was a young man from southern Italy. In our first session he asked, "Are you like a factory psychologist? Is it your job to get me to go back to work?" I had not thought of myself in this way before. I thought of myself as being paid by a relatively benign third party and I was sure there were at least some nurturant motives for the establishment of a university counseling center. Yet there were also the motives of containment and control. I began to wonder if I was being politically naive.

Over time, my patient described the culture of southern Italy. At one point he asked, "Do you like to work? Where I come from no one likes to work. People try their hardest not to work," and I was reminded of a chapter in Simon's (1984) book on Italy in which she described an elderly man, a count I think, who would appear each day at midday on the balcony of his ill-kept palace in his threadbare and only suit, to show those around that he did not need to work. And this reminded me of my mother talking about her brothers, my uncles, and their similar behavior. I then went into a fog, whose connection to preceding events was only much later recognized. I found my patient impossible to understand. And I mumbled more than usual so that he found it difficult to understand me.

I concluded that the reason I could not understand this patient was that his primary language was not English, and I further wondered if it made sense for me, or anyone, to treat patients in other than their primary language. I went on wondering this for some time, even while I was simultaneously working well with patients from Korea, Spain, and India. After discussing my difficulty with several colleagues, I began to think more about my own ethnic-linguistic past and to understand what led me to assume incorrectly that it was my not being able to work in my patient's mother tongue that created the foglike distance.

Both of my parents spoke several Eastern European languages, in addition to Yiddish. They argued and spoke privately in Hungarian. They spoke to us, the children, however, only in English. I never have been able to learn a single word of Hungarian, but fantasied discovering in analysis that I was fluent in it. That never happened. I also realized in thinking about this patient that I liked going to countries in which I could barely speak the language, in part in order to recreate an early, more peaceful state, before I could understand my mother's words.

Now it is clear that my Italian patient did want to keep me at a distance and treated me with a measure of contempt (which also played into my maternal countertransference reaction), and it is true to some degree that he used his language difference to help create this distance. However there is now no doubt in my mind that the main impediment to my dealing with this issue was an unanalyzed countertransference conflict centering around my own need not to understand.

Freud wrote that psychoanalysis is a cure through love. We are limited in our ability to work psychoanalytically with people only by or in our inability to love and be loved by them. People have loved and have been loved across all boundaries of culture and class. The question of analyzability then becomes a question of the analyst's capacity to understand the other, to be able to enter into the patient's psychic world. To the extent that a life can be understood, it can be analyzed. Each analyst can learn not who is analyzable, but, to paraphrase Green, "who is analyzable by me?"

REFERENCES

Abend, S. M., Porder, M. S., and Willick, M. S. (1983). *Borderline Patients: Psychoanalytic Perspectives.* New York: International Universities Press.
—— (1988). A response. *Psychoanalytic Inquiry.* 8 (3):438–455.
Abrams, S. (1992). Ambiguity in excess: an obstacle to common ground. In *The Common Ground of Psychoanalysis*, ed. R. S. Wallerstein. Northvale, NJ: Jason Aronson.
Ainslie, R. (1995). *No Dancin' in Anson: An American Story of Race and Social Change.* Northvale, NJ: Jason Aronson.
Aron, L., and Harris, A., eds. (1993). *The Legacy of Sandor Ferenczi.* Hillsdale, NJ: Analytic Press.
Bachrach, H. M., Galatzer-Levy, R., Skolnikoff, A., and Waldron, S. (1991). On the efficacy of psychoanalysis. *Journal of the American Psychoanalytic Association* 39(4): 871–916.
Bachrach, H. M. and Leaff, L. A. (1978). Analyzability: a systematic review of the clinical and quantitative literature. *Journal of the American Psychoanalytic Association* 26: 881–920.
Bergman, A. (1985). From psychological birth to motherhood: the treatment of an autistic child with follow-up into her adult life as a mother. In *Parental Influences in Health and Disease*, ed. J. Anthony and G. Pollack, pp. 91–121. Boston: Little Brown.
—— (1993). Ego psychological and object relational approaches—is it either/or? Commentary on Neil Altman's "Psychoanalysis and the Urban Poor." *Psychoanalytic Dialogues* 3:51–67.

Boyer, L. B., and Giovacchini, P. (1967). *Psychoanalytic Treatment of Characterological and Schizophrenic Disorders.* New York: Science House.

Brenner, C. (1976). *Psychoanalytic Technique and Psychic Conflict* New York: International Universities Press.

Ellman, S. J. (1991). *Freud's Technique Papers: A Contemporary Perspective.* Northvale, NJ: Jason Aronson.

Erle, J. B., and Goldberg, D. A. (1984). Observations on assessment of analyzability by experienced analysts. *Journal of the American Psychoanalytic Association* 32(4):715–737.

Fanon, F. (1967). *Black Skin White Masks.* NY: Grove.

Ferenczi, S. (1931). Child analysis in the analysis of adults. In *Final Contributions to the Problems and Methods of Psycho-Analysis*, pp. 126–142. London: Karnac, 1980.

Freud, S. (1905). On psychotherapy. *Standard Edition* 7:257–268.

Gedo, J. E., and Gehrie, M. J., eds. (1993). *Impasse and Innovations in Psychoanalysis: Clinical Case Seminars.* Hillsdale, NJ: Analytic Press.

Glover, E. (1955). *The Technique of Psychoanalysis.* New York International Universities Press.

Gray, P. (1994). *The Ego and the Analysis of Defense.* Northvale, NJ: Jason Aronson.

Green, A. (1972). *On Private Madness.* Madison, CT: International Universities Press.

Holmes, D. (1992). Race and transference in psychoanalysis and psychotherapy. *International Journal of Psycho-Analysis* 73:1–11.

Jacoby, R. (1983). *The Repression of Psychoanalysis.* Chicago: University of Chicago Press.

Josephs, L. (1996). The fantasy of optimal session frequency. *Psychologist Psychoanalyst.* 16:26–28.

Mays, V. M. (1985). The black American and psychotherapy: the dilemma. *Psychotherapy* 22:379–387.

Moskowitz, M. (1995). Ethnicity and the fantasy of ethnicity. *Psychoanalytic Psychology* 12:547–556.

Patterson, C. H., and Hidore, S. (1996). *Psychotherapy: A Unitary Theory.* Northvale, NJ: Jason Aronson.

Richards, H. (1993). *Therapy of the Substance Abuse Syndromes.* Northvale, NJ: Jason Aronson.

Rothstein, A. (1994). A perspective on doing a consultation and making the recommendation of analysis to a prospective analysand. *Psychoanalytic Quarterly* 63:680–695.

Schachter, J., and Butts H. (1968). Transference and countertransferenee in interracial analyses. *Journal of the American Psychoanalytic Association* 6:792–808.

Searles, H. (1965). *Collected Papers on Schizophrenia and Related Subjects.* New York: International Universities Press.

Seligman, M. E. P. (1995). The effectiveness of psychotherapy: the *Consumer Reports* study. *American Psychologist* 50: 965–974.

Simon, K. (1984). *Italy: The Places In Between.* New York: Harper and Row.

Sue, S. (1977). Community mental health services to minority groups: some optimism; some pessimism. *American Psychologist.* 32: 616–624.

—— (1988). Psychotherapeutic services for ethnic minorities: two decades of research findings. *American Psychologist.* 43:301–308.

Sue, S., McKinney, H., and Allen, D. (1976). Predictors of duration of therapy for clients in the community mental health system. *Community Mental Health Journal* 12:365–375.

Vaughns, K. (1994). *Race, does it matter? Notes from the supervisory underground.* Presentation at *Culture and Context: Psychoanalysis in a Changing World.* Psychoanalytic Society Biennial Conference, New York, March 5.

Waldhorn, H. (1960). Assessment of analyzability: technical and theoretical observations. *Psychoanalytic Quarterly* 29: 478–506.

Wallerstein, R. S. (1992). Psychoanalysis: the common ground. In *The Common Ground of Psychoanalysis.* Northvale, NJ: Jason Aronson.

White, K. (1987). *Bi-racial psychoanalysis: a consideration of dissociated across-race identifications.* Presented at the William Alanson White Society, February 11.

10

The Accommodation of Diversity in Psychoanalysis

Neil Altman, Ph.D.

INTRODUCTION

In the first century of psychoanalysis, there has been strikingly little interest in social class, race, and ethnicity as these relate to analytic work. Freud's Jewishness has been examined as an influence on his theory (Gay 1987, Klein 1985) and on his sense of the marginality of the psychoanalytic movement, the degree to which he anticipated resistance and struggle for acceptance. By and large, however, Freud did not situate his own theory in its cultural context, or develop the specific ways in which cultural difference played a role in clinical work.

To some degree one might regard Freud's seeming obliviousness to ethnicity as a reflection of the way he managed being a Jew in late nineteenth-century Vienna. The Austro-Hungarian empire of the time was a multiethnic environment in which some, such as Theodor Herzl, the founder of Zionism, developed a distinctly Jewish consciousness. Many Jews, Freud included, downplayed their differences with the non-Jewish majority in their struggle for acceptance and professional success. Gilman (1993) points out that Jews had only recently been accepted for medical training at Freud's time, and then with the understanding that they would treat only Jews. Freud, Gilman believes, may have steered clear of consideration of the cultural specificity of his theory for fear that it would be considered a Jewish psychology. Developing a psychology with universal applicability would help Freud transcend the status of "Jewish doctor."

We in the late twentieth-century United States live in quite different times. On one hand, the American aspiration to become a melting pot has stimulated a vision in which cultural differences would disappear or become irrelevant. The recent suburbanization of much of the country has allowed many people to live in situations of cultural homogeneity. On the other hand, the United States is diverse, and becoming increasingly so, ethnically, socioeconomically, and racially. Recent immigrants have often wanted to hold on to their native cultures, languages, and traditions, so that we have begun to talk of a mosaic rather than a melting pot. Traditional democratic values have led many Americans to be uncomfortable with exclusionary or elitist positions. We have had a civil rights movement, a feminist movement, a gay rights movement, a concern with multiculturalism in many areas. In addition, among intellectuals there has been extensive interest recently in the deconstruction and interrogation of our previously taken-for-granted categories in the spheres of gender, race, class, culture, ethnicity, and nationality (see Bhabha 1990, Butler 1990, Dimen 1993, West 1993).

When psychoanalysis moved to the United States as the Nazis took power in Germany, it first underwent a process of increasing homogenization. The medicalization of psychoanalysis and the development of ego psychology put the therapeutic focus on adaptation, a notion analogous to the "melting pot" aspirations of the immigrants of the time. Psychoanalysts with politically radical positions, such as Otto Fenichel (see Jacoby 1983), felt compelled to downplay these positions for fear of encountering hostility or even deportation. Economic self-interest, in a capitalist context, led psychoanalysts to focus on private practice with fees that ensured that patients would come from only the upper socioeconomic strata, which often led to racial and cultural homogeneity. Training in psychoanalysis was so expensive and time-consuming that few beyond the upper classes could afford it.

In more recent years, there has been increasing diversity among psychoanalytic patients and practitioners. The community mental health movement has provided opportunities for psychoanalytically oriented practitioners to work in lower socioeconomic status communities. The recent tendency toward erosion of private practice has created a need for clinicians to work in community clinics, and to accept into their practices an increasingly diverse clientele. Psychoanalysts have found themselves confronted with a degree of difference between themselves and their patients for which their training has poorly prepared them. They have become increasingly aware of the culturally embedded nature of the theory and practice in which they have been trained. A need has been created to develop a perspective on our field, to situate it culturally, so as to enable clinicians to orient themselves to difference.

My thesis in this chapter is that a one-person model in psychoanalysis, derived from Freudian drive theory, is limited in its capacity to accommodate difference—racial, cultural, or socioeconomic—in the psychoanalytic dyad. I argue that a two-person or three-person, relational model is necessary for taking account of such differences psychoanalytically, as well as for taking account of the community or clinic context in which psychoanalytic work with a diverse clientele often takes place. My effort is to examine the parallels between the kind of theory and practice we have developed, and the socio-cultural-political context in which we are working. I believe that we cannot simply tinker with traditional psychoanalysis in order to accommodate diversity and difference. We must be prepared to look at psychoanalysis with new eyes, so as to reconstitute our theory and practice to be relevant for our contemporary lives.

CHANGING MODELS IN PSYCHOANALYSIS AND THE ACCOMMODATION OF DIVERSITY

Freud struggled at various points in his writing with the integration of one-person and two-person psychoanalytic models. His early seduction model was dyadic in its etiological focus on what happened between two people, that is, the seduction of children. When Freud shifted the focus to oedipal fantasy as etiologically primary, he moved in a one-person direction. Freud continued to try to accommodate the interaction of psychic reality and external reality through his concept of the "complemental series" (1916–1917). With respect to the clinical psychoanalytic situation, Freud's commitment to an objective stance for the analyst predisposed him to conceive of the analytic situation in one-person terms; that is, Freud positioned the analyst outside the field being observed, which, within the one-person drive theoretical model, consists of the intrapsychic world of drives and defenses. Abstinence and anonymity as technical principles serve to ensure the analyst's nonparticipation within the field. Freud continued to separate out the nontechnical human relationship with the patient from the technical relationship, however, so that his behavior was never thoroughly abstinent and anonymous—take for example his well-known feeding of the Wolf Man. (See Gill 1982, and Lipton 1977 for extended discussions of this point.) Such thoroughgoing reserve was adopted only by Freud's later followers, who conceived of all analyst behavior as governed by technical principles. In any case, although Freud, as well as many of his contemporary followers, does not adopt a one-person model in a rigid way, one can speak of the model in abstract terms and trace the ways in which the influence of the model affects classical theory and practice. One such influence can be seen in the way transference has often come to be viewed as distortion, in the sense that the term refers to the patient's intrapsychic world projected onto an essentially blank screen analyst.

Relational models in psychoanalysis (Mitchell 1988) are two-person models. That is, the field is constituted by two people in interaction. The implications for the psychoanalytic situation are sharply divergent from the implications of a one-person model. The analyst is considered an inevitable participant, while remaining an observer, of the interpersonal field. Object-relations theories, in general, attempt to take account of the interaction of the intrapsychic organizations of each of the participants in an interaction, as well as the events that take place between them. Transference is not seen essentially as distortion, but as a personal interpretation of the events taking place in the interpersonal field. As a full participant in the interpersonal field, the analyst's subjectivity is a relevant, even crucial element in some versions of a two-person model (Aron 1991, 1992). The analyst's subjectivity may be subject to scrutiny equally with the patient's.

Three-person models in psychoanalysis (see Greenberg 1991) attempt to take account of the context in which the dyad functions. A three-person model would take into account, for example, the impact of a public clinic context for psychoanalytic work (see Altman 1993, 1995).

Drive theory seeks to view all psychological phenomena as transformations of drives and defenses against those drives. Within a drive-theoretical, one-person model, then, material related to race, culture, or class is viewed as the surface manifestation of deeper drive–defense conflicts. Race, culture, and class concerns are seen as enlisted by the patient in the service of the expression of unconscious conflict. By contrast, consider a two- or three-person model that accommodates the analyst's subjectivity as part of the field as well as the patient's. From such a perspective, both patient's and analyst's attitudes and feelings related to race, culture, and class become analytically significant parts of the field in their own right.

A CLINICAL EXAMPLE

I will now present some very brief clinical material in order to provide a concrete focus for a discussion of these psychoanalytic theoretical models in relation to racial, class, and ethnic differences between patient and analyst.

A 40-year-old upper-middle-class African-American man comes for a consultation to a white male analyst with a similar social class background. In the course of the consultation, the prospective patient indicates a desire to work with the analyst. In the next session, the analyst inquires about the relevance of race in the patient's choice of analyst. The patient replies that he prefers a white analyst. He says that he knows some black psychotherapists and that he anticipates that if he worked with a black person, there would be pressure on him to focus on issues of oppression, identification, and solidarity with lower-class black people, and anger at white people.

The analyst's reaction to this communication was complex. On one hand, he felt a sense of security engendered by the alliance the patient was making with him. He wanted to work with this patient, and he wanted the patient to want to work with him. He found himself secretly allying with the patient in disdain for those African Americans who sought a simple solution for social and personal problems in hatred of whites. He also felt relieved to be let off the hook as a white person. This particular black man will not treat me with hostility, he thought; he will not be suspicious of me, will not find my hidden racism.

On the other hand, the analyst felt uneasy that this alliance was based on creating a common "enemy." The dynamic seemed too similar to what the patient was describing in terms of black people forging solidarity out of hatred of whites. Further, he wondered if he were not being asked to collude with the patient's defensive denial of his own anger, his own sense of being oppressed, his own multifaceted identification with black people and/or lower socioeconomic status people. Finally, the analyst wondered if he were not being asked to collude with a denial of *his* racism, as if the two of them could create a black–white partnership that would be devoid of mistrust and hostility. The patient seemed to be stimulating the analyst's racism while simultaneously inviting him to deny the existence of such feelings between the two of them. Class solidarity, perhaps, was being used to deny racial difference and potential discordance.

THEORETICAL PERSPECTIVES

Consider how this clinical vignette can be understood from one-, two-, and three-person models. A one-person model would focus our attention on the patient and his defensive activity with respect to aggression in the transference. In what way is the patient expressing and/or defending against aggression and/or sexuality through his choice of a white therapist, and through the way he is interacting with him? From a drive-theoretical perspective, the racial content of the discussion would be regarded as manifest content, covering over a more basic conflict over sexuality and/or aggression. The analyst's concordant racist and classist thoughts and feelings would be seen as pathological countertransference, to be set aside or done away with.

A two-person perspective, by contrast, focuses our attention on the interpersonal field. The important questions from this point of view have to do with how two subjectivities are interacting. What are the various personal meanings that blackness and whiteness, as well as class categories, have to each person? What does each assume these categories mean for the other? What are the various dynamics of the interpersonal interaction? Is the patient trying to probe the analyst's racism and classism? Is he trying to assess the degree to which the analyst will avoid highlighting the patient's anti-black and anti-white racism? When we raise such questions as analytically significant without reference to drive issues we are operating in a relational, two-person framework; from this point of view, the analyst's own racist, classist, and other reactions are crucial aspects of the field. The patient's possible concerns about the analyst's racism do not derive solely from his fantasy life. They may be plausible hypotheses about the analyst, which may be explored from that point of view. The analyst may learn something about himself, in fact, and about his own reactions to racial and social class-related material in the course of this exploration.

The various meanings "black" and "white," as well as class categories, have for patient and analyst, as well as their expectations of each other, are impossible to understand fully without reference to the American sociopolitical, historical context. When we take account of these factors we are operating in a three-person framework. The patient's and analyst's preconceptions of each other are conditioned by societally based stereotypes and expectations. Black and white people in the United States have a plausible basis to be concerned about racist attitudes in each other.

There is an ongoing history of oppression of blacks by whites in this country, which is an inevitable background element as patient and analyst begin to interact. Taking account of such contextual elements requires a three-person view of the analytic situation.

I believe that most clinicians, of whatever theoretical persuasion, do take account of many of these interpersonal and sociopolitical factors in their work with patients. My point is that in taking account of these factors, one is not staying within the one-person framework that has significantly informed the classical Freudian point of view. Technical and theoretical confusion results if one fails to take account of the theoretical shift one has made. I can easily imagine a clinician with a Freudian orientation exploring the patient's perception of the analyst's racism with seriousness and respect. To the extent that such a clinician wishes to maintain consistency with a one-person, drive-theoretical perspective he must, however covertly, regard these perceptions, if they are to be analytic material, as reflecting transference distortion. (If the analyst does indeed harbor or exhibit racism, these feelings would be thought to contaminate the analytic field and render the transference unanalyzable.) From my own two-person perspective, I would assume that this overt or covert stance on the part of an analyst who does not believe he is manifesting racism would have its own effect on the patient, who might feel invalidated or disqualified in some subtle way. A clinician with a traditional perspective might respond: "Of course, the analyst treats the patient's concerns about the analyst's racism with full respect. The analytic meaning of these concerns is only one aspect of their meaning. To consider the way in which these racial concerns may be enlisted in the service of transference distortion does not deny that the patient may be fully entitled to his concerns about the analyst as a human being." From my point of view, such a division between the analyst as analyst and the analyst as human being is a necessary aspect of the abstinent analytic stance traditionally prescribed. A two-person perspective calls one's attention to how the patient reacts to the analyst as a complete human being regardless of how the analyst defines his or her role. If one says to the patient, "Yes, I can appreciate your concerns about my racial attitudes, but in our analytic work together we must turn our attention to the unconscious meaning this has for you," the patient may feel dismissed in a way which, from an interactional perspective, becomes important analytic material in its own right.

From a two-person point of view one may also discover a variety of ways in which race, for example, is imbued with sexual and aggressive significance. The difference from a drive-theoretical, one-person model is in the way in which these levels of meaning are layered. Within the drive-theoretical, one-person model the sexual and aggressive issues are seen as more basic, both because they are *drive* issues, and because they are *intrapsychic* issues. The two-person model is capable of maintaining a circular, fully interactive relationship between these various levels of meaning. That is, one's sexual and aggressive feelings and impulses may be as likely to be influenced and structured by their association with race as vice versa. Intrapsychic meaning and interpersonal interaction can be seen as feeding one another, with neither more basic than the other.

With this perspective in mind, let us consider some previous discussions of race in the literature. Holmes (1992) criticizes approaches that "do not fully interpret intrapsychic conflicts in the face of racial explanations offered by therapy patients." She believes that "white therapist guilt, black therapist over-identification with the downtrodden . . . and warded-off aggression in patients and therapists" account for this tendency. She advocates the attempt to "expand the patient's understanding once the racial component has been acknowledged" (p. 1). I agree with Holmes, and would add that there is the opposite danger, that one would fail to explore the racial aspect fully once the intrapsychic component is acknowledged.

Holmes goes on to point out that the therapist's race does not limit the patient's transference. Within a white patient–black analyst dyad, for example, there may develop a transference configuration in which patient is seen as black and therapist as white, just as the female gender of the analyst, for example, does not exclude the development of paternal transference. I believe Holmes is emphasizing the intrapsychic component to attitudes about race as a reaction to what she sees as an overvaluation of the manifest in some of the literature. I suggest that the "latent" can also be overvalued, and that the actual race of patient and analyst are also important elements in the analytic field.

Holmes criticizes approaches that see discordance between patient and therapist around race as negative factors. Thus, some authors' primary focus is to advocate education of the therapist to be more understanding of the racially or culturally different patient. Holmes states: ". . . discovering more about the culture of the racially different patient may inadvertently foster too much distance from the scary and warded-off drive derivatives of patient and therapist, which, in both, may initially have given rise to racially-based prejudice" (p. 2). Again, I concur, adding that what is scary and warded-off can be the prejudice itself, in both participants.

Consider now some of Holmes's case material. Miss A., a black woman, was assigned to a black therapist (Holmes herself) after forming a positive connection with a white female psychiatrist intake worker. The patient was sullen throughout her first hour with the therapist, communicating great disappointment and anger. When the therapist inquired about these feelings, the patient responded "You're black, you're a woman, and you're a psychologist!" (p. 3). Holmes's understanding of what had developed is as follows: ". . . the race, gender, and professional status of the therapist served as points of contact for the patient's transferences of defense. That is, she came to understand her protestations as warded-off self loathing, which itself was in part a defence against recognition of her rage, the threatened eruption of which had brought her to treatment" (p. 3).

Holmes notes Evans' (1985) comment that patients' racist remarks in therapy should be interpreted as defense and resistance. She justifies not having immediately made such an interpretation in this case by arguing that the defense is best interpreted after having been fully expressed. Holmes stays within a one-person model by justifying her decision to allow the patient to attack her as thus necessary for elaboration of the defense. From a two-person perspective, one might want to listen to this "manifest" content because one takes it as analytically important material on any number of levels. For example, one might wonder whether the patient is exploring her therapist's ability to survive attack, or her tendency toward retaliatory rage. Or perhaps she was trying to provoke her therapist into a protest against this racially based self-loathing, thus expressing her need for a black therapist who would stand up for herself. Holmes, in fact, notes that she did feel "burdened and disconsolate" as a result of the patient's attack, and that her supervisor did not encourage her to explore the relevance of these feelings. Although she does not say so, my impression is that Holmes sensed that her subjectivity, in its interaction with the patient's, contained important analytic material. If so, one would want to encourage the patient's unimpeded expression of her feelings in order to understand the kind of subjective reaction in the analyst, and interaction between the two of them, which the patient was unconsciously inducing.

I would now like to turn to the paper by Schachter and Butts (1971) on transference and countertransference in interracial analysis. They state: "The catalytic effect of the analyst's race upon the transference occurs when the racial stereotypes are concerned with the same affects and conflicts as the transference" (p. 803). We have here a one-person model, in which racial stereotypes are seen as preorganized imagos that may or may not fit with the transference configurations the patient brings to treatment. In their case material, Schachter and Butts include a great deal of countertransferential material, which allows one to construct a picture of a two-person interaction. They regard countertransference as a pathological impediment to the analytic process, however, thus retaining their one-person theoretical position.

In one case example, a white man is seeing a black male analyst. This man had difficulty maintaining a relationship with a woman, and had recently developed a sexual problem, premature ejaculation. He was insecure at work, ingratiating with fellow employees, fearful of losing control of his anger. He saw black men as aggressive and sexual in contrast to his sense of himself as weak and impotent. He had, according to the authors, a fantasy of magical repair, the black analyst seen as the possessor of the sexual potency he hoped to achieve.

At one point, ten months into the treatment, the patient had intercourse with a woman, and he came to his analyst seeking recognition or praise for his accomplishment. The authors state that the analyst experienced "mild disbelief in the therapeutic significance of the patient's achievement," which was evidently communicated to the patient in some way, because, they say, it ". . . reinforced the patient's stereotyped perception of the Negro as a virtual sexual superman, thus widening the gulf between patient and analyst" (p. 797). The authors note another aspect of this interaction between patient and analyst: they say that the analyst's difficulty acknowledging his patient's achievement may also represent the analyst's "need to disclaim his therapeutic power to achieve such a great effect with the patient. This problem was rooted in the analyst's insecurity about his effectiveness, which was combined, however, with a need to assert his greater power over the patient" (p. 797). Later, the authors state that this analyst's "need to deny his anxiety about sexual competitiveness merged with the racial stereotype to impede the progress of the analysis," and: "the confluence of countertransference and stereotypes serves to delay the analysis" (p. 807).

I believe that the authors' view of the countertransference as having interfered with the analysis derives from their one-person model, in which the analyst's job is to remain neutral, in the sense of being unaffected by the transference images projected onto him. From a two-person, interactional perspective, however, one would take for granted that the analyst would meet the patient's stereotypes and preconceptions with his own. The analytic field would then consist of the interaction of these two sets of preconceptions and organizing principles, along with the joint efforts of patient and analyst to gain perspective on their interaction. From this point of view, the analyst's countertransference described by Schachter and Butts is a fascinating combination of what Racker (1968) called *concordant* and *complementary identifications*. The concordant identification, with the patient's conscious self-image, has the analyst feeling insecure and ineffective. The complementary identification, which Racker describes as an identification with the patient's internal objects, is with the imago of the sexual superman, or the one who cannot tolerate any competition from the patient. From this point of view, these reactions are regarded in two ways: as part of the analyst's own organizing principles that he brings to the interaction, and as induced by the patient. The patient's perception of the analyst as sexual superman must now be regarded not only as a projection of a preexisting transference configuration, but also as a commentary on the actual interaction as he observes it. The analyst's countertransference, from this point of view, is not a pathological interference with the analytic process, but an inherent aspect of the analytic process itself. This is not to say that having become aware of his own organizing principle the analyst may not want to change it. In fact, hearing the patient's commentary on their interaction, the analyst may find a new perspective on himself for his own self-analytic use. This beneficial impact of the patient on the analyst may itself have a therapeutic impact on the patient (Searles 1979).

PUBLIC CLINICS

Most interracial, intercultural, and interclass psychotherapeutic work takes place in public clinics, community mental health centers, or hospital clinics. In this section, I argue for the utility of a two- and/or three-person psychoanalytic model in this context.

The one-person model's requirement that the analyst be anonymous does not fit with the conditions of work in a public clinic. In most clinics, therapists are expected to fulfill multiple roles in relation to their patients. Therapists may be expected to function as advocates for their patients with social service agencies; they may have to make decisions about whether their patients are entitled to emergency cash, food, or carfare; they may be expected to work with more than one member of a family; or to function as both individual and group therapist to a patient. If we hold to a definition of the analytic role that is inconsistent with such functions, we may rule out the possibility of psychoanalytic work in public clinics, and thus with most lower socioeconomic status patients of all racial and ethnic groups.

An ego psychological version of a one-person model may exclude work with patients in public clinics for other reasons. Such patients may be considered to lack the ego resources necessary to be psychoanalytic patients. They may be assumed to be preoccupied with concrete bread-and-butter issues, not sufficiently psychologically minded, not sufficiently educated. They may be thought to lack the tolerance for frustration entailed by an abstinent analytic stance, given the overall deprivation of their lives.

As I have written elsewhere (Altman 1993, 1995) the criteria for analyzability in two-person object relations theories are broader and more inclusive than in ego psychological theories. Two-person approaches do not prescribe an abstinent analytic stance and so do not require the patient to tolerate that particular kind of frustration. Criteria of analyzability in two-person models have more to do with the capacity to use an interpersonal relationship in flexible ways, as opposed to the capacity for verbal articulation and insight. Since the analyst is assumed to be a participant in the analytic field, there is less potential for inconsistency with the multifaceted role of therapists in public clinics. In short, two-person psychoanalytic models open up the public clinic as a potential arena for psychoanalytic work.

Consider, now, some clinical material that is typical in important ways of public clinic practice.

A 20-year-old Puerto Rican woman was referred to a public clinic's Child and Adolescent Division because she was found to have physically abused her son over a period of time. The local child protective service had decided to leave the boy with his mother while assigning a child abuse prevention worker to the family. This worker was to make frequent and regular home visits and be available around the clock. The prevention worker referred the patient and her son for psychotherapy.

The patient was a very intelligent and attractive woman who had been severely abused physically by her own mother and a succession of stepfathers. She was currently involved with a boyfriend, considerably older than she was, who showered her with expensive clothes and a car. When she began seeing her male therapist she came with her son, escorted to the clinic by the child abuse prevention worker. In sessions, however, she generally ignored her son and talked about herself. She described her anger at her boyfriend for being overly possessive, and her aspirations to complete high school and go on to college. She wanted nothing to do with her mother, who lived in the neighborhood. After some time, she placed her son in a nursery school during the day, and began coming alone and unescorted to the sessions. She frequently "forgot" her weekly sessions, but always maintained contact with the therapist. After some months she enrolled in a high school equivalency course and got a job as a waitress. The child abuse prevention worker visited less frequently, reassured that the danger of abuse had passed.

In the second year of this treatment, the therapist decided to leave the clinic, having obtained another job. He told the patient some weeks in advance. She reacted unemotionally, saying she knew the therapist had to pursue his own career advancement. She failed to show up for her sessions, however, for the next several weeks. Calls and letters to the patient went unanswered. Concerned that he would not have even a single final session with the patient, the therapist called the child abuse prevention worker asking if she could encourage the patient to come for a final session. On the therapist's last day in the clinic, the patient came with her son, escorted by the child abuse prevention worker. Her son had an obvious bruise on his face. The patient was furious that the therapist had called the child abuse prevention worker, because now a new child abuse report was about to be made against her. She felt that she would now be under renewed scrutiny, and that her progress in life would be undone. The patient was unwilling to discuss what any of this might have to do with the termination of the therapy.

In discussing this case, I want to focus, first of all, on the role assumed by the therapist. The therapy was initiated in connection with a child abuse prevention project, the culmination of a child abuse report and subsequent investigation. This process has the potential for being seen as persecutory by patients, although in some cases it can also be seen as supportive of the patient's wish not to abuse her child. In this case, the patient seemed to view both her prevention worker and her therapist as supportive, and she responded, in general, by thriving. I believe that the patient's transferential view of the therapist cannot be fully understood without taking account of this context.

The therapist's departure from the clinic, however, caused the entire project to become a persecutory one in the patient's mind. The patient withdrew her cooperation from the therapeutic project, to which the therapist reacted by mobilizing the prevention worker to take on the function, previously adopted by the patient herself, of bringing her to the clinic. The patient was now put in the role of an uncooperative child who needed an adult to bring her to the doctor's appointment. By abusing her child in this context, the patient might be plausibly understood to be doing any or all of the following: she destroys or undoes the therapeutic work, she reproaches or attacks the therapist for leaving her, she turns him into a persecutory object, she highlights her ongoing need for support, she denies the goodness of the therapist in her life as he leaves her, she displaces her rage onto her son.

I want to emphasize the necessity of adopting a three-person, systemic perspective in considering this clinical material. The therapist–patient relationship is situated in a child abuse prevention project in the minds of both patient and therapist. The supportive and persecutory aspects of this project frame positive and negative transference reactions as they unfold in the therapy. In contrasting this approach to a one-person model, I emphasize that it is not simply a matter of analyzing the patient's superego projection onto the therapist, or of the therapist's pathological, countertransferential collusion with this projection by calling the child abuse prevention worker, for example. Rather, from my point of view, the situation pulls for superego projection on the part of the patient, and a superego stance on the part of the therapist. What is required from a two- or three-person perspective is the exploration of the interpersonal field created by the interaction of the situation with the psychic organizing principles brought to the situation by both participants.

CONCLUSION

I have tried to demonstrate the utility of a two- and/or three-person psychoanalytic model for taking account of race, culture, class, and public clinic context in psychoanalytic work. Without such a model, these factors are inevitably reduced to relatively superficial reflections of deeper unconscious conflict. With such a model, we can take account of these factors as important elements of the psychoanalytic situation in their own right, without denying the importance of related unconscious organizing principles.

REFERENCES

Altman, N. (1993). Psychoanalysis and the urban poor. *Psychoanalytic Dialogues* 3(1):29–50.

—— (1995). *The Analyst in the Inner City: Race, Class, and Culture through a Psychoanalytic Lens*. Hillsdale, NJ: Analytic Press.

Aron, L. (1990). One-person and two-person psychologies and the method of psychoanalysis. *Psychoanalytic Psychology* 7:475–485.

—— (1991). The patient's experience of the analyst's subjectivity. *Psychoanalytic Dialogues* 1(1):29–50.

—— (1992). Interpretation as expression of the analyst's subjectivity. *Psychoanalytic Dialogues*. 2(4):475–508.

Bhabha, H. (1990). *Nation and Narration*. New York: Routledge.

Butler, J. (1990). *Gender Trouble*. New York: Routledge.

Dimen, M. (1993). Anxiety and alienation: class, money, and psychoanalysis. Paper presented at the spring meetings of the Division of Psychoanalysis, American Psychological Association, New York: April.

Evans, D. (1985). Psychotherapy and black patients: problems of training, trainees, and trainers. *Psychotherapy: Theory, Research, and Practice* 22:457–460.

Freud, S. (1916–1917). Introductory lectures on psychoanalysis. *Standard Edition* 15,16:1–463.

Gay, P. (1987). *A Godless Jew: Freud, Atheism, and the Making of Psychoanalysis*. New Haven, CT: Yale University Press.

Gill, M. (1982). *The Analysis of Transference*, vol. 1. New York: International Universities Press.

Gilman, S. (1993). *Freud, Race, and Gender*. Princeton, NJ: Princeton University Press.

Greenberg, J. (1991). *Oedipus and Beyond: A Clinical Theory*. Cambridge, MA: Harvard University Press.

Holmes, D. (1992). Race and transference in psychoanalysis and psychotherapy. *International Journal of Psycho-Analysis*. 73(1):1–11.

Jacoby, R. (1983). *The Repression of Psychoanalysis*. New York: Basic Books.

Klein, D. B. (1985). *Jewish Origins of the Psychoanalytic Movement*. Chicago: University of Chicago Press.

Lipton, S. D. (1977). The advantages of Freud's technique as shown in his analysis of the rat man. *International Journal of Psycho-Analysis* 58:255–274.

Mitchell, S. A. (1988). *Relational Concepts in Psychoanalysis*. Cambridge, MA: Harvard University Press.

Racker, H. (1968). *Transference and Countertransference*. London: Maresfield Reprints.

Schachter, J., and Butts, H. (1971). Transference and countertransference in interracial analysis. *Journal of the American Psychoanalytic Association*. 6:792–808.

Searles, H. (1979). The patient as therapist to his analyst. In *Countertransference and Related Subjects*, pp. 380–459. New York: International Universities Press.

West, C. (1993). *Prophetic Thouqht in Postmodern Times*. Monroe, ME: Common Courage Press.

11

Skin Color
in Psychotherapy

Addette L. Williams, M.A.

For a fifth grader, Tammy was large for her age. She was known for fighting and most of us tried to stay out of her way. When I became her next target, I found myself running home from school to the screams of "High-yellow bitch!" Perplexed and scared, I asked my chestnut brown father and golden brown mother for a translation of "high-yellow." This was my official introduction to the issue of skin color.

Skin color can evoke very powerful and painful feelings among African Americans* that strike at the core of their identity and self-esteem. The physical manifestation of African, European, and Native-American ancestry often affects familial and peer relationships. Skin color is sometimes a code that encapsulates information on a host of physical characteristics: eye color, texture of hair, and shape of features, although there is not always a direct correlation. As much as people have wished that this subject would go away, it remains a charged issue that is infrequently discussed openly but is ever present in the lives of many blacks. The fictional characters created by African-American writers like Gwendolyn Brooks—*Maude Martha* (1953), Toni Morrison—*The Bluest Eye* (1970), and Dorothy West—*The Wedding* (1995), to name a few, have been important vehicles through which African Americans have been able to address this topic. Although the importance of skin color for blacks has its roots in the larger racism that plagues our society, I believe what makes this such an uncomfortable topic for most African Americans is that confront-

---

* In this chapter I use African American and black interchangeably.

ing and understanding this issue involves looking critically at one's own family and community.

What follows is a historical overview of African Americans and skin color in the United States, examples of how it is brought into psychotherapy, implications for transference and countertransference, and questions and issues that come to mind for further inquiry. This chapter focuses primarily on American black–white or black–black dyads and all case material presented is from female patients. Many of the issues may be similar for other ethnic groups but it would be careless to make such generalizations without proper research.

HISTORICAL OVERVIEW

According to Bennett (1982), before slavery became firmly established, white colonists, most of whom were indentured servants, held the same inferior status as black servants and slaves. With this shared experience of oppression, there was intermingling, and relationships developed. Both Bennett (1982) and Myrdal (1962) have noted that the black and white female populations were small, suggesting that miscegenation occurred also to continue the species. As the economic gains that slavery could provide became more clear, laws were made to create and enforce a separation between blacks and whites.

In the antebellum south, white slaveowners and their overseers often forced female slaves to have sex with them, producing what some called mulatto offspring (although the "one-drop rule" [which means that a single drop of "black blood" makes a person black (Davis 1991)] would eventually overlook this biracial heritage). While many female slaves were violated, it is believed that some consented with the hope that the status of their children would improve (Bennett 1982). To some extent their status did improve. The prevailing assumption was that whites were intellectually superior to blacks, so mulattos were accorded higher status positions than blacks, like house servants (sometimes called "house niggers") and skilled laborers. Additionally, this alleged genetic superiority was reflected in a greater value on the slave auction block (Bennett 1982). As late as the 1920 United States census, mulattos were counted as a separate racial category (Williamson 1980).

This preferential system had direct implications for social and economic class. Darker blacks became associated with lower status and lighter blacks with higher status. Neal and Wilson (1989) state: "The segregated relationship between the races seemed to sharpen divisions within Black Americans themselves, and skin color played an integral role in determining the various classes of distinctions" (p. 325). A vocabulary developed to articulate these distinctions: fair, bright, high-yellow, yellow, half white, café au lait, jet black, ink spot, blue-black, shine, in-between, tan, bronze, brown skin, red, red-bone, olive, with "black" and "yellow" representing the most derogatory terms (before "black" replaced "negro"). Within this skin color hierarchy the ideal is to be neither "too" light nor "too" dark but light brown. Additionally, there are words to describe someone who makes distinctions based on color, "partial to color," and those who prefer light-skinned people, "color struck" (Neal and Wilson 1989, Russell et al. 1992).

Russell and colleagues (1992) contend that "after the Civil War the mulatto elite no longer had the distinction of freedom to separate them from the dark-skinned masses" (p. 24). During Reconstruction, social groups—such as the Bon Ton Society of Washington, D.C. and the Blue Vein Society of Nashville—formed, mainly among the higher status light-skinned black females who sought to reinforce their position. Those who had been free, in some cases for several generations before the war, referred to themselves as the "bona fide" free so as not to be confused with the recently emancipated blacks. Passing the renowned brown bag test—when compared to a brown paper bag the skin should not be darker, and the location by a panel of "judges" of the purplish and green veins in the wrist, helped gain admission to these elite groups (Gwaltney 1980, Neal and Wilson 1989, Okazawa-Rey et al. 1987). Okazawa-Rey and colleagues (1987) note that even the black church made distinctions based on color and class, with color often determining class affiliation. *The Color Complex* (Russell et al. 1992) describes the use of the paper bag test by color-conscious congregations and the light shade of brown painted on church doors to determine who would have to attend church services elsewhere. Hair was sometimes subjected to its own test. If the fine-toothed comb that hung on a rope near the entrance of some churches did not flow through the hair with ease, admission was denied. Ironically, even the black church, the foundation of the black community and its most powerful institution, was party to the divisive effects of colorism.

Lincoln (1967) reports that during World War II and for years after, so-called passport parties were held on some college campuses. Male escorts paid a color tax based on the skin color of their dates; if light enough, she meant free admission. It is interesting to note that in the literature reviewed, skin color variations among African-American men are not mentioned, yet the skin color of women is reported to have been used by men to negotiate social and economic status.

During the 1950s and '60s, overt favoritism based on skin color seemed to lessen because of the civil rights movement. With this came a celebration of African heritage, and blacks began to question the white standard of beauty. Hair was worn in its natural state and black became beautiful. Okazawa-Rey and colleagues (1987) have noted that the "black is beautiful" rhetoric did not preclude some revolutionaries' preference for light-skinned black women. Writer Bonnie Allen, a former Black Panther member who attended a rally at the Oakland, California courthouse to free Huey Newton, was warned by two male Panthers that "things are going to get rough, so you'd better go home. You're too pretty to get your face messed up" (Allen 1982, p. 67). She did not detect a similar concern for her darker "sisters."

Okazawa-Rey and colleagues (1987) believe that by the mid-1970s, the failing economy and unemployment caused a shift in the priorities of many blacks from social concerns to more individualistic ones, with a new focus on attaining the dominant culture's standard for economic and social success. This shift in focus for many meant a shift in consciousness. Given this link between skin color and economic and social class, one would expect that skin color may become a particularly volatile subject during times of economic hardship.

In the 1990s the legal system ushered in a new twist on skin color. In February 1990, Tracy Morrow, a light-skinned black woman, filed a lawsuit against her former supervisor at the IRS, a dark-skinned black woman (Associated Press 1990a,b). Ms. Morrow testified that her former supervisor, Ruby Lewis, had made demeaning references to her skin color, like "You need some sun," and "You've had it too easy." Although the federal judge ruled that Ms. Morrow was dismissed because of poor performance and attitude, it signaled to blacks that skin color is still very much a relevant issue.

In another case of the same year, Ms. Rashid, an African-American woman who considers herself dark-skinned, filed discrimination charges against the Morehouse School of Medicine. She alleged that her superior, a lighter-skinned African American, Janet Allen, assigned her an unusually heavy workload and constantly harassed her. In the affidavit, Ms. Rashid stated that her superior ". . . is prejudiced against attractive, dark-skinned/brown-skinned African-American women" (Hardie 1990 B, 2:3). Additionally, Ms. Rashid signed affidavits from three former employees who agreed with her allegations.

Many African Americans' preoccupation with skin color and the desire to change it has created a large market for skin bleaching creams. A myriad of home remedies has also been used, sometimes with quite deleterious effects. In the novel *The Blacker the Berry . . .* (1929), Wallace Thurman details Emma Lou's elaborate application of creams and potions to her dark-brown skin and her hope that they may someday make a difference. Perhaps not much has changed, even sixty years later. According to Russell and colleagues (1992), roughly $44 million worth of skin bleaching products were purchased in 1990.

SKIN COLOR IN PSYCHOTHERAPY AND EARLY RELATIONSHIPS

Before looking at how the issue of skin color is raised in treatment, it is important to note that almost all the patients described in the relevant literature are female. Neal and Wilson (1989) suggest that "although these concerns affect both men and women, psychologically these effects appear to be stronger for females, who regardless of race, have had to traditionally concern themselves more with appearance" (p. 324). While Russell and colleagues (1992) do remark that the African-American prison population is predominantly dark-skinned, little has been written exclusively on black men. It is important to find out how African-American men experience skin color apart from its reported role in object choice or as a means of transcending social and economic class barriers.

The experience of being "different" from the white ideal of beauty and sometimes "different" from one's family has had a profound effect on many dark-skinned women, who are considered to be at the bottom of the color hierarchy (Neal and Wilson 1989). This has caused many of them to doubt their physical attractiveness and experience anger, resentment, and rejection by those who prefer their lighter-skinned sisters.

For lighter-skinned women their color may arouse feelings of superiority or guilt about the possibility that they have benefited from a certain status their color affords. Lighter skin may be a reminder of the repeated violation women endured in slavery. Often this white lineage is what darker-skinned African Americans use to question their authenticity as African-American women, regardless of how they self-identify. A light-skinned woman may experience rejection by her family because her skin color is thought to have given her greater personal freedom to achieve (see Thompson Chapter 6, this volume).

In group therapy, Boyd-Franklin (1991) has noted that skin color is a recurring theme in the treatment of African-American women. The variation in skin color, hair texture, and body type of the group members and leader encourage the emergence of transferential processes within the group and provide a context in which each woman can work through her own version of this issue. She points out the shame and secrecy attached to skin color, and that for many women the group experience was the first time they had expressed such feelings in public, since "airing dirty laundry" is a common concern in the black community.

Underlying the clinical experience are the primary experiences with mother or caretaker, in which ethnocultural values are transmitted to their children. Traditionally, African-American female primary caretakers have had the task of racial socialization, which undoubtedly is informed by their own sociocultural, economic, and racial environment (Greene 1990a,b). Greene refers to Collins (1987) and Joseph and Lewis (1981), who contend that the role of mother for African-American women has additional tasks that are not required of their white counterparts. Black caretakers are faced with teaching their children about racism and preparing and warning them of dangers and potential disappointments in a way that is not overwhelming or overprotective. While a mother's warnings to her dark-skinned child not to play in the sun because she will get too black, or not to wear certain colors, such as red, may be well-intentioned, they nevertheless convey the message that her color is not okay. During a group discussion on race relations in which the author was a co-facilitator, a young light-skinned African-American man mentioned that his light-skinned mother had always told him not to socialize with or befriend darker blacks. When he was caught doing so he was verbally reprimanded. Despite this, he said he does not allow his mother to choose his friends. He later offered that his father is much darker than his mother.

Findings from mother–infant attachment research show that the way the mother was parented affects her parenting style and the kind of attachment she forms with her own child. It would seem, then, that the mother's experiences of skin color and what was transmitted to her from her own mother will impact on her own child, and certainly part of this information would include the mother's own possible conflicts about skin color (Greene 1990a). Although considered a shameful topic to mention, for some expectant parents and their families there is color anxiety prior to the birth of a baby. Dr. Harrison-Ross has observed the difference in the way that white and black parents responded to their newborn infants. Before speculating about who the baby resembles, African-American parents are often concerned *first* with skin color (Harrison-Ross and Wyden, 1973). There is even folklore about forecasting the "true" future color of the child by looking inside the infant's ears.

What is it like for mother and child who are distinctly different shades of brown? "How does the mother respond to comments and questions about the child's color?" (Greene 1990a). Thompson (1995) states that skin color becomes a factor that can either impede or enhance the caretaker's mirroring function. Myers (1977) describes how his black analytic patient, while associating to the colors black and white in a dream, recalled becoming aware of the difference in skin color between herself (dark-skinned) and her mother (light-skinned), while taking a bath. With this new awareness of difference came the fantasy "that if she scrubbed her skin hard enough, she would clean off the brown dirt and would look like the clean, white, idealized mother" (p. 168). The patient said that her mother had explicitly connected her rejection of her daughter to the daughter's dark skin. The identification with the mother's conflicts about color encourages the splitting of self and object representations according to the meanings of black and white, or dark and light (Myers 1977).

Greene (1990a) suggests that "another relevant line of inquiry is related to the question of whether or not a black mother is predisposed to be more protective of her darker-skinned children either as a result of her own conflict about skin color or perhaps the realistic notion that the dominant culture will be even less hospitable to these children" (p. 222). Greene (1990a) offers the psychoanalytic explanation that the protectiveness and concern black caretakers have for their dark-skinned children may be a reaction formation to defend against the caretakers' unconscious hostility and other negative feelings for the child. She encourages therapists to consider a range of possible clinical meanings for the caretakers' feelings and behavior. While Thompson (this volume) acknowledges the self-hatred in making distinctions based on skin color, she believes skin color is also seen as a source of hope and optimism for the future generation. I would add that another useful line of inquiry would be the way African-American caretakers talk about skin color with their light- and dark-skinned children, and the overall approach whole families take in discussing the matter when members—as is often the case—represent the skin color spectrum of very light to dark brown.

TRANSFERENCE AND COUNTERTRANSFERENCE—SKIN COLOR IN THE CONSULTING ROOM

Given the charged nature of this subject and the difficulty discussing it with peers and family, it would seem that skin color may not be an easy subject to raise in therapy. According to Boyd-Franklin (1991), the issue is often not raised in cross-racial treatment. Although in a black intraracial dyad, the patient may feel more comfortable broaching the topic, the therapist's skin color will affect how the patient discloses information and how the transference unfolds. Comas-Diaz and Jacobsen (1991) have outlined ethnocultural transference and countertransference paradigms focusing on *intra*ethnic and *inter*ethnic dyads. This within-group and between-group model may provide a starting point for understanding the transferential reactions that may develop when skin color is a point of noticeable difference or similarity in the therapy dyad. In this model variations in skin color represent, in a sense, different ethnic sub-groups.

A therapist and patient with distinct differences in skin color may have an *inter*ethnic experience with regard to skin color. For example, a patient may be overcompliant, particularly if the patient feels there is a power differential, which skin color connotes for some people. Others may want to deny anything that calls attention to difference because it involves a confrontation with one's own subculture of skin color. Ambivalence may be another prevailing characteristic of the *inter*ethnic transference, wherein the patient struggles with both positive and negative feelings toward the therapist. A patient may struggle both consciously and unconsciously with the question, "What does it mean to identify with and internalize someone whose skin color represents envy or oppression?"

In dyads of the same or similar skin color, there may be an *intra*ethnic experience. The shared skin color may elicit an omniscient-omnipotent transference in which the patient experiences the perfect, ideal parent. There may be an overidentification with the therapist, the thinking being "you understand what it is like to be in my skin." Other patients may actively dislike a therapist of their own skin color, evoking an autoracist transference, that is, powerful negative feelings toward the self regarding skin color may be projected onto the therapist. Having split off and projected such negative attributes and feelings toward the therapist, the patient has difficulty seeing the therapist as benign and well-intentioned. These by no means exhaust the transference reactions that might arise because of skin color. One can also imagine the types of countertransference that correspond to the different transferences. Both patient and therapist are likely to have very definite feelings about their respective experiences of skin color with family and the larger society.

Proponents of intersubjectivity or a two-person psychoanalytic model, such as Hoffman (1983), Aron (1991, 1992), and Greenberg (1991), have challenged the blank screen concept and argue instead that there is a constant interaction between patient and therapist. The therapist is not simply an observer of the transference that unfolds independently of him or her. The transference is not reduced to a distortion or derivatives of early relationships. Transference, according to radical critiques of the blank screen ". . . always has a significant plausible basis in the here-and-now" (Hoffman 1983, p. 393).

Thompson (Chapter 6) and others who have written about the therapist's own subjectivity as it is evoked by the patient in the room illustrate the mutual influence inherent in the psychotherapeutic relationship. Aron (1991) aptly comments that "some of the observations that patients make about their analysts are likely to be unpleasant and anxiety provoking. Therefore, analysts might back off from exploring the patient's resistances because of their own anxieties and resistances" (p. 35).

Comas-Diaz and Jacobsen (1991) present a vignette in which an Anglo-Mexican female was in therapy with a white female therapist. The therapist asked the patient how she felt about their differing ethnic backgrounds and the patient responded, "It doesn't matter, I am also half Anglo" (p. 400). After exploring her overcompliance with the therapist, whom she perceived as an authority figure and member of the dominant society, and realizing her own authoritarian identification with her Anglo side with regard to her relationships with her Mexican and Hispanic friends, discussion followed about her ethnic ambivalence. The patient felt that her skin was not light enough and that she was "too Mexican looking." She had been blond during childhood and in Mexico she had been called La Gringa. She perceived the Hispanic and Anglo men she had dated as always abandoning her for "tall, blond, Anglo women." The patient was aware that her therapist was a tall, blond, Anglo woman and she became mistrustful. Comas-Diaz and Jacobsen assert that the therapist's initial countertransference reaction of pity did not facilitate an exploration of the patient's ambivalence about her ethnic background.

Over time, a patient's increased self-awareness affords him or her an awareness of others, in particular, the analyst's character structure with its limitations and strengths (Wolstein 1983). This awareness may lead to questions for the analyst as the patient attempts to cope with aspects of the analyst's unconscious psychology. No matter how well-analyzed and careful the analyst may be, even quite disturbed patients will experience the analyst's subjectivity. Our interpretations, one of the hallmarks of psychoanalytic work, invariably reveal some parts of ourselves. Aron (1991) points out that this private realm is exactly where we want to connect with people—it is where they live emotionally. Such an attempt at connection, however subtle or unconscious it may be, is akin to the way that children are motivated to explore their parents' inner worlds (Aron 1991). An analyst who thinks about transference and countertransference this way and remains open to hearing the patient's observations of the analyst may gain some insight into how the patient gleaned information from early caretakers regarding skin color. Certainly, in a therapeutic setting with an African-American dyad of distinctly different hues, each member will have his or her own fantasies about the other with regard to skin color, and will have formulated hypotheses about the other's perceptions and feelings as well.

Much of the discussion about skin color thus far has explored the experience of skin color differences within ethnic groups and the transference and countertransference reactions that occur. The following excerpt from a case presented by Fischer (1971) adds another perspective—the perception of skin color and its effect on countertransferential reactions when the therapist is from a dominant group.

The patient was a very light-skinned black woman whose family cherishes and worships whiteness. In the white analyst's presentation of the case to a senior colleague, the analyst noted that he had repeated several times how light-skinned the patient is and how easily she could pass for being white. The analyst emphasized that the patient was almost the same color as himself. Later he noted that he had inadvertently omitted the patient's race in a report of the case. He recognized that unconsciously he was trying to deny the patient's blackness. The analyst had come to associate his own sexual and aggressive fantasies with the blackness of his schoolmates in a predominantly black area of Philadelphia where he lived during his youth. This raises the issue of what blackness connotes for many people in our society—aggression, poverty, lack of education, ugliness. This example challenges the notion that sensitivity to skin color variations in African Americans is only an *intra*group issue.

Our language and literature reflect these dynamics of color and race. There seems to be no shortage of phrases like "black sheep of the family," "blacklist," and "black humor" where *black* is used to connote something illegal, unacceptable, or perverse. As Fanon (1967) puts it, " . . . whether concretely or symbolically, the black man stands for the bad side of the character" (p. 189).

Although Fanon's observations were made in the context of the colonial relationship between white Europeans and black Africans in Algeria, the American institution of slavery involved a similar type of power relationship. In the process of adapting to the norms of the dominant culture, many of the people of African descent in the United States have internalized the values of the dominant culture, in a sense an identification with the aggressor. Toni Morrison eloquently explains in *Playing in the Dark, Whiteness and the Literary Imagination* (1992) that the projection of the not-me, which she calls the Africanist persona, has served the collective need to justify and rationalize the exploitation of the other. Morrison contends that one of the distinguishing features of American literature is the Africanist presence, even in novels where there seem to be no African-American people.

SUGGESTIONS FOR FURTHER RESEARCH AND LITERATURE

There are other thus far unexplored aspects that add to the complexity of a person's experience of skin color. Despite the nomenclature that has evolved to describe skin color, the brown bag tests and vein "examinations," skin color can be very subjective. What is light-skinned or dark-skinned? Certainly there is more agreement about extremes but the point remains that while the distinctions are not always clear the consequences may be profound.

The classification of skin color is contextual; its significance only becomes relevant and meaningful in the context of other people, which means that in a sense, skin color is not static. A woman typically considered medium-brown in one setting may appear light-skinned in comparison to others in a particular group, while feeling dark in comparison to her very light family in which some members passed for white. I would also argue that skin color has different implications depending on one's geographical location in the United States, which may further complicate the experiences of people who live and move in distinctly different areas of the country. Is it merely coincidence that the plaintiffs in the lawsuits mentioned earlier live in the south? Or do differences in skin color have a particular importance in that region?

An important caveat in thinking about this issue is that one should not assume that a person experiences his or her skin color according to the stereotypes that light and dark represent. For example, a dark-skinned woman may well have been the preferred child over lighter siblings.

Noticeably absent from the literature reviewed, which focuses on heterosexuals and their relationships, is how colorism affects black lesbians and gays. Is it simply that the same dynamics are involved in object choice, or are there additional factors? Given that homosexual relationships are not accorded the same status in our society as heterosexual ones, is skin color still thought to be a way to improve one's social and economic class position in homosexual contexts?

Greene (1985) asserts that "color can be seen as a salient and usually obvious physical characteristic of a black person and a variable which can often predict where that person will work, live, socialize, attend school, receive health care, and how much money they may earn." (p. 390). Although Greene's use of color in this context refers to the darker color of African Americans in general, as compared to the dominant group, skin color has historically been an equally salient characteristic for many people. If one accepts the poignant nature of this issue, its exploration in psychotherapy or psychoanalysis is essential. Therapy across skin color lines (however nebulous they may be), depending on the personal experiences of the therapist and patient, may become a cross-cultural endeavor. As in all cross-cultural treatment, there is potential growth and understanding for both patient and therapist.

REFERENCES

Allen, B. (1982). It ain't easy being pinky. *Essence*, July, p. 68.

Aron, L. (1991). The patient's experience of the analyst's subjectivity. *Psychoanalytic Dialogues* 1:29–51.

—— (1992). Interpretation as expression of the analyst's subjectivity. *Psychoanalytic Dialogues* 2(4):475–507.

Associated Press. (1990a). Atlanta trial focusing on color-bias charge. *The New York Times*, February 1, p. A, 20:4.

—— (1990b). Racial suit by a black against a black fails. *The New York Times*, July 16, p. A 18:2.

Bennett, L., Jr. (1982). *Before the Mayflower, A History of Black America*, 5th ed. Chicago: Johnson

Boyd-Franklin, N. (1991). Recurrent themes in treatment of African-American women in group therapy. *Women and Therapy* 11(2):25–40.

Calnek, M. (1970). Racial factors in the countertransference: the black therapist and the black client. *American Journal of Orthopsychiatry* 1:39–46.

Collins, P. (1987). The meaning of motherhood in black culture and black mother–daughter relationships. *Sage: A Scholarly Journal on Black Women*, 4:3–10.

Comas-Diaz, L., and Jacobsen, F. M. (1991). Ethnocultural transference and countertransference in the therapeutic dyad. *American Journal of Orthopsychiatry* 61:392–402.

Davis, F. J. (1991). *Who Is Black? One Nation's Definition.* University Park, PA: Pennsylvania State University Press.

Fanon, F. (1967). *Black Skin White Masks.* New York: Grove.

Fischer, N. (1971). An interracial analysis: transference and countertransference significance. *Journal of the American Psychoanalytic Association* 19:736–745.

Gatewood, W. (1990). *Aristocrats of Color.* Bloomington, IN: Indiana University Press.

Greenberg, J. (1991). Countertransference and reality. *Psychoanalytic Dialogues* 1:52–73.

Greene, B. (1985). Considerations in the treatment of black patients by white therapists. *Psychotherapy* 22(supp.):389–391.

—— (1990a). What has gone before: the legacy of racism and sexism in the lives of black mothers and daughters. *Women and Therapy* 9(1–2):207–230.

—— (1990b). Sturdy bridges: the role of African-American mothers in the socialization of African-American children. *Women and Therapy* 10(1–2):205–225.

Gwaltney, J. L. (1980). *Drylongso, A Self-Portrait of Black America.* New York: Vintage.

Hardie, A. (1990). Morehouse med school faces EEOC complaints. *Atlanta Constitution*, February 23, pp. B, 2:3.

Harrison-Ross, P., and Wyden, B. (1973). *The Black Child–A Parents' Guide.* New York: Peter H. Wyden.

Hoffman, I. (1983). The patient as interpreter of the analyst's experience. *Contemporary Psychoanalysis* 19(3):389–422.

Joseph, G., and Lewis, J. (1981). *Common Differences: Conflicts in Black and White Feminist Perspectives.* New York: Doubleday.

Lincoln, C. (1967). Color and group identity in the United States. *Daedalus* 96:527–541.

Morrison, T. (1992). *Playing in the Dark, Whiteness and the Literary Imagination.* New York: Vintage.

Myers, W. (1977). The significance of the colors black and white in the dreams of black and white patients. *Journal of the American Psychoanalytic Association* 16:163–181.

Myrdal, G. (1962). *An American Dilemma, The Negro Problem and Modern Democracy.* New York: Harper & Row.

Neal, A., and Wilson, M. (1989). The role of skin color and features in the black community: implications for black women in therapy. *Clinical Psychology Review* 9(3):323–333.

Okazawa-Rey, M., Robinson, T., and Ward, J. V. (1987). Black women and the politics of skin color and hair. *Women and Therapy* 6:89–102.

Russell, K., Wilson, M., and Hall, R. (1992). *The Color Complex, the Politics of Skin Color among African Americans.* New York: Anchor.

Thompson, C. (1995). Self-definition by opposition: a consequence of minority status. *Psychoanalytic Psychology* 12:533–546.

Thurman, W. (1929). *The Blacker the Berry . . . A Novel of Negro Life.* New York: Macmillan.

Williamson, J. (1980). *New People, Miscegenation and Mulattoes in the United States.* New York: Free Press.

Wolstein, B. (1983). The pluralism of perspectives on countertransference. *Contemporary Psychoanalysis* 19(3):506–521.

12

In Search of Repressed Memories in Bilingual Individuals

Rafael Art. Javier, Ph.D.

Memory reconstruction in the analysis of bilingual patients entails a unique set of complications that result from the patients' having more than one linguistic code to process and organize the events, perceptions, and experiences in their lives. The nature and extent of the retrievability of a memory is greatly affected by the quality of the individual's linguistic and psychic organization (Javier 1989). This has been observed empirically (Javier and Marcos 1989, Javier et al. 1993) and in psychoanalytic work with patients whose treatments were characterized by complex displays of linguistic switching as important traumatic memories were being dislodged from the control of the repressed, leading to a different organization of their psychic structures (Buxbaum 1949, Greenson 1950, Javier 1995).

In this chapter, I discuss issues pertaining to the different levels of memory organization possible and the nature of the process of repression in the context of a bilingual linguistic organization. It is my belief that the quality and nature of the psychoanalytic treatment may be compromised in substantial ways when the patient under consideration possesses two linguistic organizations in his or her experience. Only by incorporating analyses of these linguistic processes as part of the analytic equation can we obviate the danger of what Judith Welles (1993) has called "counterfeit analyses: maintaining the illusion of knowing." These situations are counterfeit because they leave essential aspects of the individual's psychic structure connected to his or her unique relation to languages out of the psychoanalytic situation. For these individuals, linguistic codification can become intertwined with intrapsychic phenomena and hence complicate the nature of the analytic data and their interpretation.

THE FALSE MEMORY CONTROVERSY

But there is a more basic issue that needs to be addressed before we can embark on a discussion of memory reconstruction in bilinguals. This issue is at the core of the false memory controversy. When we talk about memory reconstruction it is assumed that an event or experience has in fact occurred and, due to a mechanism of forgetting, is no longer a part of conscious memory. While there may be less question with regard to experiences that took place in late childhood and adulthood, there is more controversy with regard to young children. There are a number of studies that suggest a high level of suggestibility in children or a tendency to "confabulation" and "false recognition" (Cohen 1989, Loftus 1993, Schacter et al. 1995). Young children were found to have difficulties encoding and/or retrieving the source of acquired information, and also to have a greater tendency to forget sources of information faster than older children. Several reasons have been suggested as to why very young children cannot remember early experience. It is not because repression is in operation but rather because

1. they lack the neurological maturity to encode adequately their experiences;
2. they lack the linguistic ability to encode their experiences verbally;
3. they lack the schemas within which they can represent and organize event memories (Cohen 1989, Schachtel 1947);
4. they may have been using encoding strategies that do not help them to elaborate and enrich the memory representation with semantic association; and finally,
5. they may be encoding memories in ways that are inappropriate for the retrieval processes used at a later age, and thus it becomes a matter of inappropriate encoding strategies rather than memory loss (Cohen 1989, Winograd and Killinger 1983).

Loftus (1979) was even able to demonstrate how children's memories for details of an event could be easily modified by misleading information presented during the retention interval.

Research evidence supporting the view that childhood memory could be subject to distortion by external influences has been used to question the extent to which childhood memories of a traumatic event, such as sexual and physical abuse, could also be affected in the same manner. But, according to Riccio and colleagues (1994), only when the stimulus attributes, which provide specificity to a memory of an event, are forgotten, is it possible for a memory to become malleable. Forgetting of stimulus attributes, or specific defining characteristics of the experience under consideration, tends to increase with time and hence distortion and false memory then become more possible (Cohen 1989). Similarly, it appears that a child's temperament could impact on the malleability of memory. Inhibited children were found to be more susceptible to suggestion when asked about a past event than uninhibited children (Schacter et al. 1995).

In psychoanalytic thinking, when we refer to memory reconstruction, we are not suggesting the creation of a memory that never occurred, but the reconstruction of a memory that, while remaining inaccessible due to psychic factors, has influenced the nature of the individual's psychic experience. An essential aspect of psychoanalytic exploration is the search for what the experience is all about, where it took place, who was involved in the experience, and when it occurred. These are the kinds of experience attributes that make it possible to establish the memory of an experience with some degree of certainty (Wagenaar 1986). A repressed "false" memory is less likely to withstand the power of psychoanalytic scrutiny.

However, the emphasis of psychoanalytic scrutiny is on the examination of an individual's character structure, which has been influenced by infantile conflictual memories, and the examination of these memories without concern for the extent to which they resemble objectively proven reality. That is, we are concerned with psychic reality—a mental set created by persistent unconscious conflictual factors (Arlow 1985). It is not possible to prove with any degree of certainty the extent to which early memories of past events are accurate with regard to the "who," "when," and "where." According to Cohen (1989) and Wagenaar (1986), only "what" the experience was all about, what happened, seems to provide a categorical organization of the experience that is likely to be remembered more accurately.

We recognize that an experience can be distorted at various levels. Therefore, tremendous caution is maintained as to its objectivity unless it can withstand the full power of psychoanalytic inquiry.

BILINGUAL ORGANIZATION,
MEMORY DEVELOPMENT,
AND INTRAPSYCHIC PHENOMENA

Language develops and acquires its meaning in relation to important people in our lives and in the context of historical, political, socioeconomic, and ecological conditions that characterize the lives of those on whom we depend emotionally. Our relationship with the environment, the smell of the land, our mother's caresses, her responses to our calls for food or warmth, the harsh or sweet and embracing sounding voices of our grandparents, the taste of food and succulent juices of fruits, the smell and beauty of the beach, the hot and dry summer, the rhythmic sound of music—such experiences, and the different emotions associated with them—are normally represented and stored in what Bucci (1985) calls the *perceptual channels*. They become part of a comprehensive memory matrix against which other data are assessed and processed. It is in this context that we acquire a sense of ourselves and our connection to the world as our psychic structure is formed. These are the data that Winnicott (1965), Sullivan (1953), and Kohut (1977) found so crucial for the development of psychic formation and that become ingrained in the individual's self representation.

When verbal codification is used to mediate these experiences the linguistic channel becomes the mode of memory representation. Words learned in that context become a powerful symbolic means to organize these experiences. The texture of these experiences and memories, the quality of the introjects and identifications thus developed, may then become more closely connected to that specific language function ("the mother tongue") although some of the experience may have been organized at the nonverbal level.

Although psychoanalysis relies heavily on the vicissitudes of verbal expression, it is clear that only when the analysis is successful in allowing the quality of experience that has been organized at the perceptual channel to emerge, can the experience be more fully expressed and hence become part of the interpretative matrix. Depending on the extent to which linguistic approximation is found for information organized along the perceptual channel, memories associated with these perceptually coded experiences could be, in part, verbally retrieved. I say in part because the extent of approximation depends on the quality of what Bucci (1985) called *referential activity*, which varies between individuals "as a matter of competence, and may vary within an individual over time as a function of external context or inner state" (p. 589).

In the bilingual case, I suggest that the individual's relationship to his or her languages may also determine the mode and extent to which these memories may be accessed linguistically. It has been found that bilinguals do develop different linguistic organizations depending on the level of linguistic proficiency and on the way the languages were learned (Ervin and Osgood 1954). It has been suggested that when the individual learns and becomes proficient in a second language later in life, the two languages remain separately organized in the brain, each with its own phonemic, syntactic, symbolic, ideational components and memory structure. A coordinate linguistic organization is thus said to have taken place. A compound bilingual organization is said to have taken place when the languages are learned at the same time, spoken by the same people, and used to refer to the same experiences (Ervin and Osgood 1954, Javier and Marcos 1989). In such cases both languages are assumed to be organized along a common unitary linguistic structure.

A coordinate linguistic organization, by definition, implies that the two languages remain relatively independent of one another—hence the term *language independence phenomenon* (Javier and Marcos 1989, Marcos and Alpert 1976), while compound linguistic organization allows for more interplay between or among the languages. That this is the case was amply demonstrated by the psycholinguistic work of Lambert (1972), Ervin (1963), Marcos and Alpert (1976), Ojemann and Whitaker (1978), Albert and Obler (1978), and by my own work (Javier 1983, Javier and Marcos 1989). Findings from these investigations suggest that even in the case of a compound bilingual organization, most individuals develop a coordinate bilingual organization for some of their experiences and a compound organization for others. Part of the reason for that has to do with the specific semantic, phonemic, and grammatical structures of the languages involved, which make one-to-one relationship between or among the languages impossible. Some languages, for instance, may even lack certain concepts altogether or have specific concepts much more developed than others, as in the well-known case of the Eskimos whose concepts for snow surpass those of other languages in their specificity. According to Kolers (1968), however, it is more likely for concepts related to affective state (love, hate, frustration) and abstract formulations (such as freedom, country) to remain language-specific than concepts related to concrete experiences. This may explain

why some bilinguals may find it easy to curse in one language and difficult to do so in another, or why they may find that their associations to
dream material could be easier and more fluid in one language, but not
necessarily the language of the dream. In a recent presentation by Schlachet
and Aragno (1994) a patient was unable to associate to the "bear" of his
dream; his associative process became liberated when translation into the
Spanish "oso" was made, which was associated with conflictual memories of an abusive father.

From this perspective, we can see how the accessibility of memory
developed in relation to one of the languages depends on the nature and
quality of the patient's linguistic organization in addition to the individual's psychic state. The problem, however, is how are we to have access
to the kinds of earlier experiences that are organized around nonverbal
representations and thus become lodged in a perceptual mode of memory
organization? Are we to assume, in keeping with previous comments, that
the language that developed closer in proximity to the experience will
be the language of preference for accessing memories associated with
these experiences? The question then becomes how to understand the
amply demonstrated role of intrapsychic structure in language development (see Buxbaum 1949, Foster 1992, Greenson 1950, Javier 1989,
1995, Krapf 1955, Marcos 1976). We must consider the interplay of intrapsychic structure and language representation and how language could
become subservient to psychic demands (see Figure 12–1). Moreover, we
also need to consider the possibility that an experience that is not accessible in one language may be accessible in another and hence the concept of repression proper may not apply (Javier 1995).

I suspect that all our experiences are organized along sensory-percep-
tual and linguistic channels to various degrees (a dual linguistic channel
in the case of the bilingual) and that unconscious forces become increasingly more influential in these experiences' ultimate organization along
these channels, as suggested in Figure 12–1. That the intrapsychic structure could affect the perceptual channel processing has been demonstrated by patients whose ability to perceive and feel is distorted due to
anxiety. In extreme cases, it can be seen in patients suffering from hysterical blindness, pseudocyesis, paralysis, sexual dysfunction, and dyspnea
(Freud 1896). Examples of the extent to which language function can be
affected by intrapsychic conflict can be seen in patients suffering from
speech disturbances due to anxiety and unconscious conflicts, as has been
described by Greenson (1950) and Buxbaum (1949). The extent to which

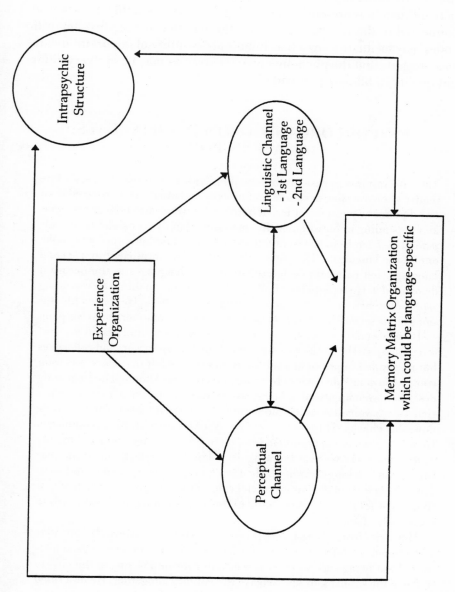

Figure 12–1. Personal Experience Organizational Matrix

the different channels for organizing an experience shown in Figure 12–1 may ultimately represent different degrees of accessibility of memories connected to these experiences, and the fact that having two linguistic codes may facilitate as much as hinder accessibility of important memories, suggests that the phenomenon of repression may have a very different quality in bilingual individuals.

PSYCHIC ORGANIZATION IN BILINGUALS: A CASE IN POINT

Take, for instance, a case of a bilingual individual who spent his early formative years traveling to various countries as his father was transferred from one diplomatic post to another. At home there were various languages spoken depending upon whether the immediate family was alone or accompanied by friends and acquaintances or family members who only spoke one of the languages. The patient, having become proficient in a second language, felt comfortable interchanging his languages as the occasion demanded it. He reported not finding much pleasure in things he was doing especially when he felt that he was obliged to do them. He started his sessions in his second language, speaking in a precise manner about his pain.

He was a talented young man in the arts and sports and also in his chosen profession. He was frequently admired by his supervisors and colleagues but responded to praise in a mixed manner as he felt that more was soon going to be demanded of him by those praising him. Although he frequently described what appeared to be intense feelings in reference to these experiences, his voice remained monotonic, even when tears started to come down his cheeks. There was a quality of detachment in his presentation. He had a sense of depression in him, often finding himself sad and moody as if about to cry without knowing why. This was, in fact, one of the reasons for his seeking treatment. He came to his sessions on time and dutifully lay on the couch, but it was clear that he did not feel comfortable. At times he would even become mute in the analysis, unable to find words to describe his feelings.

Memories from his past were presented factually and devoid of any personal texture, after which he would start to sob. He often verbalized feelings of not being sure whether it was better for him to stay in the city, to move to the suburbs, or just to leave the country altogether. He described himself as terribly afraid of airplanes and of the dark and as walking around with a general feeling of catastrophe.

What really transpired in this patient's past so as to give him this sense of fragmentation and general feeling that he was not quite where he is supposed to be? To answer that question we need to undertake a careful reconstruction of his past by a systematic analysis of his personal history and early memories.

Indeed, memory reconstruction and its related phenomenon, repression, constitute the cornerstone of psychoanalytic conceptualization and practice (Freud 1914). In Freudian conceptualization, ordinary perceptions, thoughts, motivations, fantasies, wishes, dreams, and memories of events, as well as the individual's relationship with him- or herself and others are influenced by the vicissitudes of unconscious fantasies and conflictual demands made by id-ego-superego processes on the mental life of the individual (Brenner 1979, Bucci 1985, Freud, 1940). As stated before, this is what has been referred to as psychic reality, or the mental set created by persistent unconscious fantasies (Arlow 1985, Freud 1896, 1905, 1940).

It is against this mental set that "the data of perception are perceived, registered, interpreted, remembered, and responded to" (Arlow 1985, p. 526). In this context, neurotic processes, and for that matter transference manifestation, can be said to represent how the "individual misperceives, misinterprets, and misreponds to the data of perception in terms of the mental set created by persistent unconscious fantasies" (p. 526). Indeed, neurotic process and transference manifestations represent the work of repressed memories which find expression through these means.

Freud (1940) recognized that, because of the quality and nature of mental representation, and the possibility for distortion due to the work of the unconscious, it is difficult and even impossible to accurately and objectively ascertain with any degree of certainty a mental representation's real components. Thus, his reliance on inferences and interpolations constituted the basic elements of his psychoanalytic method as the technique that provides the best opportunity to reach repressed memories of events.

In the case of our patient, it was clear by the nature of his complaints and the symptomatic transformations (phobias) reported, as well as his linguistic history, that a sense of the nature of his psychic reality could be reconstructed in the context of his multilinguistic reality. It was also clear that although the patient only remembered having experienced these types of symptoms for the last few years, the quality of the symptoms could not be explained unless they were seen in the context of his much earlier experiences.

> He was able to speak about a number of apparently important experiences he had while living in other countries: his piano and art lessons, the friends he made along the way, his language teacher, the many hours he spent alone in his room, the time his father never made it to his recital and his relief when he finally saw his mother in the audience. The patient was surprised that he would feel irritable after expressing these types of experiences and his behavior following these sessions would be characterized by silence and a reluctance to get into anything "heavy." He would then apologize.
>
> The patient was unable to bring any understanding to bear regarding his feeling of irritability, other than saying that these were very personal moments that he had not discussed with anybody. Nevertheless, he was very respectful with me and very eager to please me by trying to give whatever association he thought I wanted from him. And even after these types of sessions, he would frequently verbalize his satisfaction with the work of the analysis.

Were we in the midst of a resistance, or was the patient attempting to communicate another important aspect of his experience in which compliance was the safest way of being? His satisfaction in this context was a way of expressing that it was a familiar position, although the nature of this was not totally within his awareness.

Jones's (1993) excellent discussion on the evolution of the concept of repression can be instrumental in helping us understand the different levels of repression (or inaccessibility of experience) in our patient. She examines the evolution of the concept of repression from its description of the more normal process to its elaboration of repression proper, or "complete and persistent inaccessibility of representations, resulting from their association with anxiety and other painful affect" (Bucci 1985, p. 590). In this context, Jones eloquently discusses various kinds of possible repression, each with its own implications for psychoanalytic conceptualization. Of those discussed, four seem to be most relevant for our discussion: Preverbal Infantile Repression, Postverbal Infantile Repression, State Dependent Repression, and Repression Proper, which could occur as part of an Automatized Suppression mechanism or as part of a Conditioned Repression mechanism.

The term *preverbal infantile repression* refers to those experiences, feelings, and wishes that were encoded in a nonverbal form (or perceptual-sensory channel) and are thus not accessible to verbal, that is, conscious, recall. According to Jones (1993), "the nonverbal memory whose reemergence is stimulated by the evolution of the transference finds its way to verbal representation in a highly disguised form, similar to dream representation. The complex feelings surrounding the traumatic event are then able to be worked through verbally in the analysis" (p. 86).

Postverbal infantile repression, on the other hand, refers to a condition in which "certain experiences, affects, or drive derivatives are nevertheless experienced and encoded in nonverbal form" (Jones 1993, p. 86), although development of language has already taken place.

State Dependent Repression is said to be in place when "an experience, feeling, or wish occurring in the past may be inaccessible to consciousness because the individual was in an altered state of consciousness at the time of its occurrence" (p. 87). With regard to the bilingual process, a kind of altered state of consciousness develops when a patient processes aspects of a traumatic experience in a specific linguistic mode (one of the languages), with the experience remaining inaccessible to consciousness until the patient returns to that linguistic state of mind.

Unlike in the previously described repressions, the crucial element of repression proper is a condition in which feelings, wishes, and fantasies that had been at one point unquestionably in conscious awareness and accessible to verbal representation are now inaccessible "due to the mobilization of guilt, shame, or disgust" (Jones 1993, p. 88).

Jones's discussion of different kinds of repressive experience allows us to put into perspective the nature of our patient's experience. For instance, the fact that he registered irritability and then was unable to free his associative process suggests that we may have been dealing with repressed memories of a preverbal infantile nature—a state-dependent condition, or at the very least with an experience that has remained organized at the perceptual channel associated with postverbal infantile repression. If that is the case, how are we to help the patient gain access to the information? We suspect that the success of the analysis of this patient would depend not so much on the language utilized (he is proficient in all his languages) but on the extent to which the patient is able to return to the state of psychic representation associated with the conflictual experience under discussion. Let us examine the patient's very strong response to my (manifestly) inadvertent introduction of his primary language into a session. This occurred at a beginning of a session following a number of sessions in which the patient appeared rather detached while talking about his father.

> During these sessions the patient described his father as removed and uninvolved with the family affairs, but he also remembered feeling close to him while he was small. Details of these experiences, however, were vague and sketchy. His description of his mother, on the other hand, was much more vivid and present: he recalled her driving him to school, her involvement in his piano and art lessons, the food she prepared, her responses to his illnesses, and so on. The feeling of irritability would emerge after these sessions.
>
> After my unplanned introduction of his primary language—I asked the patient to come in in his primary language—a much more complex sense of his father emerged. Although he remembered his father as someone who in social meetings was always entertaining and, when at home, retreated to his study room alone to unwind, he still harbored a great deal of admiration for him. He felt that he resembled his father in many of the things he did. He described himself as a thinker like his father and it was clear that he had been favored over his sister. He remembered with great longing a time at the beach, playing ball there when he was 5 years old. His father had taken two weeks off before being transferred to another country and the family went away together to the beach. Although the patient had been at the beach several times with his mother, he remembered this time the most vividly: the salty and warm water, the white sand, the kiosk by the water where he ran with his father to buy a vanilla ice cream. This was a vivid description of a time when his relationship with his father was the most rewarding, and after this recollection the patient felt a sense of warmth toward his father.
>
> Following these verbalizations, the patient again reported feeling in a bad mood at work and at home. He felt both angry at his father and depressed, because these types of experiences were few and far between, and because he remembered always waiting for his father to come home from work and finally falling asleep without seeing him. After only a few sessions of speaking in the primary language, the patient decided to return to the second language, abruptly stating that he did not feel comfortable speaking in the first language, "that it was not appropriate." I suspected that the patient was getting in touch with his rage toward his father and desperately needed to gain some distance, which the second language provided, in order to preserve his image of him.

This patient became petrified and overwhelmed with emotion when he heard his first language being spoken by the analyst. Until this point the patient had been able to talk in detail about a number of important memories, but there was a sense that something was missing from the memories, especially with regard to his father. His descriptions were stale, as if missing texture and warmth. After allowing memories from the first language to emerge, his verbalization in the second language also became characterized with a kind of richness and texture not felt until then. This phenomenon has been experimentally demonstrated in a psycholinguistic study (Javier et al. 1993). For this patient, as with previous ones, we could see the interplay of language and psychic state and hence the importance of submitting both to the same kind of analytic inquiry.

The extent to which the patient was able to speak of his conflictual experience with his father without being fully aware of the range of his affective responses suggests that repression in the form of isolation of affects had taken place. But the extent to which the shifting of the language allowed for a fuller expression of the experience suggests that a "State Dependent Repression" had taken place. However, the fact that the patient seemed to lack the linguistic symbolism to relate his early experience with his father in a vivid manner in his second language, but was able to do so in the first language, suggests that a combination of State Dependent Repression and Preverbal Infantile Repression, or perhaps a Postverbal Infantile Repression, may have been in operation. Inaccessibility of an experience does not in itself reflect the work of repression proper since such an inaccessibility could be linguistically based, although for some material repression proper may also be involved.

It could be said then that for a bilingual individual such as our patient, in the case of some experiences, the richness of the memories may emerge more clearly when the language closer to the original experience is in operation. With other experiences, it may be possible for the assumed repressed memories to find ways of expression in the context of the analysis even in the language originally most distant from the experience. In a case of a bilingual who is deficient in a second language, however, this may be much more complicated, as repression of the experience may be further exacerbated in the second language (Marcos and Alpert 1976) because the individual may not possess the adequate linguistic symbols to communicate the experience.

TECHNICAL CONSIDERATIONS

In view of the complexity of the linguistic and psychic process, it would be difficult to provide specific technical recommendations for the treatment of bilingual patients. I have tried to advance the proposition that the treatment of individuals who have more than one language to organize and communicate their experiences cannot be understood outside the context of each individual's personal psychology, or the nature of his or her unique psychic reality. What is important is to reach with the patient a state that Wolff (1988) has termed *transforming dialogue*. Such a process is elaborated by Freedman (1983) who suggests that all listening involves a sequence of rhythmic alternation of two phases: receiving and restructuring. During the phase of receiving there is "an openness to the intent of the other . . . a tolerance for multiple alternatives . . . an emphasis on subjectivity, that is, a suspension of the need to objectify or symbolize" (p. 409). During the phase of restructuring, on the other hand, there is "a narrowing of attention, a reduction of the possibilities aiming toward consolidation and synthesis, and emphasis on objectification and symbolic representation" (p. 409). For a proper receiving phase to occur, the analyst should be able to form clear mental images (not concepts) from the patient's verbalization, including the affective components of the experience(s) verbalized by the patient. The restructuring process should only begin when the image is securely fixed and vividly in place in the analyst's mind.

To the extent that the analyst succeeds in establishing this kind of dialogue with a bilingual patient, and the patient's linguistic behavior is seen in the context of the linguistic characteristics and nature of this patient's psychic condition, the treatment is likely to progress and the danger of a counterfeit analysis will be avoided. Additionally, Foster's (Chapter 13) approach to the assessment of the patient's personal experience in the context of his or her linguistic history provides a more concrete, powerful tool for reaching important memories in the patient's personal history.

CONCLUSION

Memory reconstruction and its related phenomenon, repression, constitute the cornerstone of psychoanalytic conceptualization and practice (Freud 1914). Indeed, it is the role of analytic treatment to help the patient reclaim past memories and thus establish a different and more co-hesive and integrated view or personal narrative that incorporates the past with the present (Arlow 1985, Freeman 1985, Wallerstein 1985). This process involves the working through of repressed painful memories, which could result in a different reorganization of the psychic structure under more conscious control. Thus, the analysis of superego functions and the vicissitudes of the id and its derivatives, the analysis of transfer-ence and countertransference, and dream interpretations all serve im-portant roles in the search of the repressed. In the particular case of the bilingual patient, an analytic treatment that does not also include the role of language in the quality of the psychic structure can only lead to a coun-terfeit analysis.

REFERENCES

Albert, M., and Obler, L. (1978). *The Bilingual Brain: Neuropsychology and Linguistic Aspects of Bilingualism.* New York: Academic Press.

Arlow, J. A. (1985). The concept of psychic reality and related problems. *Journal of the American Psychoanalytic Association,* 33:521–535.

Brenner, C. (1979). The components of psychic conflict and its consequences in mental life. *Psychoanalytic Quarterly* 48:547–567.

Bucci, W. (1985). Dual coding: a cognitive model for psychoanalytic research. *Journal of the American Psychoanalytic Association* 33:571–608.

Buxbaum, E. (1949). The role of the second language in the formation of ego and super-ego. *International Journal of Psychiatry* 18:279–289.

Cohen, G. (1989). *Memory in the Real World.* Hillsdale, NJ: Lawrence Erlbaum.

Ervin, S. (1963). Language and TAT content in bilinguals. *Journal of Abnormal and Social Psychology* 68:500–507.

Ervin, S., and Osgood, C. E. (1954). Second language learning and bilingualism. *Journal of Abnormal and Social Psychology* (Supplement) 49:139–146.

Foster, R. M. (1992). Psychoanalysis and the bilingual patient: some observations on the influence of language choice on the transference. *Psychoanalytic Psychology* 9:61–76.

Freedman, N. (1983). On psychoanalytic listening: the construction, paralysis, and recon-struction of meaning. *Psychoanalysis and Contemporary Thought* 6:405–434.

Freeman, M. (1985). Psychoanalytic narration and the problem of historical knowledge. *Psychoanalysis and Contemporary Thought* 8:133–182.

Freud, S. (1896). The aetiology of hysteria. *Standard Edition* 3:189–221.

—— (1905). Fragment of an analysis and a case of hysteria. *Standard Edition* 7:3–122.

—— (1914). On narcissism: an introduction. *Standard Edition* 14:69–102.

—— (1940). An outline of psycho-analysis. *Standard Edition* 23:141–207.

Greenson, R. (1950). The mother tongue and the mother. *International Journal of Psy-chiatry* 31:18–23.

Javier, R. A. (1983). The effect of stress in the language independence phenomenon in coordinate bilinguals. *Dissertation Abstracts International* 43:238b.

—— (1989). Linguistic considerations in the treatment of bilinguals. *Journal of Psychoanalytic Psychology* 6(1):87–96.

—— (1995). Vicissitudes of autobiographical memories in bilingual analysis. *Psychoanalytic Psychology* 12:429–438.

Javier, R. A., Barroso, F., and Munoz, M. A. (1993). Autobiographical memory in bilinguals. *Journal of Psycholinguistic Research* 22(3):319–338.

Javier, R. A., and Marcos, L. (1989). The role of stress on the language-independence and code-switching phenomena. *Journal of Psycholinguistic Research* 18(5):449–472.

Jones, B. P. (1993). Repression: the evolution of a psychoanalytic conception from the 1890s to the 1990s. *Journal of the American Psychoanalytic Association* 41(1):63–93.

Kohut, H. (1977). *The Restoration of the Self.* New York: International Universities Press.

Kolers, P. A. (1968). Bilingualism and information processing. *Scientific American,* March, 79–86.

Krapf, E. E. (1955). The choice of language in polyglot psychoanalysis. *Psychoanalytic Quarterly* 24:343–357.

Lambert, W. (1972). *Language, Psychology, and Culture.* Stanford, CA: Stanford University Press.

Loftus, E. F. (1979). *Eyewitness Testimony.* Cambridge, MA: Harvard University Press.

—— (1993). The reality of repressed memories. *American Psychologist* 48:518–537.

Marcos, L. R. (1976). Bilinguals in psychotherapy: language as an emotional barrier. *American Journal of Psychotherapy* 30:552–560.

Marcos, L., and Alpert, M. (1976). Strategies and risks in psychotherapy with bilingual patients: the phenomenon of language independence. *American Journal of Psychiatry* 133:1275–1278.

Ojemann, G. A., and Whitaker, H. A. (1978). The bilingual brain. *Archives of Neurology* 35:409–412.

Riccio, D. C., Rabinowitz, V. C., and Axelrod, S. (1994). Memory: when less is more. *American Psychologist* 49(11):917–926.

Schachtel, E. G. (1947). On memory and childhood amnesia. *Psychiatry* 10:1–26.

Schacter, D. L. , Kagan, J., and Leichtman, M. D. (1995). True and false memories in children and adults: a cognitive neuroscience perspective. *Psychology, Public Policy, and Law* 1(2):411–428.

Schlachet, P. J., and Aragno, A. (1994). *The accessibility of early experience through the language of origin: a theoretical integration.* Paper presented at the Seventh Biennial Conference, the Psychoanalytic Society of the Postdoctoral Program, New York University, March.

Sullivan, H. S. (1953). *The Interpersonal Theory of Psychiatry.* New York: Norton.

Wagenaar, W. (1986). My memory: a study of autobiographical memory over six years. *Cognitive Psychology* 18:225–252.

Wallerstein, R. S. (1985). The concept of psychic reality: its meaning and value. *Journal of the American Psychoanalytic Association* 33:555–569.

Welles, J. K. (1993). *Counterfeit analyses: maintaining the illusion of knowing.* Presented at the APA division (39) Spring meeting, New York.

Winograd, E., and Killinger, W. A. (1983). Relating age at encoding in early childhood to adult recall: development of flashbulb memories. *Journal of Experimental Psychology: General* 112:413–422.

Winnicott, D. W. (1965). *The Maturational Processes and the Facilitating Environment.* New York: International Universities Press.

Wolff, P. H. (1988). The real and reconstructed past. *Psychoanalysis and Contemporary Thought* 11(3):379–414.

13

Assessing the Psychodynamic Function of Language in the Bilingual Patient

RoseMarie Pérez Foster, Ph.D.

Therapists in the United States, who for the most part conduct their work in English, are likely in the course of their careers to treat a patient who, while fluent in English, is not a native speaker. This includes those patients who learned their English later in life in the United States, or as children and adolescents in their own countries. While our assumption tends to be that inner psychic life, historical experiences of the past, and active expressions within the therapeutic relationship can be simply and directly expressed in the second language of a proficient speaker, there is fascinating evidence that bilingual speakers may in fact use their dual (or multiple) language systems in the service of psychodynamic and defensive operations. The literature suggests that the different languages of the multilingual speaker are powerful organizers of cognitive and affective experience: they can be used to express, repress, isolate, and dissociate affect-laden content (Amahti-Mehler et al. 1993, Buxbaum 1949, Greenson 1950, Javier and Marcos 1989, Krapf 1955), as well as to organize inner representations of early self–other interactions (Foster 1992, 1996a,b, Marcos 1976). Within the dynamics of the treatment situation, the bilingual's language choice can become an integral part of the resistance (Buxbaum 1949, Greenson 1950), as well as a powerful venue through which transference phenomena are evoked (Foster 1992, 1996a, Krapf 1955).

Bilinguals are people who possess two language codes with which they can think about themselves, express ideas, and interact with the people in their lives. In the tradition of the early linguist, Whorf (1940), one might say that bilinguals possess dual symbolic templates through which they shape and organize their world, as well as dual sets of verbal symbols through which they codify their experiences and give voice to their expression. In the clinical situation this duality also impacts on how bilingual patients go about narrating their life story in the treatment process. While bilinguals function with varying levels of proficiency in the English-speaking workaday world, or the English-speaking treatment situation, they may in fact dream, express surprise, curse their neighbor, make love, or soothe a child all in their native tongue. These particular activities tap at the quick of inner impulse life and primal relational experience; however, their soulful meaning is often lost in the translated utterances of a second language that are far removed from the sensuality of the original lived experience. Indeed, the native tongue has been described in the analytic literature as the repository of early infantile striving, and the language system that holds the fullest complement of sensorial, affective, and cognitive elements related to early experience (Amahti-Mehler et al. 1993, Buxbaum 1949, Greenson 1950, Loewald 1980).

The purpose of this chapter is twofold: (1) to describe the current thinking on the psychodynamic operations of language in the multilingual speaker, underscoring for the clinician the role that language may play in manifest symptoms, defensive operations, self-experience, and the clinical process (that is, transference and resistance) and (2) to offer an organized system of inquiry for the monolingual clinician to assess these phenomena in their bilingual patients. The Psycholinguistic History is a format of inquiry that I have organized especially for the clinician who has no knowledge of the patient's native language (see Table 13-1, p. 255). It offers an entré into the multilingual speaker's psyche, evaluating how language may have been used to organize early developmental experience, as well as whether language plays a role in current psychic functioning.

PSYCHODYNAMIC OPERATIONS
IN BILINGUALISM

Though very much unacknowledged, the issue of bilingualism in psychoanalysis is as old as the field itself. German was a second language for many of Freud's early patients. They included the Wolf Man, Lucy R., and many of the Americans who went to Vienna for analysis with Freud (Flegenheimer 1989, E. Menaker, personal communication 1990). It was not until 1949 and 1950, however, that the first works appeared on the inherent problems of treating a patient in his or her second language. Edith Buxbaum (1949), Ralph Greenson (1950), and Eduardo Krapf (1955) are credited with the seminal observations in this area. They proposed that the mother tongue is the unconscious repository of early infantile wishes. Their reports commonly noted that treatment in a patient's second language—a code learned at a later psychosexual period—would render certain areas of intrapsychic experience consciously unavailable to the clinical work. Working from a classical drive/conflict model, they basically argued that treatment in a non-native tongue avoids the early language of key fantasies and memories. A second language offers the patient a ready defense system for warding off old psychic structures, helping to repress feelings associated with early life. Greenson (1950) described the analytic treatment of a bilingual German/English woman. At one point in the process the patient, on finding that the analyst was also bilingual, refused to speak in German, claiming, "I have a feeling that talking in German I shall have to remember something I want to forget" (p. 19). This patient also described herself differently in the two languages: "In German I am a scared dirty child—in English I am a nervous, refined woman" (p. 19).

According to this viewpoint, then, childhood memories become uniquely alive in the treatment when the actual lingual expressions of that period are used. This is very similar to the early observations made by Ferenczi about the use of childhood "obscene words" in treatment. He noted that words in their unique infantile form carry the most affective and potentially regressive power (Ferenczi 1911). The native language is seen as a vehicle for reviving the past, presumably releasing unconscious wishes into consciousness accompanied by their fuller affective complement.

The early observations on bilingualism carried important implications for both the technical and theoretical applications of the psychodynamic approach to the bilingual mind. They illustrated that multilinguals can use language in the service of psychic repression. They also showed that language can play a key operational role in both the release of unconscious material as well as in the concordant resistance to that material. They further suggested that different language codes could be associated with difference experiences of self (Greenson 1950).

Krapf, the multilingual analyst working and reporting from Argentina in 1955, noted that his multilingual patients often chose the language in which they could speak about charged topics with the least amount of anxiety. Later reports by other authors elaborated on how the words of a language learned in a later developmental period, while potentially quite efficient at semantic description, are devoid of the sensorial, affective, and semiotic accompaniments these same words have in the native tongue. Marcos (1976), Marcos et al. (1973) and Rozensky and Gomez (1983) have all described how the second language is frequently used to intellectualize emotional material, isolate affect, and split off anxiety-ridden components of internal fantasy. As clinicians in the United States who are working with diverse patient populations and often treating non-native English speakers, we must likewise consider how the bilingual patient's use of English in the treatment might serve as an inadvertent avoidance of deeper feelings and early experiences.

In the 1960s and 1970s, Luis Marcos, a Spanish psychoanalyst trained in the United States, published a series of papers on his work with Spanish/English patients. In addition to supporting the work of the early writers, Marcos and his co-authors integrated their clinical observations of bilingual functioning with findings about language-related phenomena from other disciplines. They noted research from clinical neurology, which indicated that the bilingual's languages are cortically represented in clearly distinct (and some overlapping) parts of the brain (Albert and Obler 1978, Ojemann and Whitaker 1978, Paradis 1977). This was found to be particularly true of those who learned second languages at a later developmental period. Marcos and colleagues also borrowed from information processing research, which shows that for the bilingual the same word in each language has the same central denotive meaning, but will generate separate chains of associations, idiosyncratic meanings, and specialized affects (Diller 1974, Ervin and Osgood 1954, Kolers 1963). In addition, Marcos referenced work from clinical psychology, which indicates that on projective testing bilinguals can manifest different character traits (Findling 1969), recall different sets of past experiences, and display different types of ideational and emotional material (Ervin 1964), all according to which language they are being tested in.

Marcos concluded that there must exist some kind of language independence phenomenon—and that this was true especially for those proficient bilinguals who learned their two languages in different acquisitional contexts. Each language system would seem to have the ability to code, organize, and store experience. But the fascinating relationship between the two language systems, their relative insulation versus interaction, is the interface that psychodynamic clinicians need to study. For, as has been so interestingly pointed out by every writer in this area, the possession of a dual linguistic system seems to be used in the service of psychodynamic operations.

Recently, Javier and colleagues (1993) reported on how a bilingual's languages impact on the recollection of experience. They found that memories recalled in the actual language of an experience, whether that language is the mother tongue or not, are reconstructed with much more detail, vividness, and affective attunement than when they are recalled in another language. In light of Javier's description of this process (Chapter 12), however, we make note of important questions such as how deeply early childhood trauma can be worked through in a second language. Javier (1989) also proposed that the option of a language choice for the bilingual can function as a coping mechanism under psychic distress. He described a Spanish/English patient who suffered physical trauma during childhood and refused to speak Spanish (his first language) in session during a period of possible psychotic decompensation. The author argued that English, the patient's second language, served an adaptive coping function, fending off both the affective components of early trauma and further psychotic disorganization.

Those of us in the New York area who conduct and report on bilingual psychoanalysis where two languages are used as an integral part of the protracted therapeutic work corroborate Javier's findings (see Foster 1993, Jaffe 1993, Stern 1993, Sternberg 1993). We are all aware of the defensive coping function served by the second language in forestalling varying degrees of anxiety and ego disorganization.

My own work and thinking about bilingual phenomena has been influenced by developments in contemporary psycholinguistics and object relations theory. The psycholinguistic body of work has provided psychoanalysis with needed structure on the process of how language is acquired and what role it plays in the symbolization of external experience and internal self states. The current work of Bloom (1973), Bruner (1977, 1981, 1983), Dore (1975), and the revival of Vygotsky's thinking from the early 1900s (1962, 1978, 1981, 1988), consistently show that the child's ever-evolving experience with interpersonal events is an essential key to understanding how language is acquired. These authors maintain that language develops in the matrix of caretaker and child being with each other. The meanings ascribed to words, the link between language code and a real event in the world, are things that adult and child produce in the context of their mutual and shared experiences.

In the course of my bilingual psychoanalytic work conducted in Spanish/English, I have previously reported how a patient's language switching in the treatment is often accompanied by a concurrent shift in the transference–countertransference paradigm (Foster 1992, 1996a). As the patients shift the lingual aspect of their narrative over a sustained period of time, so do they seem to shift the specific aspect of the self that is speaking and the object (vis-à-vis the analyst) that is being spoken to. My signal that this has taken place is not only the music, mood, and meaning of the new language, but often my own transformation upon entering the patient's new language space. In a seemingly linguistic instant both the interpersonal and the intersubjective communication shift to different speaking terms, as if the language has sculpted both patient and therapist into different objects. Integrating these observations with thinking in contemporary psycholinguistics (that language learning is a social function that occurs within the relational context of the child and other), I came to believe that condensed within each language are both the verbal symbols and the representation of the primary "other" who offered those symbols. Alive within each symbol is its semantic meaning and the interiorized versions of the self and that other who shared common experiences and gave them a name. I have proposed that early object relations, and the specific language they are coded in, are critically yoked or intertwined, and as such interiorized within the complex matrix of self presentations. Each language gives voice to the relationship with important others (and their cultural world) who offered particular verbal symbols for the shaping of both external experience and the internal experience of self (Foster 1996a,b).

For multilingual individuals, potential linguistic divisions in self representation (based on language-specific self–other interactions) are a vital organizational dynamic to identify. In addition, as noted by earlier authors, differences in ways of being and experiencing can also provide the mechanism for defensively isolating or dissociating deep levels of psychic conflict—a process that must be kept in mind by anyone working with a multilingual patient.

CASE ILLUSTRATION

The following is case material of a bilingual Spanish/English-speaking patient with whom I conducted a bilingual analysis for five years. This patient's treatment was marked by alternating changes in differential language usage. I am aware that bilingual analyses are not particularly common procedures and that, in the main, clinicians will be confronted with treating patients in English whose native language they do not know. However, this case is presented for the purpose of demonstrating the psychodynamic operations of language in the bilingual speaker. I will track language-related shifts in affective experience, memory reconstruction, associational flow, and self–object reenactment through the transference. I will then address how monolingual clinicians can assess these language-related phenomena in their bilingual patients.

A 40-year-old Cuban woman,[1] mother of two, sought consultation with me for depression and outbursts of verbal rage toward her children. Yulie has been married for fifteen years to an extremely successful, also Cuban, corporate lawyer who is in practice with two partners. Yulie and her husband are urban, socially ambitious, and active in local politics. She is extremely proud of her position on the community board of her district, a post for which she actively campaigned. Yulie is her husband's office manager. She handles all billings and support staff, has designed a new suite of offices for the practice, and recently transferred all office business onto a computer software system, which she taught herself to operate. She has a high school equivalency diploma.

Yulie migrated to this country at the time of the Castro revolution at age 6. In Cuba, her father had been an engineer and her mother a school teacher. Both parents bitterly opposed the communist occupation in their country, vowing never to return until Castro was overthrown. Yulie describes her parents during the early years in the United States as consumed with politics and the bitter downgrade in their socioeconomic status. Indeed, Yulie's father, portrayed as an opinionated and fearless man, took part in the abortive Bay of Pigs invasion (1961) in which he died. Yulie speaks of her father in heroic terms: "Papi left us, but he died for Cuba."

At our first meeting, the patient is gracious and poised despite her nervousness. She is groomed in a distinctly American, tailored style, but her social manner is rather courtly in an old-fashioned Caribbean sort of way, which is familiar to me. She calls me "doctora," mentions that I have been well-recommended, asks permission to be seated, and states that we Latins should get along well. Our conversation to this point has all been in Spanish, including the initial phone contact. I deliberately followed Yulie's language lead, as is my custom with bilingual patients. Thus in Spanish, she

---

[1] The case was previously reported by the author in *Psychoanalytic Dialogues* (1996) 6(1): 99–121. Copyright © 1996 *Psychoanalytic Dialogues*. Used by permission.

willingly shares the unhappiness of her present marriage. Her husband is domineering, demeaning, and never fails in an argument to remind her of her inferior education. In her frustration, she has been exploding at the children and seeks therapy to "control my temper."

Yulie struggles to compose herself. Now about twenty minutes into this first session, the patient asks if she can continue the session in English. She says, "It is just that in English I can express myself so much better. I know exactly what I want to say. English is my strong language because I went to school here." "It's okay," I say, then at a later point I ask her, "In what language do you live with your husband?" She says, "Oh, in Spanish only." I begin to wonder here what role Yulie's language may play in her sense of self and relational mode with others.

Yulie begins to see me twice weekly. She continues to speak only English. In the ensuing months she talks of the tumultuous and chaotic adolescent years after her father's death:

> My mother cried all the time, never slept, and lost 60 pounds. She heard my father's voice. She hardly took care of us. This went on for years. I was no angel when I got older. I gave my mother a lot of grief. I went out with one boy after another. She called me a tramp. We were killing each other. She would lock me out of the house. Finally I ran away with my boyfriend at 16. But it didn't work out after a year. My mother wouldn't let me come back home—she said I was no good. I lived with my aunt, got my act together, started getting good jobs—then I met Orlando. My mother couldn't believe that an educated man would want to marry me. She tells me to put up and shut up with him. After all—he's my only hope to be a decent person. I should remember how lucky I am that he married me.

At this point in the work (about six months later), Yulie brings in a dream: she is in the playground with her children, other mothers are sitting on park benches. They are talking and their voices get louder, and now the women are turning into *cacatúas*. She uses this Spanish word for a type of Caribbean parrot. I ask her in what language she has had the dream. "I always dream in Spanish," she says. I ask her to continue telling me the dream in this language.

> Las mujeres se vuelven cacatúas. Es increible. Empiezan a volar alrededor de mí. No se callan. Quieren que yo no hable. Estan gritando; pajaros feos. Corro pero no las puedo escapar. Yo me despierto en una pesadilla con pánico.
>
> (Translation) The women are turning into cacatúas. It's incred-

ible. They start to fly toward me. They don't quiet down. They don't want me to say anything. They are screaming—the ugly birds. I run away, but can't escape them. I wake up in a nightmare, in a panic.

In the following sessions, Yulie continues to talk of the dream and its associations to her mother. For the first time since the initial twenty minutes of our first meeting, she uses Spanish in session, at times alternating with English, but now seemingly drawn to speaking her native language as she begins painfully to recount her mother's verbal abuse and abandonment.

I also notice something else happening at this juncture. Yulie begins to assume a much more comfortable, settled-in position with me. Around this time she switches from the formal "usted" to the more familiar "tu" in addressing me. I see this as a sign—of something. The language has drawn us closer—possibly. But then she begins to be late for sessions. First a few minutes, then up to fifteen minutes. She is breezy about this, at times not even explaining. I find myself annoyed at her attitude. On another occasion she has her receptionist call to cancel her session. I'm starting to steam. On another occasion she brings two friends who sit and wait outside during the session. I grumble to myself, "What is this, a public waiting room?" Finally one day she pays my bill (late) with a crumpled check dug out of the bottom of her bag. Is this a shabby check for shabby service? I'm really steaming now!

I could go on, but the countertransferential process has become palpably clear. Subjectively I have become an unwitting partner in Yulie's very personal drama. She has successfully transformed me into a hacking Caribbean bird who wants nothing more than to squawk at her, keep her in line, and make her behave. My first attempts to interpret this transference are met with anger and accusations. "You are just like everyone else trying to tell me what to do. You just sit there and don't say much, then when you do, it is to criticize me. What are you doing in this kind of work anyway—Latin women can usually never keep their mouths shut!" (I believe that Yulie is pointedly interpreting here a dimension of my own bilingual self split).[2] The mother tongue has indeed transformed us both!

Yulie is fighting and working. It is tough going. We live almost entirely in Spanish now. She speaks in English seemingly to rest, and I must say that I feel relief at these times. In the months and years to come we get to

---

[2] An unexplored aspect of bilingual psychoanalysis is the analyst's own language-related self-experience. A recent paper by M. Stern (1993) points to changes in both the analyst's mood and analytic technique upon shifting to his or her own native language in the treatment. This observation carries significant import, for it suggests the potential for tremendous variegation and complexity in transference—countertransference phenomena, all of which can become active material for the analytic work.

know that her mother's grief and agitated depression were probably of psychotic proportions, and that she harbored the jealous resentment that Yulie had been the light of her father's eyes.

As we came to reconstruct, Yulie's development in the English-speaking American world served a dual function. After her father's death when she was 12, she had immersed herself in all things American with a vengeance: absolutely perfecting her English, excelling in school, and allowing herself to be "adopted," (as she called it), by several American teachers with whom she came to identify strongly. Thus on the one hand the English code became developmentally the second symbolic medium through which she conducted particular relational experiences and came to evolve complex, creative, and adaptive functions in her self development. On the other hand, the English allowed her to ward off and efficiently encapsulate—as might any well-articulated characterological defense—the anguish of her early psychic life. This was the life and trauma with primary objects that she had internally organized in a different language: the actual loss of her father, and the psychic loss of her mother and motherland. At the most deeply feeling moments of "living" in her Spanish world in the treatment, Yulie came to reexperience herself as the girl child who had been punished and banished by her mother for the oedipal crime of adoring her father. Yulie's heroic Americanized adage: "Papi left us, but died for Cuba," simply became the mournful: "Papi se me fué," (Daddy left me). Linguistically, to be noted here is Yulie's use of the reflexive form of the verb "go" in Spanish, a form that does not exist in English syntax. It denotes that the verb has had a uniquely intimate and personal impact on the subject (the self) in the sentence, suggesting something like: Daddy has gone on me.

Yulie would also come to understand that at the core of her manifest marital difficulties was a torturous and complex dual transference to her husband as both idealized paternal figure and castigating, envious mother. It was these two self–object configurations, these modes of being with another, that were so deeply symbolized in her Spanish, so cleverly guarded by her English, and so dramatically revived in the "theater" (McDougall 1989) of her bilingual analysis.

As in the reports of early authors, the patient's eventual use of her native tongue in treatment undoubtedly released richer and more affect-laden material; this was the language medium of her primary object world. Operationally, the second language served as a coping or defensive operation against the significant losses and anguish symbolized by her mother tongue. This case of a bilingual speaker shows how language can be used dynamically to mediate the conscious availability of internal-conflictual material, as well as the concordant dissociation from that material. In addition, the description of language-related transference–countertransference shifting is suggestive of language's deep symbolic capacity to represent internalized object relational experiences. For condensed within each of the patient's languages were both the verbal symbols and the object relations within which these symbols were learned. Using these new symbols in the analysis gave them and the related interiorized versions of self and other fresh descriptive-semantic meanings; these are the related interiorized versions of the self and the primary other who once mutually shared and negotiated common experiences, and in the context of their relationship (and the language culture at large), gave them a symbolic name.

Now, fortunate indeed is the bilingual like-matched therapeutic dyad, which, as argued, can more efficiently access early intrapsychic material, as well as offer enhanced transformational possibilities for transference enactments. But we are more commonly faced with treating a patient whose native language we do not know. How can a monolingual therapist find an entrée into the language-related psychodynamic processes of their bilingual patients? How does the clinician begin to evaluate whether the patient's current domain of English language usage may play a role in the dissociation from or resistance to important intrapsychic material? What part does language play in how a bilingual patient's psychological distress is organized and defended against? These questions can be addressed by the monolingual clinician by conducting a psycholinguistic inquiry.

THE PSYCHOLINGUISTIC HISTORY: A FORMAT OF INQUIRY INTO THE PSYCHODYNAMIC OPERATIONS IN BILINGUALISM

The argument for the psycholinguistic assessment of patients in treatment is based on the bilingualism literature discussed just above, and recent developments in contemporary psycholinguistics. As noted earlier, linguists have been studying language acquisition in a social-relational context (Bloom 1973, Bruner 1977, 1981, Dore, 1975). The conceptual core of this perspective is the early work of Vygotsky who conceived of all symbolic ideational material as modeled after social interchange with another (1981). Daniel Stern (1985) explains the phenomenon this way: meaning results from the interiorization of inter-personal negotiations "involving what can be agreed upon as shared. And such mutually negotiated meanings . . . grow, change, develop and are struggled over by two people and thus ultimately owned by [them]" (p. 170). Just as mother and child stimulate, regulate, and influence each other in the pursuit of mutuality and attunement (Beebe 1985, Beebe and Lachmann 1988, Benjamin 1990, Stern 1974, 1977, 1985), so do they subsequently strive to be together in the new shared experience of verbal symbols (Stern 1985)—a sharing of mutually created lingual meanings about personal experiences, the external world, and most important to the developing child, meanings about his or her own selfhood. As all children move beyond the primary objects, they will engage in further dialectics throughout development. Other members of their culture at large will become the new verbal mediators, who will contribute to the further layering of language meaning (Stern 1985, Wilson and Weinstein 1990).

Thus to be kept in mind by clinicians is that the building of language reflects a composite of developmental stages (psychic, cognitive, affec-tive), varied social contexts, and meaning-producing interactions with important others (Wilson and Weinstein 1990). Given that early lan-guage is learned from these important others, words can be seen as the symbolic object-relational capsules of the past. They are the voice of the self with the other. They are the potential evokers of early mean-ing in the "small two person society" (Harris 1992) of mother and child, who together begin to create verbal symbols for describing experience.

The bilingual speaker possesses not only dual sets of symbols for re-ferring to internal states and the external world, but two different chains of meaning-producing self–object interactions and developmental con-texts. Whether a second language has been acquired in a different envi-ronment or in a different developmental period (in school, upon migra-tion), or whether a second language has simply been taught in early life by another caretaker, each code system will represent a separate com-posite of unique relational-contextual experiences. At the level of neuro-cognitive organization, the literature reviewed earlier suggests that many of the cognitive and affective components of these experiences will have been processed and stored in memory along language-specific organiza-tional schema. At the level of psychodynamic organization, these language-specific object experiences may come to be associated with different modes of being, different modes of interacting with another, different modes of discharge, and different modes of experiencing oneself. Clinical reports suggest that the relative isolation or interaction of these language-related states is often titrated by their conflictual valence.

The Psycholinguistic History is a format of inquiry into these dynamics (see Table 13–1). It explores two spheres of language operation in the bilingual speaker:

1. *Psycho-Developmental Factors* surrounding each language acquisition: These are the cognitive, affective, behavioral, and object-relational factors associated with the learning of each language. This information can elaborate the role that each language has played in the patient's developing psychic operations, for example, defensive formations and organization of self experiences.
2. *Current Usage Factors*: This is information on the current domains of language use, regarding how, when, where, and with whom the

Table 13–1. Psycholinguistic History©

I PSYCHO-DEVELOPMENTAL FACTORS

1. Age at acquisition of each language.
2. Nature of relationships with people from whom languages were learned.
3. Social/cultural/environmental context of each language acquisition.
4. Psycho-developmental phase, or special psychodynamic issues surrounding acquisition of each language.
5. Domain or context of each language's early usage.

II CURRENT USAGE FACTORS

1. Current domain or context of respective language usage.
2. People to whom languages are spoken.
3. Experience of self when speaking each language.
4. Language of dreams and internal self-talk.
5. Language of sexual fantasies.

Copyright © RoseMarie Pérez Foster, Ph.D., 1996.

patient's idioms are currently used. This line of inquiry begins to delineate how present language choice is associated with conscious expression of psychic material and manifest personality functioning.

I would like to illustrate with a case example:

Jan is a 37-year-old Scandinavian man who came to the United States on a graduate fellowship at age 25 and never returned home. He eventually acquired a Ph.D. in epidemiology and married an American woman. His English is perfect. He is a respected researcher in his particular area, but is also involved in commercial real estate investments from which he makes a substantial income. He is part of a business consortium with fellow countrymen. Jan presented with intense hypochondriasis, fear of death, and the compulsion to check his heartbeat. He also complained of explosive rages toward his business partners. In time, he described his "other compulsion": frequenting prostitutes who are "putty in my hands; they are willing to silently obey all of my sexual demands." Jan began this activity shortly after divorcing his first wife.

The patient is the second oldest of five children. He has an older brother and three significantly younger sisters. He remembers his father as emotionally removed and unapproachable. His mother was his everything. "She was my world—I could not live or breathe without her." From ages 4–7, his mother would take Jan in to bathe with her. "I was imprisoned by her touches, her smells, and an excitement that I did not know what to do with. Then when I am 7, the first of three baby girls is born, and she drops me like I am a nothing. I didn't know whether to feel relief or like murdering her."

Early latency years are difficult for Jan. He is shy and has trouble separating from mother and home. He idolizes his older brother and male cousins; however, they call him sissy and do not include him in their games. Around age 10 Jan begins to come into his own, excelling at school and making some friends. Adolescence proves difficult, however, as his mother is experienced as intrusive and demanding. "She chases away my girl friends." At university, Jan again excels in the academic sphere, but is inhibited in his social relationships. He blames this on the fact that he still lives at home with this family. Upon graduation, he is offered a fellowship by an international health organization to pursue epidemiologic research in the United States. "I have my chance to finally get away from my mother. I come to America and never go back."

Jan's Psycholinguistic History

Developmental Factors

The first four items of this section of the history can be explored jointly.

1. The ages of language acquisition
2. The relationships to the people who taught each language
3. The social/cultural/environmental context of each language acquisition
4. Any remarkable psycho-developmental issues surrounding the language acquisition periods

Jan learns his first language from his mother. It was the language of his early infantile developmental life, his intimate relationship with his mother, and the protracted period of overstimulation with her. An important addendum is that English is spoken by the father and older brother, but mainly reserved for use outside the home in business and academic domains.

At age 10 Jan also acquires English. He is fluent in only eight months' time. The circumstances surrounding his English acquisition are quite notable. Jan develops a warm paternal relationship with his English instructor, who tells him that he will excel in the new language and possibly become more fluent than his brother. From this moment on, Jan vows to speak only English, to think in English, and to count in English. Indeed he does this. The patient claims that this single statement from his instructor was the turning point of his life.

(5) *The domain of early language usage*

Jan reserved his new English for use at school and newfound interchange with his brother and father. "Through English I finally excelled, felt manly and became like my brother. It was the one way in which I could compete." As Jan worked with these issues in treatment, he came to realize that English was a vehicle he used to identify with the men in his life. But at an even deeper level, thinking in a newfound English speaking world—a world uncontaminated by his mother's tongue—seems to have also offered Jan a fairly comprehensive defensive framework through which he could isolate and split off his early trauma with her. Thinking in a new symbolic system was not unlike a dissociative mechanism. Thus maintaining the psychic disruption of his early years at bay, he managed to use his latency years in the service of developing functions and skills that would serve him in later life. We note here the powerful role that language plays for this patient in the development of defensive structures and the organization of his self-experience.

Current Language Usage

The reader is reminded that this patient eventually left his motherland, trained as an academic researcher in the United States, and came to live an Americanized lifestyle. What is the fate of the patient's language usage within his current adult adjustment, and what part, if any, does it play in how he organizes the expression of his psychic distress? This section of the Psycholinguistic History will assess the patient's current language choice and contextual usage.

1. In what domains are Jan's languages currently used?
2. To whom are the languages spoken?
3. What is Jan's experience of self speaking and negotiating life in each language?
4. In what language does he dream?
5. In what language does he sexually fantasize?

Regarding Jan's (1) present language usage and (2) the people with whom the respective languages are spoken, Jan lives a tightly constructed English-speaking life with his current second wife and American friends. He writes for English language scientific journals. His spoken English is precise and accompanied by polished manners and emotional restraint. He uses his native language *only* when conducting business with his investment partners. Here his interactions are marked with more spontaneity, lack of verbal caution, and above all verbal rages when he does not get his way. In fact this has become a problem—aggressive negotiating has turned into bullying and near physical fighting. "I will let no one take me for a sucker," he says.

(3) Language-related experience of self

In his English-speaking world, Jan consciously feels quite a success, proud of his American life, social status, and the elitism of his academic circle. However, it is in his native language that the deep emotional doubts about his worth and manliness are keenly experienced and acted upon. The patient and I have come to understand the fighting in the work place as the transference of the aggressive struggle with his brother and father. It is his rage at their shunning him and leaving him to be sissified and exploited by his mother. He wants to kill them for this still. Speaking in the native tongue with his countrymen consistently evokes this transference. The music, mood, and meaning of the first language pulls Jan closest to the lived experience of feeling like an unmanly child. In the second language he is able to defensively avoid these painful aspects of his self experience, by both the real competitive success that his English-speaking life affords, and the second language's powerful defensive ability to affectively neutralize, intellectualize, and/or isolate the early conflictual experiences he "lived" in the mother tongue.

(4) and (5) Language of dream and internal fantasy

Turning to Jan's internal life, simple inquiry into the language of his sexual fantasies reveals that they are always in his native idiom. Most of his fantasies are organized around the sexual trauma with his mother. On the English-speaking surface his interpersonal and sexual approach to his wife is tentative. However, internally it is only the voices of his early life that fully arouse him as they depict some configuration of a physical sadomasochistic fantasy. Indeed, his activities with prostitutes who are "putty in my hands," are a repetitive enactment of his mother holding him captive in the bath—this time with Jan as the captor.

In summary, Jan is a complicated man whose early developmental trauma has deeply affected his object relations, impulse control, and organization of self. Indeed, his presentation of sexual and physical enactments (hypochondriasis, rages, sadomasochistic enactments) embodied repetitive and desperate efforts at self-restoration (Stolorow and Atwood 1991). His analysis will have to proceed like any other: with an ultimate understanding of his deep desires, a working through of his traumas and their impact on his self and relational worlds, and the ultimate elaboration of new psychic mechanisms. However, from his psycholinguistic history we learn that his most conflictual desires and traumata are deeply associated with his infantile language. They are embedded in his mother tongue and he relives these experiences in his native language still: when he rails at his colleagues or fantasizes and acts out a sadomasochistic encounter.

Interpreting to him that he uses English to guard against these deep and dangerous feelings is effective and useful. But the real question in this treatment, and that of any other bilingual patient, is to what depth Jan can work through this early material in English, the language of his resistance. In effect, we will have to crack open the early language code. We have thus far attempted various ways of doing this: Jan has begun to tell his dreams and to recount his rages in his native language (which he later translates). The level of clear emotion that this evokes has been very fruitful for the work. The patient has also used another more unique vehicle for exploring his early language. Initially unaware of the determinism behind his actions, Jan began a research project that involved a population from his own country: the study of sexually transmitted diseases in young children. This work basically involved reading the Scandinavian journal reports of children who had been sexually abused. It was through this unique project that Jan was finally able to enter his mother's language, as well as her bath, ultimately reconstructing the repressed memories of his sexualized experiences with her.

Jan has become increasingly aware of the duality that exists in his psychological life. The therapeutic work thus far has made him quite conscious of the role that his English life plays in binding his anxiety and diffusing his impulses. It has taken years for him to utter the words of his first language in session. When he does so now, he will often stop abruptly saying: "It's too much like this—too powerful." He then goes back to English. I believe that the "power" he speaks of is not only the affective accuracy and intensity of the mother language, but the potential strength of the transference enactment that might be evoked when he enters the primal sensorial space of his mother's speech. Thus far the patient and I have been coasting productively on the positive wave of being two brothers, analyzing and telling stories in English—Jan's language of being adult, equal, and productive. But there are other unspoken dimensions of coexperience brewing between us. I can feel Jan bristle when I remind him about a late payment. Also, I experience my countertransference as I resist his petulant demands for time changes and make-up sessions. I know that I am fighting against becoming "putty in his hands." I have recently brought this case into supervision.

I would like to conclude by making several points. Language is a powerful organizer of experience. It becomes intimately yoked to the objects associated with the language learning, to the environmental ambience in which the language learning took place, and to the internal psycho-developmental state of the child at the time of acquisition. When several languages are acquired, and especially when they are learned within different relationships and different developmental contexts, each *language code* becomes a kind of signifier for that set of lived experiences. As we saw with Jan, who acquired his second language under very special developmental circumstances, English became a powerful signifier of new identifications, ego ideals, defensive structures, and autonomous ego functions. One might say that in the multilingual individual, language can serve as a characterological organizer. In the face of early trauma or unresolved early conflict, the clinician must also be aware that bilingualism can serve a highly dynamic and defensive function, for a second language system is a formidable binder of anxiety that can effectively isolate and dissociate affect initially experienced in another language system.

Foreign-born patients who enter our consulting rooms citing the often-heard immigrant's adage: "starting a new life in a new country," are wiser and more complex than we give them credit for. However, monolingual clinicians can now begin to access their patients' language-related identifications, defensive functions, relational experiences, and modes of organizing psychic distress through inquiry into their psycholinguistic histories.

REFERENCES

Albert, M. L., and Obler, L. K., eds. (1978). *The Bilingual Brain: Neuropsychological and Neurolinguistic Aspects of Bilingualism.* New York: Academic Press.

Amahti-Mehler, J., Argentieri, S., and Canestri, J. (1993). *The Babel of the Unconscious.* Madison, CT: International Universities Press.

Beebe, B. (1985). Mother–infant mutual influence and precursors of self and object representations, In *Empirical Studies of Psychoanalytic Theories*, vol. 2, ed. J. Masling, pp. 27–48. Hillsdale, NJ: Analytic Press.

Beebe, B., and Lachmann, F. (1988). Mother–infant mutual influence and precursors of psychic structure. In *Frontiers of Self Psychology*, vol. 3, ed. A. Goldberg, pp. 3–25. Hillsdale, NJ: Analytic Press.

Benjamin, J. B. (1990). An outline of subjectivity. *Psychoanalytic Psychology*, 7 (Suppl): 33–46.

Bloom, L. (1973). *One Word at a Time: The Use of Single Word Utterances Before Syntax.* Hawthorne, NY: Mouton.

Bruner, J. S. (1977). Early social interaction and language acquisition. In *Studies in Mother–Infant Interaction*, ed. H. R. Schaffer, pp. 271–289. London: Academic Press.

—— (1981). The social context of language acquisition. *Language and Communication* 1:155–178.

Buxbaum, E. (1949). The role of the second language in the formation of the ego and superego. *Psychoanalytic Quarterly* 18:279–289.

Diller, K. C. (1974). "Compound" and "coordinate'" bilingualism: a conceptual artifact. *Word* 26:254–261.

Dore, J. (1975). Holophrases, speech acts and language universals. *Journal of Child Language* 2:21–40.

Ervin, S. M. (1964). Language and T.A.T. content in bilinguals. *Journal of Abnormal and Social Psychology* 68:500–507.

Ervin, S. M. and Osgood, C. E. (1954). Second language learning and bilingualism. *Journal of Abnormal and Social Psychology* 49:139–146.

Ferenczi, S. (1911). On obscene words. In *First Contributions to Psychoanalysis*, trans. E. Jones. New York: Brunner/Mazel.

Findling, J. (1969). Bilingual need affiliation and future orientation in extra group and intragroup domains. *Modern Language Journal* 53:227–231.

Flegenheimer, F. A. (1989). Languages and psychoanalysis. The polyglot patient and the polyglot analyst. *International Review of Psycho-Analysis* 16:377–383.

Foster, R. P. (1992). Psychoanalysis and the bilingual patient: some observations on the influence of language choice on the transference. *Psychoanalytic Psychology* 9:61–75.

—— (1993). *The bilingual self.* Paper presented at the thirteenth annual spring meeting of the Division of Psychoanalysis (39) of the American Psychological Association, New York, NY, April.

—— (1996a). The bilingual self: duet in two voices. *Psychoanalytic Dialogues.* 6:99–121.

—— (1996b). The bilingual self: notions of a scientific positivist or pragmatic psychoanalyst? A reply to Massey. *Psychoanalytic Dialogues* 6:141–150.

Greenson, R. R. (1950). The mother tongue and the mother. *International Journal of Psycho-Analysis* 31:18–23.

Harris, A. (1992). Dialogues as transitional space: a rapprochement of psychoanalysis and developmental psycholinguistics. In *Relational Perspectives in Psychoanalysis*, ed. N. Skolnick & S. Warshaw, pp. 119–145. Hillsdale, NJ: Analytic Press.

Jaffe, S. (1993). The inner world of words: crossing the language barrier in psychoanalytic treatment. Panel introduction presented at the thirteenth annual meeting of the Division of Psychoanalysis (39) of the American Psychological Association, New York, NY, April.

Javier, R. A. (1989). Linguistic considerations in the treatment of bilinguals. *Journal of Psychoanalytic Psychology* 6:87–96.

Javier, R. A. and Marcos, L. (1989). The role of stress on the language independence and code-switching phenomenon. *Journal of Psycholinguistic Research* 18:449–482.

Javier, R. A., and Munoz, M. A. (1993). Autobiographical memory in bilinguals. *Journal of Psycholinguistic Research* 22:319–338.

Kolers, P. A. (1963). Interlingual work association. *Journal of Verbal Learning and Verbal Behavior* 2:291–300.

Krapf, E. E. (1955). The choice of language in polyglot psychoanalysis. *Psychoanalytic Quarterly* 24:343–357.

Loewald, H. (1980). Primary process, secondary process and language. In *Papers on Psychoanalysis.* New Haven, CT: Yale University Press, 1976.

Marcos, L. R. (1976). Bilinguals in psychotherapy: language as an emotional barrier. *American Journal of Psychotherapy* 30:195–202.

Marcos, L. R., Alpert, M., Urcuyo, L., and Kesselman, M. (1973). The effect of interview language on the evaluation of psychopathology in Spanish-American schizophrenic patients. *American Journal of Psychotherapy* 130:549–553.

McDougall, J. (1989). *Theaters of the Body*. New York: Norton.

Menaker, E. (1990). Personal communication.

Ojemann, G. A., and Whitaker, H. A. (1978). The bilingual brain. *Archives of Neurology* 35:409–412.

Paradis, M. (1977). Bilingualism and aphasia. In *Studies in Neurolinguistics*, vol. 3, ed. H. Whitaker, and H. Whitaker, pp. 65–121. New York: Academic Press.

Rozensky, R. H., and Gomez, M. Y. (1983). Language switching in psychotherapy with bilinguals: two problems, two models, and case examples. *Psychotherapy: Theory, Research and Practice* 20:152–160.

Stern, D. N. (1974). The goal and structure of mother–infant play. *Journal of the American Academy of Child Psychiatry* 13:402–421.

—— (1977). *The First Relationship: Infant and Mother*. Cambridge: Harvard University Press.

—— (1985). *The Interpersonal World of the Infant*. New York: Basic Books.

Stern, M. (1993). The subjective and intersubjective experience of switching languages in analytic treatment. Paper presented at the thirteenth annual spring meeting of the Division of Psychoanalysis (39) of the American Psychological Association, New York, NY, April.

Sternberg, S. (1993). La mère et la mer: hidden meanings in the mother tongue. Paper presented at the thirteenth annual spring meeting of the Division of Psychoanalysis (39) of the American Psychological Association, New York, NY, April.

Stolorow, R. D., and Atwood, G. E. (1991). The mind and the body. *Psychoanalytic Dialogues* 1:181–196.

Vygotsky, L. S. (1962). *Language and Thought*. Cambridge: M.I.T. Press.

—— (1978). *Mind in Society: The Development of Higher Psychological Processes*. Cambridge: Harvard University Press.

—— (1981). The genesis of higher mental functions. In *The Concept of Activity in Soviet Psychology*, ed. J. V. Wertsch, pp. 114–188. Armonk, NY: Sharpe.

—— (1988). Thinking and speaking. In *The Collected Papers of L. S. Vygotsky*, ed. R. W. Rieber and A. S. Carton, pp. 39–288. New York: Plenum.

Whorf, B. L. (1940). Science and linguistics. *Technology Review* 44:229–242.

Wilson, A., and Weinstein, L. (1990). Language, thought and interiorization. *Contemporary Psychoanalysis* 26:26–40.

INDEX